Workplace Skills

Reading for Information

Career Readiness Preparation

DISCARDED
NATIONAL CITY LIBRARY

THIS BOOK IS THE PROPERTY OF
THE NATIONAL CITY PUBLIC LIBRARY
14. NATIONAL CITY BLVD
NATIONAL CITY, CA 91950

McGraw Hill Contemporary

The McGraw·Hill Companies

www.mhcontemporary.com

 **Contemporary**

Copyright © 2011 by The McGraw-Hill Companies, Inc.

All rights reserved. Except as permitted under the United States
Copyright Act, no part of this publication may be reproduced
or distributed in any form or by any means, or stored in
a database or retrieval system, without the prior written
permission from the publisher, unless otherwise indicated.

Printed in the United States of America.

WORKKEYS® is the registered trademark of ACT, Inc.
The McGraw-Hill Companies, Inc. have no affiliation with
ACT, Inc., and this publication is not approved, authorized
or endorsed by ACT, Inc.

Send all inquiries to:
McGraw-Hill/Contemporary
130 East Randolph, Suite 400
Chicago, IL 60601

ISBN 978-0-07-655574-1
MHID 0-07-655574-7

Printed in the United States of America.

5 6 7 8 9 QDB 16 15 14 13 12 11

 The **McGraw·Hill** Companies

Contents ...

Introduction

Today's employers want to know if you have the skills and knowledge needed to be productive in the 21st Century workplace. *Workplace Skills* is designed to help you to certify the career readiness skills that you already have and to help you to improve your skill levels for greater career success and mobility. By completing this series, you will be better prepared to take a career readiness test and receive a Career Readiness Certificate.

The *Workplace Skills* series provides instruction and practice in three skill areas identified by employers as holding the key to your success in more than 85 percent of current and emerging careers. These areas are: Applied Mathematics, Reading for Information, and Locating Information. The questions you are asked in each of these areas are taken from actual workplace situations. They are designed to help you to identify, understand, and solve problems that you may encounter on the job.

Each book contains lessons that include a step-by-step example to introduce the skill and *On Your Own* problems to practice the skill. The lessons in the book will guide you through progressively higher skill levels, from those needed for entry-level employment to those required in higher-level jobs. Foundational skills are listed in the *Remember!* notes included in each lesson. *Performance Assessment* problems with answers and explanations at the end of each skill level allow you to review and assess your mastery of the skills at that level. In each of the three subject areas, employers have determined the skill level required for a job, and you may ask for that information from your instructor.

Workplace Skills: Reading for Information

Signs, directions, safety instructions, bulletin boards, notices, regulations, e-mail, contracts, and memos—in today's workplace, written materials are everywhere. In a world where we are increasingly expected to coordinate and communicate through written text, employers need to know that employees can read, understand, and use the information communicated in these materials.

Workplace Skills: Reading for Information will help you develop and improve your reading skills. All examples in this book are based on actual workplace documents. As you work through the lessons and performance-based assessments, you will develop problem-solving skills that you can apply to the understanding of any written document.

Two-Step Approach

Knowing how to approach Reading for Information problems will give you confidence when solving them. Though different problems will require application of different skills, the problem-solving process can be summarized in two essential steps.

 Step 1 Understand the Problem

Before approaching any problem, you must be sure you understand what you are being asked to do. You can use the *Plan for Successful Solving* to help you organize the information presented in a problem and then plan how to solve it. The plan includes five questions:

Plan for Successful Solving	
What am I asked to do?	Determine what answer you are being asked to find. This is usually found in the question posed at the end of the problem.
What are the facts?	Identify what information is provided within the document. Identify the document's main idea and details.
How do I find the answer?	Determine where the information needed to solve the problem is located within the document.
Is there any unnecessary information?	Scan the document to determine if any information is not needed. Some details may not be needed to answer specific questions.
What prior knowledge will help me?	Think about personal background knowledge and experience you have that might help you better understand the question and what steps are needed to find an answer.

Remember!

The content of this book assumes foundational skills in reading that are required at the pre-employment level. These are often listed in the *Remember!* notes of each lesson.

In every skill lesson, the *Plan for Successful Solving* is modeled to help you see how to apply the two-step approach to any workplace situation, regardless of the skill or skill level needed.

Think and Ask Questions About Text

Answering questions that require you to read for information can be like decoding a message or solving a puzzle. You must determine what information is needed to answer the question. Below are four key skills that you should use when reading workplace documents. For each skill, there is a set of questions that will help you better understand and use the information that you read.

Skill	Key Questions
Identify main idea and details	· What is the main point of the paragraph or document? · Which details support the main idea and clarify the purpose of the document?
Determine the meaning of unfamiliar words	· Is the definition of the word directly stated in the document? · How is the word used in the passage? · Is the word similar to another word whose definition I know?
Follow a series of steps	· What is the goal or end result of following these steps? · Are the steps listed in a specific order? Are they numbered?
Apply instructions	· Under what circumstances should I follow the instructions? · Are there conditions for which different actions should be taken depending on the outcome of an earlier step?

Step 2 — Find and Check Your Answer ■ ■ ■

Sometimes finding the right answer may require you to adjust your initial plan. It is important to review all answer choices to be sure that the answer you have selected is the best option. Once you have identified the best answer choice, it is a good idea to review the original question to be sure your understanding of what you are being asked to do is correct and that your answer makes sense. If you determine that your answer may be incorrect, you should look back at your plan and revise it. Then perform the steps needed to arrive at and check your revised answer.

The two-step approach to problem solving is an easy-to-follow model for you to use as you develop the confidence needed to successfully approach problems you will encounter both in the workplace and on a Career Readiness Certificate test. *Do not worry yet about memorizing the steps.* With practice, you will naturally learn and remember this extremely useful approach. Over time, learning this model and using it carefully in your preparation for the test will provide you with a reliable approach to problem solving.

Remember!

If necessary, revise your *Plan for Successful Solving.*
· Determine and apply your solution approach.
· Check your answer.
· Select the correct option.

Level 3 Introduction ▪ ▪ ▪

The lesson and practice pages that follow will give you the opportunity to develop and practice the comprehension skills needed to answer work-related questions at a Level 3 rating of difficulty. The *On Your Own* practice problems provide a review of key reading skills along with instruction and practice applying these skills through effective problem-solving strategies. The *Performance Assessment* provides problems similar to those you will encounter on a Career Readiness Certificate test. By completing the Level 3 *On Your Own* and *Performance Assessment* questions, you will gain the ability to confidently approach workplace scenarios that require understanding and application of the reading skills featured in the following lessons:

Lesson 1: Identify Main Idea and Details

Lesson 2: Choose Correct Meanings of Words

Lesson 3: Define Common Workplace Words

Lesson 4: Follow a Series of Steps

Lesson 5: Apply Instructions to a Situation

These skills are intended to help you successfully read and understand workplace documents such as procedures, policies, bulletins, and other publications. Reading these types of documents often requires the ability to:

▪ understand what the information tells you to do,

▪ identify information you need from clearly and directly stated text,

▪ identify the main point of the passage,

▪ understand how to apply instructions to various situations.

Through answering document-related questions at this level, you will begin to develop problem-solving approaches and strategies that will help you determine the correct answer in real-world and test-taking situations.

Lesson 1 ▪ ▪ ▪
Identify Main Idea and Details

Skill: Identify main ideas and clearly stated details

When reading business documents such as company policies, procedures, and memos, you need to be able to identify the main idea of each paragraph. You also must recognize the details in the paragraph that support the main idea. The main idea explains what the paragraph or document is about. The details provide more information to explain and support the main idea.

Remember!

A well-written paragraph often includes a topic sentence that clearly states the main idea. The other sentences within a paragraph should provide details that help support or explain the main idea.

Skill Examples

Example 1
Identify a main idea when stated in the topic sentence.

Please read the following new guidelines for processing online orders. Customer Service has received several complaints about wait time. We must reduce this time to keep our customers happy. By making the changes below, we will reduce the amount of time between orders being placed and customers receiving their products.

The topic sentence identifies that the main idea of this memo is to explain how to make shipping times to customers faster. The details provide information about why making this change is important.

Example 2
Identify clearly stated details.

First check that the claim is covered by the owner's policy. Then ask for forms of documentation. Check the accuracy of the amount of damage and the cost of repair. These steps will help our division avoid processing false insurance claims. This will help save both time and money.

This paragraph begins with details. These details clearly list how to process an insurance claim. The main idea in this example is located near the end of the paragraph.

Skill Practice

To: Supply Clerk
From: Office Manager
Subject: Order for next week
Please order the supplies needed for next week. First, count the supplies on the shelf. Subtract that amount from the total amount needed. Calculate the cost of all items needed. Then, enter the total cost on the bottom line.

Use the e-mail to the left to answer the following questions.

1. You are a supply clerk responsible for carrying out the instructions in the e-mail. What is the main idea?

   A. There is an extra order next week.

   B. You must order supplies.

   C. Count the supplies on the shelf.

   D. Subtract the total cost on the bottom line.

   E. Do not order additional items for next week.

2. Which detail describes what you should do after you calculate the cost of all items?

   F. Subtract the cost of all items.

   G. Enter the total cost on the bottom line.

   H. Subtract the number of items on the shelf.

   J. Add the cost of all items.

   K. Enter the cost of the items on the shelf.

Try It Out! ■ ■ ■

As a medical transcriptionist at Community Hospital, you read the memo to the right. What is the main idea of this memo?

A. You will take a test that has two parts.

B. You will take a written and an oral test.

C. You must complete the test in one hour.

D. You will take a test to evaluate your skills.

E. You must understand computers to take the test.

Community Hospital

You have finished your first year as a medical transcriptionist. You will now take a skills test. The test has two parts, one written part and one oral part. In both parts, you will transcribe medical information into a computer. In the first part, you will transcribe information from written notes. In the second part, you will transcribe information from a tape. The test takes no more than one hour to complete.

Step 1 Understand the Problem ■ ■ ■

Complete the *Plan for Successful Solving*.

Plan for Successful Solving

What am I asked to do?	What are the facts?	How do I find the answer?	Is there any unnecessary information?	What prior knowledge will help me?
Find the main idea of the paragraph.	The paragraph describes a test one must take. It explains the reasons for the test and what is on the test.	Look for the answer that best explains what the whole paragraph is about.	There are some details that do not help me find the main idea of the paragraph.	The main idea identifies what a paragraph is about.

Step 2 Find and Check Your Answer ■ ■ ■

- Confirm your understanding of the question and revise your plan as needed.

- Based on your plan, determine your solution approach: *Though the first sentence provides background information, the second sentence seems to explain what the rest of the paragraph is about. The sentences that follow give details about the test. The second sentence identifies what kind of test it is. I'll select the option that best describes this sentence.*

- Check your answer. Review all answers to determine if the answer you have selected is the best possible answer.

- **Select the correct answer:** D. You will take a test to evaluate your skills. This sentence summarizes the main idea of the paragraph. The other answer options explain specific details that describe the test, but they do not fully explain the main idea of the paragraph.

Remember!

The main idea of a paragraph is usually stated at or near the beginning of the paragraph.

Problem Solving Tip

Test answer options often contain phrases or clauses that appear in the paragraph. However, just because a phrase or clause appears in the paragraph does not mean that it states the main idea. When identifying the main idea from a list of options, be sure to think about which answer option really tells what the entire paragraph is about.

DAILY UPDATE

Saturday, June 15

It is going to be busy tonight. As usual, the dining room is open for dinner. However, the reception room is closed for a graduation party of 25 people. Do not seat other customers in this room.

The party will require all workers to observe reception rules. This means new reservations and walk-in seating will be limited to the main dining room. Extra event staff will be working the reception.

Because the reception room is closed, there may be delays in seating customers. In case of delays, please ask customers to wait at the bar. Give customers whose reservations have been delayed one free drink while they wait.

---

1. You work as a hostess at this restaurant. You will be working this Saturday evening. What is the main idea being addressed in the second paragraph of the above update?

   A. The restaurant is understaffed this evening.

   B. Reception rules must be followed this evening.

   C. The restaurant is fully booked for the evening.

   D. All patrons can have a free drink at the bar this evening.

   E. Walk-ins can only be seated in the main dining room.

2. Which of the details applies to walk-in customers at the restaurant who are not part of the graduation party?

   F. Customers should be seated in the main dining room this evening.

   G. Prepare drinks for patrons waiting at the bar to be seated.

   H. The regular restaurant staff might be busy.

   J. All workers should follow reception rules.

   K. It is going to be busy tonight.

Training Manual

It is important that all employees understand the basics of our solar-powered energy systems before they begin working at our company. Solar energy uses the energy in sunlight. It is this energy that is used to generate electricity.

Solar energy (photons) shines on cells inside the solar panel. The photons move the electrons in the cells. The electrons move through conductive material. These electrons are an electric current.

The electric current travels through the material to electrical wiring. The wiring takes the current to the inverter. The current goes into the electrical outlets of a building.

3. You are a technician being trained to fix solar-powered energy systems. You must learn the information in the training manual before you can go on site. What is the main idea of the above training manual section?

    A. Solar-powered energy systems use photons that move electrons.

    B. Electrons move through materials.

    C. Solar-powered energy systems use sunlight to generate electricity.

    D. An electric current goes into the wiring of a building.

    E. Only special materials are moved by photons.

4. What detail is most helpful for a solar-power energy technician to find out how the current is carried to the inverter?

    F. Sunlight makes electricity.

    G. Photons move electrons.

    H. Solar-powered energy shines on cells.

    J. Electrons move through material.

    K. Wiring takes the current to the inverter.

Dear Dan,

Congratulations on your promotion! Your years of hard work and dedication have been noticed, and we are excited to have you start next week in your new role.

As the new janitorial supervisor you have several tasks. Your top priority is to create a daily schedule for the janitorial staff. The schedule is very important. Your second priority is to check the staff's work. You will also need to hire new staff and check their work during the first few months.

There is another task to take care of as well. We have a new janitorial supplies company. We have only worked with them for two months. We will need to make sure they are reliable. Make sure that we are receiving all the supplies we order.

5. You have just been promoted to janitorial supervisor of an industrial cleaning staff. The note above is from the building engineer where you work. What is the main idea of the second paragraph of her note to you?

    A.   Certain tasks demand top priority for the supervisor.

    B.   Checking staff's work is not a priority.

    C.   The new supplies company will check supplies.

    D.   The supplies may need to be checked in two months.

    E.   The staff work schedule is very important.

6. Which detail identifies a task that must be performed daily by the supervisor?

    F.   Your years of hard work and dedication have been noticed.

    G.   You will need to hire new staff.

    H.   We will need to make sure they are reliable.

    J.   The schedule is very important.

    K.   Make sure that we are receiving all the supplies we order.

Sunspot Solar

Welcome to the last week of training! You are part of our new sales force. You will help sell our solar-energy systems.

You have read two sets of materials during your training. The materials explained that most people do not understand solar technology. The first set of materials explained solar energy. A good salesperson should understand the science of solar energy. The other set of materials explained solar-energy installations and their cost.

The training materials are important. They have answers to many questions customers will ask you. Customers will want to know how solar energy works. They will then ask how much it will cost to install their system. You should have an estimate at your first meeting. The training materials you have will help you do this.

7. You are a new salesperson for the solar energy company Sunspot Solar. You are finishing your job training. What is the main idea of the second paragraph of the company letter?

   A.   You will read two sets of training materials before your training.

   B.   Sales people should have an estimate at the first customer meeting.

   C.   Customers need to know about solar energy installations and their cost.

   D.   The information will help you become a good salesperson.

   E.   The materials explain that most people do not understand solar technology.

8. Which of the details contained in the letter apply to a salesperson's responsibilities to the customer?

   F.   Solar technology is explained in the training materials.

   G.   Potential customers will want to know their system's cost.

   H.   The materials explain solar-energy installations to customers.

   J.   The sales force will help sell solar-energy systems.

   K.   This is the last week of training.

Procedure Manual — Dental Technician

Our company makes dental crowns, bridges, and dentures. The dental technician is responsible for making these products for our clients. As a dental technician, it is your job to follow the procedures that make the highest quality devices.

- The dentist sends a mold of the patient's mouth. Use the mold to make a plastic model of the patient's teeth and mouth.
- When the plastic is hard, check the model. Check the size and shape of all teeth. Measure the gum line.
- Make the customized product based on your measurements.
- Apply porcelain in layers. Continue until size and shape are correct.
- The tooth can be shaped until it is the same as the original tooth.

9. As a dental technician, you are responsible for making customized products for customers. What is the main idea expressed in the first paragraph?

    A. Dental crowns, bridges and dentures are devices.

    B. The dental technician makes products.

    C. Specific procedures make the best quality devices.

    D. The company makes crowns, bridges, and dentures.

    E. Clients make the devices.

10. Which detail in the manual supports the idea that the dental technician makes customized products?

    F. Apply porcelain in layers.

    G. The tooth can be shaped until it is the same as the original.

    H. Dental technicians are responsible for making devices.

    J. The company makes crowns, bridges, and dentures.

    K. When the plastic is hard, check the model.

Employee Handbook

As a semiconductor processor, you will make microchips. These are used in electronic products. Only skilled workers can make microchips. Workers must follow these strict procedures:

Chips are made in a cleanroom. The cleanroom is a space that is free of dust. You will be allowed to enter the space only when wearing the protective outer clothes that cover you completely. This is called a "bunny suit." It is easy to work in.

If you work on the initial stage of the process, you will operate the machine that slices bulk silicon into thin wafers. Then, you will work with the machines that polish the wafers. After that, you will be in charge of having wafers washed in a chemical bath. This smooths them. Then the wafer is cut by machine into individual chips. These chips are sold to manufacturers.

11. You are a semiconductor processor making chips for electronics manufacturers. What is the main idea of this section in the employee handbook?

   A. Microchips are used in many electronic products.

   B. Machines slice silicon into thin wafers.

   C. The cleanroom is free of dust and easy to work in.

   D. Skilled workers must follow strict procedures in making microchips.

   E. The chips are sold to manufacturers.

12. What is a detail that supports the idea that special care is needed when making microchips?

   F. The cleanroom is a space that is free of dust.

   G. "Bunny suits" are easy to work in.

   H. Machines polish the wafers.

   J. Thin wafers are made from bulk silicon.

   K. Wafers are washed in a chemical bath.

Answers are on page 251.

Lesson 2 ▪ ▪ ▪
Choose Correct Meanings of Words

Skill: Choose the correct meaning of a word that is clearly defined in the reading

When reading documents that contain new or unfamiliar words, you sometimes can use clues within the document to determine the words' meanings. By understanding how to identify when words are clearly defined within workplace documents, you can learn how to locate clues that help determine the meanings of unfamiliar words.

Remember!

Depending on the content of a document, definitions of words may or may not be clearly stated. If a workplace document is about common, everyday procedures, then it is unlikely that definitions of words will be provided. This is because it is expected that employees fully understand their everyday procedures. If a document deals with something new—such as new software, a change in procedures, or employee training—then it is possible that definitions will be provided for any new terminology that is introduced.

Skill Examples

The company is instituting, or starting, a new procedure for office closings during snowstorms. We are starting this new set of steps to avoid the confusion caused by the old system. The procedure requires all employees to call a special office number during a snowfall or the days after a snowfall. There will be a recorded message telling you if the office is closed.

Example 1
Identify a word's meaning when its definition is directly stated.

In the first sentence of the memo, the term *instituting* is introduced and defined immediately following its first use. Often the stated definition is set off by commas and linked to the word using the word *or*. In the example above, "or starting" refers to the term *instituting* and provides the reader with a direct reference to the term's meaning.

Example 2
Identify a word's meaning when its definition is not directly stated.

In the first sentence, the term *procedure* is introduced and defined in the sentence that follows its first use. This is a common technique used by writers to clarify the meanings of words that might be unknown to the reader. In the example above, "this new set of steps" refers to the term *procedure* and provides the reader with an indirect reference to the term's meaning.

Break Procedures

Every employee is entitled to one 15-minute break before lunch and one 15-minute break after lunch. Breaks may be taken only in the lounge or outside in the courtyard. Note that smoking is prohibited inside the building. As smoking is not allowed indoors, employees who wish to smoke must take their break outside. Please use only the designated areas set aside for smoking.

Skill Practice

Use the procedures document to the left to answer the questions below.

1. What is the meaning of the word **designated** in the passage?

   A. set aside
   B. encouraged
   C. allowed
   D. not allowed
   E. not advised

2. What is the meaning of the word **prohibited** in the passage?

   F. discouraged
   G. limited
   H. allowed
   J. not allowed
   K. not advised

Try It Out! ■ ■ ■

You are a medical assistant who has started training on new computer software. The software will help you organize patient files. Based on the information given in the third bullet point, what is the meaning of the word **correlated**?

A. useless

B. matched

C. too expensive

D. rarely prescribed

E. out of date

Memo

To: All medical assistants

Re: New software

In an effort to quickly transfer patient records into the new software system, please review the following important features:

- How to complete personal information for every patient
- How diagnoses are added to a patient's chart via the software
- What medications the patient is taking and how these are correlated, or matched, to the diagnoses by the software
- How to recognize software alerts that warn about actual or potential danger from pharmaceuticals that should not be combined
- How to recognize software alerts that warn if a drug is not recommended due to a condition that makes the drug unsuitable or dangerous for a particular patient

---

 Step 1 **Understand the Problem** ■ ■ ■

Complete the *Plan for Successful Solving.*

Plan for Successful Solving

What am I asked to do?	What are the facts?	How do I find the answer?	Is there any unnecessary information?	What prior knowledge will help me?
Find the meaning of the term *correlated.*	New software analyzes medications that a patient takes to see how they affect one another.	Look at the bulleted list, especially the item that contains the word *correlated.*	The other bullets that do not help explain what *correlated* means are not necessary.	I know to look for the words *or* or *is* to see if a word is defined within the text.

 Step 2 **Find and Check Your Answer** ■ ■ ■

- Confirm your understanding of the question and revise your plan as needed.

- Based on your plan, determine your solution approach: *The third bulleted item mentions that the software correlates the medications the patient is taking. The other words in this bulleted statement tell that* correlate *refers to how medications are matched to the diagnoses. Among all the answer choices, option B means the same thing as* correlate.

- Check your answer. Review all answers to determine if the answer you have selected is the best possible answer.

- **Select the correct answer:** B. matched
  The third bullet point states that the software helps determine the medications the patient is taking and how these are correlated, or matched.

Remember!

The meaning of a word can often be found when it is restated in the same sentence in which the term is used or in the following sentence.

Problem Solving Tip

The correct answer needs to be more than just similar in meaning to the word being defined. Remember that you are looking for the word's meaning as it is used in the passage. The definition of the word is often clearly stated within the passage itself.

MEMO

TO: All Maintenance Personnel

FROM: R. Jones, Maintenance Supervisor

You may have noticed that we have purchased and installed the latest Q-10 machines. We must add these machines to our Preventive Maintenance (PM) schedule. Familiarize yourself with the instruction manual your team leader will give you. Note that these are very technical machines that require careful PM.

Your team leader will show all members of your team the PM procedures for the Q-10. You will then be assigned one part of PM for all the Q-10 machines, and your part of the PM will be listed on the complete PM schedule.

As with most PM, the Q-10 will need to be lubricated, or oiled, every day with high-grade oil to make sure its moving parts run smoothly. Because the Q-10 is a complex apparatus, the machine must be adjusted on a daily basis to make sure it performs efficiently.

The flag on the machine tells how often each PM task must be done. Your team leader will assign and schedule these tasks for team members.

---

1. As a member of the machine maintenance team for a large manufacturing company, you receive the above memo. Based on the passage, when machinery is **lubricated** it is

    A. made slippery.

    B. given fuel.

    C. moved around.

    D. started up.

    E. cleaned and washed.

2. A section of the memo explains that you must make daily adjustments to keep the apparatus performing smoothly. What is the meaning of the word **apparatus**?

    F. schedule

    G. oil

    H. team

    J. flag

    K. machine

Employee Handbook

Welcome to Z-Plastics & Molding. As a new member of our team, there are some guidelines and safety regulations you must follow. Adhering to safety regulations is one of your most important responsibilities. Be careful when working around the high-speed machines in our factory. Operators must wear protective gear at all times on the factory floor. These include safety glasses, earplugs, heat-resistant gloves, and face masks. Masks prevent the inhalation of airborne particles and dust created during the plastic-molding process.

The injection-molding machine that you will be operating heats plastic until it is liquefied, or made fluid. The machine then pours the liquid plastic into a mold. The mold then leaves the machine along a conveyor belt and is left to set until the plastic hardens and cools. Another machine then removes the molded product from the mold housing.

Your job is to make sure that your machine is working properly. You must be sure that there are no spills, stoppages, or other interruptions in the manufacturing process. It is important that you report any problems immediately to your supervisor.

---

3. You are a plastic molding machine operator. Based on its use in the first paragraph of the above passage, what is the meaning of the word **adhering**?

    A.   requiring

    B.   protecting

    C.   following

    D.   making safe

    E.   regulating

4. According to the first sentence of the second paragraph above, what is a substance like after it is **liquefied**?

    F.   molded

    G.   injected

    H.   waterlogged

    J.   fluid

    K.   spilled

Instructions for Installing a Toilet

Begin installation once the old toilet is removed. Clean the area thoroughly. Then place a thick mat on the floor of the work area.

Toilet installation is the opposite of toilet removal. Handle the new bowl with care. Carefully invert the position of the bowl. Once the bowl is upside down, place it carefully on the pad. Seal the toilet to its soil pipe flange, or rim. Do this by setting a standard toilet rubber ring, or gasket, over the bowl's outlet. The flat face of the gasket should be placed against the bowl. Follow this procedure whether using a wax gasket or a plastic gasket.

5. You are an assistant helping a master plumber install a new toilet. Your boss watches as you perform the first steps in the process. Based on the instructions above, what position is the bowl in when you **invert** it?

    A.   upright

    B.   on its side

    C.   right side up

    D.   upside down

    E.   in several pieces

6. In the second paragraph of the instructions, what is the **gasket** that is needed as a seal?

    F.   the outlet

    G.   the flange

    H.   the bowl

    J.   a wax plug

    K.   a ring of rubber

> **To:** Setters   **Date:** May 17
>
> **From:** Operations Manager
>
> **Subject:** Procedures reminder
>
> As a setter, always check the machines before the workers begin using them. Remember that precision parts are exact or refined parts, and they are made to exact size and quality. Because the parts are used in large appliances, we must check that they fit in the appliances they are used with. This is why it is so important to follow procedures.
>
> First, be sure the machines are calibrated, or measured and adjusted, to the exact part size needed. You must then start the machine for a test run. Check that the machine is making the part correctly. If the part made during this test is not correct, adjust the machine. Then make another part to determine if it is correct. Repair or clean the machine if necessary. If the machine still does not make a correct part, report the problem to the supervisor.

7. You work as a setter in a factory that makes precision parts. Based on the above e-mail, what does **precision** mean?

    A.   precut

    B.   exactness

    C.   oversized

    D.   appliance

    E.   snug-fitting

8. Based on the instructions, what do you do to a machine when you **calibrate** it?

    F.   Make it bigger.

    G.   Change the size.

    H.   Change the standard.

    J.   Repair nonworking parts.

    K.   Adjust to an exact measure.

From: Dr. Shayna Williams, MD   Sent: Tue 8/11 3:30 PM
To: Medical Billing
Subject: Billing for New Insurance

To Whom It May Concern,

I've noticed that there have been some billing irregularities since I accepted the new insurance. Don't worry...I'm not blaming you for these unusual billing items. I know it is confusing when every insurance company has different ways of doing things!

Please take some time to review the new insurance forms. Note that they require far more codes for every bit of patient care. Also notice that their codes have six numbers for each procedure, not the usual five numbers. For example, most other insurance companies code a simple office visit as 10001. The new company code for a visit is 010001. Also, the new insurance company demands a code for each part of an exam I do. Most other companies don't have this requirement. I've indicated each item of an exam on the patient chart. Please find the code for each and bill for all of them.

Many thanks. Keep up the good work!
Dr. Williams

9. You are a medical office billing administrator who has received the above e-mail from one of the doctors in your building. What does the doctor mean when she says that there have been billing **irregularities**?

   A.   The bills have not gone out on time.

   B.   The bills ignored the procedures done.

   C.   The bills did not follow normal procedure.

   D.   The bills had some unusual errors or items.

   E.   The bills were not paid by the insurance company.

10. At the end of the message, the doctor explains that not all companies have the same demands as the new insurance company. Based on this part of the e-mail, what does **requirement** mean?

   F.   necessity

   G.   coding

   H.   payment

   J.   notation

   K.   digits in a number

Employee Questionnaire

Thank you for applying for a job with Big-Breeze Wind Energy Company!

We are delighted that you want to work in the exciting field of renewable wind energy. Before completing the full, detailed application, there are a few important things we need to find out about you regarding your qualifications.

Please answer the following questions by checking "Yes" or "No" for each item. Return this form to the human resources administrator when completed.

	Yes	No
• Do you have acrophobia (fear of high places)?	☐	☐
• Do you have experience and/or training in computer systems monitoring?	☐	☐
• Do you have experience and/or training in computer troubleshooting and repair?	☐	☐
• Do you mind working outdoors in all types of weather?	☐	☐
• Do you mind driving in all types of weather?	☐	☐
• Do you own your own car or other vehicle?	☐	☐
• Do you live within 25 miles of this facility?	☐	☐
• Do you have training in aerodynamics, or air flow?	☐	☐

11. You are applying for the position of a wind-power maintenance technician at Big-Breeze Wind Energy Company. You have been asked to fill out the above questionnaire. Wind turbines are often several stories high. Why might having **acrophobia** disqualify you for this job?

   A. because it is a fear of the outdoors

   B. because it indicates a lack of relevant experience

   C. because it is a fear of being in high places

   D. because it is a fear of being outside during storms

   E. because it is a disease that is often disabling

12. By finding out about an applicant's **qualifications**, the company is learning

   F. if the applicant has the skills needed for the job.

   G. the family history of the applicant.

   H. what the applicant wants for a starting salary.

   J. how long the applicant plans to stay at this job.

   K. whether the applicant likes to drive.

Answers are on page 251.

Lesson 3 ∎ ∎ ∎
Define Common Workplace Words

Skill: Choose the correct meaning of common, everyday workplace words

When reading workplace documents, you need to be able to understand the meanings of words that are commonly used in all types of work environments. Workplace terms are often used by fellow employees, and it is expected that new employees learn these terms. By carefully reading the ways in which workplace words are used, you can learn to correctly identify their meanings.

Remember!

There are many terms that have workplace meanings that are different from their everyday meanings. For example, in business the term *minutes* refers to the notes of a meeting, while in everyday conversation it refers to a period of time. Knowing the unique meanings of common workplace words such as *minutes* is important when communicating in workplace settings.

Skill Examples

Example 1
Determine a word's meaning using related, familiar words.

> Employee safety is our primary concern. For that reason, every worker who uses welding equipment as part of his or her job is required to wear protective eyewear. You may have noticed that our safety glasses have a pull-down mask. The mask is intended to prevent injury while welding and must be down at all times.

The passage describes safety procedures for welders. From this, you may decide that the word *protective* has something to do with safety. You may also notice that the word contains the familiar, everyday word *protect*. You can therefore conclude that *protective* eyewear is gear that prevents the eyes from being injured.

Example 2
Determine a word's meaning by the way it is used.

> Patient files are ordered alphabetically and placed in the appropriately labeled file drawer. The files are organized by the first letters of the surname. If two patients have the same surname, organize the files alphabetically by the first letters of the patient's first name, or given name.

The passage contains instructions for filing patient files, as in a doctor's office. The passage tells you that the files are organized in alphabetical order. Files are organized by surname, then by first name if the surname is the same. This information gives you a hint that the term *surname* refers to a person's last name.

To: All Staff

RE: Ordering Supplies

Management has decided that it is impractical for each department to order its supplies separately and from different suppliers. We will work to consolidate this process to help make this system run more smoothly. We will eliminate unnecessary steps in the process by first having all departments place their orders through the administrative assistant to the office manager.

Skill Practice

Use the memo to the left to answer the following questions.

1. What is the meaning of the word **impractical**?

    A. confused

    B. expensive

    C. inefficient

    D. well rehearsed

    E. well informed

2. What is the meaning of the word **consolidate**?

    F. eliminate

    G. combine

    H. cheapen

    J. reduce

    K. monitor

Try It Out! ■ ■ ■

As a human resources specialist, you have received a cover letter from an applicant. Based on its description in the last sentence of the first paragraph, what does a **letter of recommendation** state?

   A. the applicant's previous hours and salary

   B. why the applicant was hired for the former job

   C. how the health clinic functioned

   D. a transcript of the applicant's school record

   E. how well the applicant worked at the former job

> To Whom It May Concern:
>
> It would be a privilege to be a medical assistant for your office. I have had previous work experience in the field. In my last summer of high school, I worked with a local health clinic. I enjoyed this work. I liked working with the patients and the doctors. I know the doctors liked my work and enjoyed having me there. Their letter of recommendation is attached. It explains how well I did my job.
>
> I am excited about having the chance to expand my knowledge as a medical assistant. I am familiar with medical charts, taking weights and heights, and medical office scheduling and billing procedures. I am also eager to learn new skills in this field.
>
> I would be happy to come in for an interview. Thank you very much for your consideration.
>
> Sincerely,
>
> Alicia Marshall

 Step 1 ## Understand the Problem ■ ■ ■

Complete the *Plan for Successful Solving*.

Plan for Successful Solving

What am I asked to do?	What are the facts?	How do I find the answer?	Is there any unnecessary information?	What prior knowledge will help me?
Find the meaning of the term *letter of recommendation*.	The letter is from the clinic she worked for. It explains that she did a good job there.	Look at the first paragraph that talks about this letter.	The second and third paragraphs do not help define the term.	I recommend restaurants and movies I like.

Step 2 ## Find and Check Your Answer ■ ■ ■

- Confirm your understanding of the question and revise your plan as needed.

- Based on your plan, determine your solution approach: *The first paragraph ends with a brief description of the letter of recommendation. It says that the letter describes how well she worked at the clinic. I know from my own experience that to recommend something means to explain why it is good or worthwhile. So a letter of recommendation must be a letter that explains how well this person performed at her former job. I'll select the option that best fits this meaning.*

- Check your answer. Review all answers to determine if the answer you have selected is the best possible answer.

- **Select the correct answer:** E. how well the applicant worked at the former job
  The letter of recommendation explains how and why the applicant was a good employee who did good work for her former employer.

Problem Solving Tip

It is important to try to connect what you read to your previous personal experience. In many instances, you may have seen or heard common workplace terms such as *letter of recommendation*. Thinking back to these references can often help you choose the correct meaning of the terms you read.

Remember!

The meaning of an unfamiliar word can often be found by reading other words in the passage that might indicate its meaning.

MEMO

TO: All new staff

RE: Jargon

It's good to have you working with us at Metro Steak House. To do a good job, you should quickly learn the jargon cooks, dining room staff, and host staff use for orders. For example, you must know how to tell the cook a customer's choice as a side of potatoes. Some customers may want french fries, others may want "bakers." These are the terms to use when placing the order with the cook.

Our restaurant also does a lot of take-out business. Be sure to tell the cook if the order is for in-house customers or take-out customers. If the meal is "on wheels," the cook will place the order in take-out containers.

We're sure you'll quickly catch on to Metro Steak House jargon. The more quickly you adapt, the better our service will be.

---

1. You are one of the newest members of the dining room staff at Metro Steak House. What does a customer who orders a **baker** at this restaurant want to eat?

    A.   french fries

    B.   a baked potato

    C.   a take-out potato

    D.   a slice of pie

    E.   cake for dessert

2. As a new member of the host staff, you are in charge of taking some orders. What type of food is ordered **on wheels**?

    F.   meals too heavy to carry on a tray

    G.   meals delivered by car

    H.   a take-out order

    J.   a children's meal order

    K.   quickly prepared meals

Pre-exam Dental Procedures

1. Remove instruments from the sterilizer. Place each in its appropriate drawer.

2. Sterilize any instruments not yet cleaned from the previous day.

3. Check that a sufficient amount of filling material is available for use that day. If there is not enough filling, be sure to get more from the supply room.

4. Make sure that the exam rooms are clean and neat. Put away anything that has been left out of its drawer.

5. Check that there are enough paper bibs for use that day for all patients. If there is not a sufficient amount, fill the bib box with additional bibs from the supply room.

6. Turn on all the lights in all the exam rooms to be sure they are all working properly.

---

3. As a dental hygienist, you are instructed to follow the list of procedures above before examining patients. What is an example of an **instrument** that you might remove from the sterilizer during the first task?

    A.   the dental chair

    B.   a dental mirror

    C.   a musical tape recording

    D.   patients' tooth molds

    E.   exam room light bulbs

4. Based on the passage, if you have a **sufficient** amount of a supply, then you have

    F.   too little of it.

    G.   the right amount of it.

    H.   far too much of it.

    J.   the wrong type.

    K.   an older version.

To: Marketing Services—All

From: Cristóbal Rivera

Subject: Executive Planning Committee Meeting Minutes

Dear Team:

Below are the notes from last week's Executive Planning Committee meeting. If you have any questions regarding this information, please feel free to ask me.

Regards,

Cris

* *

Meeting Minutes

Date: April 6

The meeting convened at 2:30 P.M.

Present: E. Blaine, president; R.S. Woolcott, vice president; V. Needham, chief financial officer; A. M. Turnbull, chief operations officer; L. Donovan, marketing director; N. O'Hara, creative director; Cristóbal Rivera, executive secretary

- V. Needham reviewed the costs and income for the last quarter. Profits were up 3%.

- M. Turnbull reported on the progress for the introduction of the new product line. The line will be ready by July to market; can begin to present to potential customers. When questioned by E. Blaine, Turnbull showed that the product can be manufactured within the cost limits previously discussed.

- L. Donovan presented a schedule of possible meetings with advertising to decide on the best roll-out for the new line.

The meeting adjourned at 3:12 P.M.

5. As a marketing assistant, you received a copy of the above meeting minutes. Based on its use above, what does the word **minutes** mean?

   A.   time

   B.   small

   C.   record

   D.   plan

   E.   discussion

6. What does the term **to market** mean in the above context?

   F.   to shop

   G.   a store

   H.   to buy

   J.   to manufacture

   K.   to distribute for sale

Replacing/Fixing a Faucet Fixture

Note: As each part of the existing faucet is removed, place it on a flat surface in the order in which it was removed.

- ☐ Be sure to turn off the water flowing to the sink.
- ☐ Remove the screws that secure the faucet to the sink. Carefully lift the faucet off the sink base and set aside.
- ☐ Look at the condition of the washers that seal the water line and the faucet. Replace cracked or damaged washers. Make sure the new washer is the same size and thickness. Often, washer replacement is enough to fix dripping faucets.
- ☐ If after replacing the faucet the drip persists, check the water line entering the faucet. Look for cracks in the line. Replace cracked lines where found.

7. You are a plumber that works for a kitchen specialty store. You must use the company checklist when replacing a faucet fixture. What does **seal** mean?

- A. a type of animal
- B. a type of screw
- C. to replace water lines
- D. to keep water out
- E. a replacement faucet

8. When the plumber replaces a **damaged** washer, in what condition is this part?

- F. broken
- G. new
- H. flowing
- J. thick
- K. dripping

Ticket Counter "Quik-List"

Quik-Air requires that all counter personnel follow these guidelines with each customer.

1. Always be friendly and polite to customers.

2. Determine the number of passengers in the party. Ask if they wish to be seated together.

3. Before issuing boarding passes, all passengers must present valid identification (e.g., driver's license, passport, other government-issued identification).

4. Every customer should be given our list of passenger guidelines. It is recommended that you explain the size limitations of bags you can carry aboard and bottles of liquid stored in those bags. If the customer seems unaware of these limitations, review the regulations regarding the types of objects that cannot be carried aboard an airplane.

9. You are an airline ticket counter agent. In step 2 of the checklist above, what does the word **party** mean?

    A. group

    B. event

    C. celebration

    D. organization

    E. political affiliation

10. What do the guidelines mean by **carry aboard** an airplane?

    F. children

    G. unruly behavior

    H. seat size

    J. take on the plane

    K. surcharge for excess luggage

Instruction Manual

Hand movers at our store handle boxes that are too small or contain products that are too fragile to be moved by machines. For this reason, it is important to plan carefully and use common sense when moving these materials from the receiving bay into the storeroom.

Hand movers use wheeled dollies to move stock. The first rule in piling boxes on a dolly is always to place the largest and heaviest boxes at the bottom. Then smaller and lighter boxes are placed on top. Always leave 2 inches of space beneath the handle so it can be grasped easily. Tilt the dolly back toward your body by placing one foot against the back of one wheel. Do not tilt the dolly at an angle greater than 45°. Slowly roll the dolly to its destination. Closely watch the boxes to make sure they remain in place.

11. You work as a hand mover in the storeroom of a large warehouse. What happens at the **receiving bay**?

    A.   Merchandise is paid for.

    B.   Boxes are packed.

    C.   Boxes are delivered and unloaded.

    D.   Machines remove large, heavy boxes.

    E.   Boxes are organized by size and weight.

12. To move stock, you have to use special equipment. What is a **dolly**?

    F.   a type of toy

    G.   a type of motorized cart

    H.   a type of delivery truck

    J.   a type of conveyor belt

    K.   a type of wheeled hand cart

Answers are on page 251.

Lesson 4 ▪ ▪ ▪
Follow a Series of Steps

Remember!

Numbered lists are not the only way in which a series of steps can be written. Bulleted lists are usually written in the order that the steps should be taken. Sometimes a series of steps isn't written as a list at all. For a series of steps that is written in paragraph form, words that signal sequence include *first, second, third, next, then, finally, following, before,* and *after*.

Skill: Choose when to perform each step in a short series of steps

When reading business documents, especially those that describe a procedure, it is important that you are able to follow the steps needed to correctly complete the task. The steps in a procedure are often numbered, and the numbers tell you the order in which the steps are performed. Sometimes, however, the steps in a procedure are shown as a bulleted list. In other cases, the steps may be described in order within a paragraph. Practicing how to identify the order of steps in a process or procedure will help you be effective in the workplace.

Skill Example

Follow a procedure when the steps are in a numbered list.

The procedure below describes how orders should be received on a receiving dock. If asked to describe what should be done before counting the items, you first go to step 4. Since this step involves counting the items, you can look to the previous steps to identify what must be done beforehand.

When working at the receiving dock:
1. Identify the company delivering the goods.
2. Enter the delivery date, time, and delivery person's name.
3. Instruct the delivery person to show or tell you the contents of each box.
4. Count the number of items in each box.
5. If the type and number of items matches the order, check off that item on the order form.

When a new patient comes to the office to see the doctor, the medical office assistant should follow the procedure below.
· Welcome the new patient.
· Inform the patient that he or she must fill out a patient information form.
· Ask the patient to bring the form to you when the form is completed.
· After the form has been returned, check to make sure every section is filled out completely.
· Ask the patient to show you his or her insurance card. Double-check the card against the form to make sure that the insurance is still current.

Skill Practice

Use the procedures document to the left to answer the following questions.

1. What does the medical office assistant do immediately after getting the form back from the new patient?
   A. Put away the pen and clipboard.
   B. Check the insurance card.
   C. Help fill out the form.
   D. Check that it is completed.
   E. Call the insurance company.

2. Why must the medical office assistant double-check the form against the insurance card?
   F. to make sure that the patient is still insured
   G. to know that the numbers were copied correctly
   H. to double-check the spelling of the patient's name
   J. to fill in the insurance part of the new patient form
   K. to make sure the insurance company will pay the doctor

Try It Out! ▪ ▪ ▪

You are an ophthalmic technician responsible for making prescription lenses for glasses. According to the checklist, in what situations must steps 3–5 be repeated?

A. when the lens grinder is not functioning

B. when the lensometer shows an incorrectly curved lens

C. when the prescription calls for bifocal lenses to be created

D. when the lensometer has not smoothed the lens sufficiently

E. when the lens does not fit the frames chosen by the patient

Step 1 Understand the Problem ▪ ▪ ▪

Complete the *Plan for Successful Solving.*

Plan for Successful Solving

What am I asked to do?	What are the facts?	How do I find the answer?	Is there any unnecessary information?	What prior knowledge will help me?
Identify when steps 3–5 must be repeated.	The steps are for making lenses. There are instances where steps 3–5 must be repeated.	The answer likely follows step 5. I should read steps 6 and 7 carefully to see if the answer is in these steps.	The steps before step 3 may not help determine when to repeat steps 3–5.	Directions that say to repeat certain steps are usually listed immediately before or after those steps.

Step 2 Find and Check Your Answer ▪ ▪ ▪

▪ Confirm your understanding of the question and revise your plan as needed.

▪ Based on your plan, determine your solution approach: *The steps are numbered and easy to follow. The question asks about repeating steps 3–5. This tells me that the answer is probably somewhere after step 5. Reading these steps carefully, I see that the information is in step 6, which tells the conditions under which steps 3–5 must be repeated. I'll select the option that best describes the information given in step 6.*

▪ Check your answer. Review all answers to determine if the answer you have selected is the best possible answer.

▪ **Select the correct answer:** B. when the lensometer shows an incorrectly curved lens

Step 6 explains that if the lens does not match the prescription, steps 3–5 must be repeated.

Lens Creation Checklist

1. Select "blank" glass or plastic lenses, as indicated on the prescription.

2. Mark the lenses to indicate where the required curves must be created, based on the prescription.

3. Place the lens in the lens grinder. Set the dials for the prescribed curves.

4. Start the lens grinder. Monitor the machine as it rotates the lens and creates the required curves on the lens.

5. Once the lens curve has been created, place the lens in the finishing machine for smoothing and polishing.

6. Check the lens in the lensometer to make sure it matches the prescription exactly. If it does not, recalibrate the curves and repeat steps 3–5.

7. If the lens matches the prescription, polish the edges and insert the lens into the glasses frame.

Problem Solving Tip

Look to see if the question refers to a particular step in the process, especially if the steps are numbered. Focusing on a particular step within the list will help you locate the correct answer. If the steps are not numbered or listed, look for key words in the question that may occur only in one or two steps of the process. The answer may be found in these steps.

Remember!

The steps in a procedure are often numbered, and the numbers tell you the order in which the steps are performed. Regardless of whether the steps of a procedure are numbered, they are typically written in sequential order.

Quicky Lube Oil and Auto Body
Oil Change Guidelines

1. With the car on the lift, locate the oil drain pan plug. Loosen the plug with a wrench.

2. Place a receptacle under the oil drain pan. Remove the plug.

   CAUTION: Be prepared for the rush of <u>hot</u> oil into the receptacle.

3. Let the oil drain completely. Wipe excess oil off the pan and plug. Replace the plug by hand to prevent damage to the threads. Tighten the plug with the wrench.

4. Locate the oil filter (usually on the side of the engine). Wipe the filter clean. If the filter shows too much oil or is clogged, mention this to the customer and explain why it should be replaced. Replace the oil filter <u>only</u> if the customer agrees to have this done.

5. With the car off the lift, open the auto's hood. Locate and remove the oil filler cap.

6. Place the funnel in the opening and add new oil. Most cars take between 4 and 5 quarts.

7. Replace the oil filler cap. Close the hood.

8. Start the car and let the engine run for one minute.

9. Shut off the engine, and use the dipstick to check the oil level. Add more oil if needed.

   NOTE: Dispose of the used oil into the recycled oil barrel.

---

1. As an auto repair technician at Quicky Lube, when must you take special safety precautions when changing oil?

   A. when driving the car on the lift

   B. when checking the oil filter

   C. when draining the hot oil

   D. when using the wrench to remove the plug

   E. when removing the oil filler cap

2. When you perform an oil change for a customer, at what point should you add additional new oil to the car, if necessary?

   F. when a new oil filter is installed

   G. after running the engine for a minute

   H. after removing the funnel from the filler

   J. when you wipe clean the oil filter

   K. after the plug is screwed back into place

Pie Crust (for 20–22 Pies)

Ingredients: 6 pounds of pastry flour

2 tablespoons salt

3 pounds solid vegetable shortening

$4\frac{1}{2}$ cups cool (not cold) water

- Mix flour and salt in a large stainless steel bowl. Make a well in the middle. Put the shortening in the well.
- Coat your hands with flour. Use your fingers to break up the shortening into tiny crumbs. Mix the pea-sized bits of shortening well throughout the flour.
- Pour half the cool water into the flour mixture. Form the mixture into a ball. Continue adding small amounts of water until the dough holds together. Do <u>not</u> knead the dough.
- Divide the dough into 10-ounce balls. Use the scale to get an accurate weight. Add or remove dough as needed for each ball. You should have 20–22 balls of dough.
- Place all the balls of dough on a tray, cover with plastic, and place in the refrigerator.
- When you are ready to make the pie crusts, flour the counter and the rolling pin. Roll out each ball of dough until it is round. Dough should be 4 inches larger than the 8- or 9-inch pie plate and less than $\frac{1}{4}$ inch thick.
- Place each rolled-out crust into a pie plate. Gently press the dough along the bottom and sides of the pie plate. Crimp the edges (if it's to be an open pie) and trim excess dough.

3. You are a commercial baker who is following the above recipe for making pie crust. At what point in the recipe should you add water?

    A.   after making the well

    B.   after weighing the balls of dough

    C.   before adding the shortening

    D.   after mixing the flour and shortening

    E.   before crumbling the shortening into bits

4. According to the recipe, when do you put flour on the counter?

    F.   when weighing the ingredients

    G.   before rolling out the dough

    H.   after trimming the edges of the pie crust

    J.   before adding the shortening

    K.   after the dough is kneaded

TO: Administrative Assistants

RE: Meeting Procedures

It is your job to make sure that department meetings are well organized and efficient. There are certain steps you should follow on the day of the meeting. (Steps 1 and 2 should be done the day before an early morning meeting.)

(1) Send an e-mail invitation to all employees who must attend the meeting. The e-mail should remind them that the meeting is taking place. It should state where and when the meeting is taking place and have a brief summary of the agenda.

(2) Prepare the conference room for the meeting.

(3) If the meeting is a video- or Web-based teleconference, make sure all needed equipment is present and in working order. Make final arrangements the day before the meeting is scheduled to make sure that the video and Internet connections are working.

(4) Make a list of everyone attending the meeting. If some employees have not arrived after 5 minutes, call their offices to remind them to come to the meeting.

(5) Finally, be available in case anyone needs you to bring supplies or information to the meeting.

5. You are an administrative assistant working for an accounting company. When do you call attendees to remind them about the meeting?

A. before the meeting starts

B. before you send them the e-mail

C. the day before the meeting takes place

D. when the teleconference begins

E. if they are late for the meeting

6. When do you make the final arrangements for a video- or Web-based teleconference?

F. the day before the meeting is scheduled

G. the day the meeting is scheduled

H. when you send the e-mail invitation

J. before you schedule the meeting

K. when you make a list of everyone attending

Attaching Limb Leads

If your EKG system uses three limb leads, place them in the order indicated below.

1. Place the black lead on the right shoulder and the white lead on the left shoulder, placing both where the shoulder connects to the torso.

2. Place the red lead on the upper thigh of the left leg.

After placing the limb leads, attach the chest leads, V1 to V6. Attach in the order indicated below.

1. Attach lead V1 immediately to the right of the sternum.

2. Attach lead V2 just to the left of the sternum.

3. Attach lead V4 along the mid-clavicle line.

4. Attach lead V3 midway between leads V2 and V4.

5. Attach lead V6 on the mid-axillary line, horizontal to lead V4.

6. Attach lead V5 midway between V4 and V6.

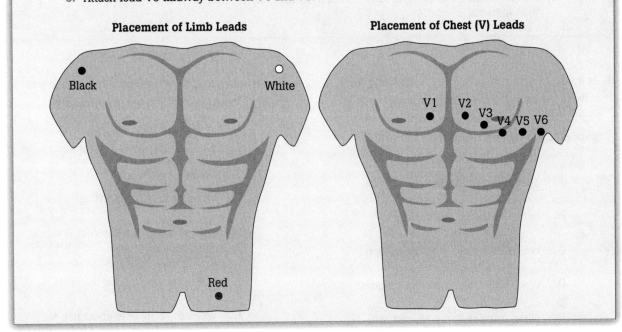

Placement of Limb Leads

Placement of Chest (V) Leads

7. You work as an electrocardiogram (EKG) technician at a local hospital. According to the list of steps above, which limb lead should you place on the body last?

    A.   lead V4

    B.   lead V6

    C.   black lead

    D.   white lead

    E.   red lead

8. Which lead should you place on the chest after placing lead V6?

    F.   lead V2

    G.   lead V3

    H.   lead V4

    J.   lead V5

    K.   lead V7

Standard Blow-in Insulation Procedures

1. Remove objects and dirt that may interfere with the process.

2. Place an attic ruler in each quadrant to be insulated. The rulers will ensure that the correct depth of insulation is added.

3. Fill the blowing machine hopper with insulating foam. Check the hopper frequently, as foam flows best when the hopper is more than half full. Add foam as needed.

4. Hold the hose parallel to the floor, with the foam falling about 1 foot away. Begin at the far wall and work your way toward the center. Always blow the foam in the direction of the joists. Walk carefully, balancing on the joists.

5. Apply the foam with a back-and-forth motion.

6. Keep the hose close to the floor when blowing the insulation under cross beams, wiring, and other obstructions.

7. Check the thickness of the insulation. Fill in all spots where insulation has less depth than it should.

9. As a home insulation specialist, you are using blow-in insulation to insulate a residential attic. Based on the instructions above, when do you place attic rulers in each quadrant of the attic?

A. after filling the hopper

B. before removing obstructions

C. before beginning to add insulation

D. when insulating under cross beams

E. when calculating the amount of insulation used

10. According to the instructions, when should you blow insulation into the center of the attic?

F. after insulating the far walls and corners

G. when hosing under wiring

H. after checking the depth of the insulation

J. once you can walk on the joists

K. when the hopper is about half full

Procedures for Electrical Systems Check

- Set the breaker on the tower to the "off" position.

- Use the multimeter to make sure that the surge-arrestor is working.

- Check the conductors on the building breaker box to make sure it is not activated.

- Disconnect the input lines on the building breaker box.

- Short three wires together on the building breaker, using a wire nut. Then insulate with electrical tape.

- Turn the tower breaker to the "on" position.

- Make sure the turbine starts within 60 seconds after turning the breaker on.

11. You are a wind turbine maintenance technician. Part of your job is to check the electrical system of the wind turbines. What do you do before checking that the building breaker box is not activated?

   A. Disconnect the box's input lines.

   B. Turn off the breaker on the tower.

   C. Connect wires with electrical tape.

   D. Wait 60 seconds for the turbine to start.

   E. Turn the tower breaker on.

12. What must be working properly before the maintenance procedure can continue?

   F. The tower breaker must be on.

   G. The input lines must be connected to the box.

   H. All electrical wires must be insulated.

   J. The surge-arrestor must be functioning.

   K. The conductors must be deactivated.

Answers are on page 251.

Lesson 5 ∎ ∎ ∎
Apply Instructions to a Situation

Remember!

"If-then" statements provide clues that there are different next steps depending on what occurs in a previous step. (Example: Check the oil levels. If the oil level is lower than 3 quarts, then add more oil.) As you can see in Skill Example 2, the word then does not always appear in "if-then" statements.

Skill: Apply instructions to a situation that is the same as the one in the reading materials

When workplace documents provide instructions for a procedure, it is expected that you will be able to learn the procedure and follow it when needed. For example, many businesses have a procedure that explains what to do during a fire drill. When a fire drill occurs, you are expected to follow that procedure.

Skill Examples

Example 1
Understand how to apply instructions to a situation that is the same as the situation in the reading passage.

> When the store has advertised a sale, display the biggest sale items up front, near the door. This will lure customers into the store. Set up other displays further into the store. This will encourage shoppers to walk through the store and view other nonsale items they might decide to buy. All sale item displays should be clearly flagged.

The instructions describe how items should be displayed when a sale has been advertised. Details are given to indicate where the biggest sale items are to be placed, as well as other sale items that have been advertised.

Example 2
Understand how to apply instructions to a situation that is conditional.

> When account clerks get a bill from a supplier, they must first check it against the order to see that it lists the correct number of items ordered. If it does not match the order, you must alert the supervisor. Confirm that the correct amount is listed on the bill and write a check for that amount. Staple the bill to the company order. Clip the check on top of both.

This passage describes the process an accounts payable clerk follows in paying a bill. Within the passage, directions are given for what should be done when the items or charges on the bill do not match the order. This helps you understand what to do when that specific condition arises.

Emergency Fire Procedures

It is extremely important to understand what to do and where to go in the event of a fire. That is why the city fire department requires us to have two fire drills every year. If you hear the fire alarm go off, immediately stop working. Calmly walk out of the office into the corridor. Locate the nearest exit. Never take an elevator!

Open the exit door and walk down the stairs until you reach the ground floor. Allow other workers from lower floors to enter the stairwell with you, but try to keep moving. Walk quickly but calmly.

When you reach the ground floor, leave the building through the exit. Walk calmly away from the building and await further instructions.

Skill Practice

Use the procedures document to the left to answer the following questions.

1. The fire alarm starts to ring. You must get out of the building as quickly as possible. What is the best way to leave the building?

    A. through the fire department

    B. through the corridors and stairs

    C. in the elevator

    D. on the escalator

    E. on the fire escape

2. What should you do if the stairwell gets crowded with other building employees?

    F. take different stairs down

    G. take the elevator down

    H. tell them to find a different stairwell

    J. allow them in while you keep moving

    K. go back to your office because it is only a drill

Try It Out! ■ ■ ■

You are a bench worker who makes pieces for a large jeweler. You and your family plan to take a two-week vacation in August. When is the latest you should request time off from your office manager?

A. in January

B. in March

C. in May

D. in June

E. in July

From: Human Resources   Date: September 22

To: All Employees

Subject: Vacation Procedures Reminder

Every full-time employee gets two weeks paid vacation. The company must have enough staff working at all times. Therefore, vacations must be scheduled in advance. The office manager must approve all vacations.

Management asks that vacation time be requested at least two months in advance. Please check with your department manager before handing in a request. Your manager will check to see that the time you are requesting has not already been given to someone else. The office manager will make every effort to approve your vacation request. Be advised that you should not make definite plans until you get written approval from the office manager.

Step 1 — Understand the Problem ■ ■ ■

Complete the *Plan for Successful Solving.*

Plan for Successful Solving

What am I asked to do?	What are the facts?	How do I find the answer?	Is there any unnecessary information?	What prior knowledge will help me?
Identify the latest date by which I should schedule an August vacation.	The e-mail describes the procedure for requesting a vacation.	I should focus on paragraph 2, which describes the procedure for scheduling a vacation.	The first paragraph does not give any specific procedures.	In the past, I have had to ask management before I could take time off.

Step 2 — Find and Check Your Answer ■ ■ ■

- Confirm your understanding of the question and revise your plan as needed.

- Based on your plan, write your solution approach: *The question asks what the latest acceptable time is for requesting an August vacation. The procedure for asking for a vacation is described in paragraph 2. It states that the company wants at least two months' notice for scheduling a vacation. That means June is the latest time to request an August vacation. I will select the option that names or is closest to June.*

- Check your answer. Review all answers to determine if the answer you have selected is the best possible answer.

- **Select the correct answer:** D. in June

  June is two months before August, which means June is the latest time to inform management that you want to take an August vacation.

Problem Solving Tip

Read the question carefully to determine what situation is being referred to. Find the paragraph that has information closely related to what you need. Read the procedure that applies to the situation described in the question. Then identify and choose the option that matches that procedure.

Remember!

Signal words and phrases can help you recognize unique situations. For example, *"if-then"* statements indicate that there are different next steps or additional steps, depending on what occurs in a previous step.

On Your Own ▪ ▪ ▪

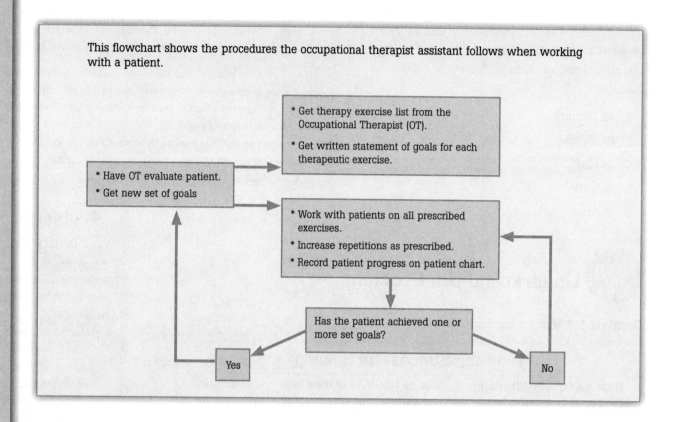

This flowchart shows the procedures the occupational therapist assistant follows when working with a patient.

* Get therapy exercise list from the Occupational Therapist (OT).

* Get written statement of goals for each therapeutic exercise.

* Have OT evaluate patient.
* Get new set of goals

* Work with patients on all prescribed exercises.
* Increase repetitions as prescribed.
* Record patient progress on patient chart.

Has the patient achieved one or more set goals?

Yes

No

1. You are an occupational therapist assistant who has been working with a patient for over a month. At what point should you consult with the OT to get new goals for the patient?

   A. when therapy begins

   B. when the patient has achieved at least one set goal

   C. when the patient has not achieved the set goals

   D. when no more repetitions can be added

   E. when every goal has been met by the patient

2. After a review of a patient's progress, it is determined that he has not achieved any of the originally set goals. As the occupational therapist assistant, what should you do next?

   F. lower his number of exercise repetitions

   G. set new goals for him

   H. continue working on his prescribed goals

   J. provide a different exercise list

   K. change the exercises based on your own evaluation

Combined Sewer Overflows (CSOs)

During combined sewer overflows (CSOs), storms and rainfall add huge amounts of water to the sewer system. This can overwhelm the facility. Conditions may get dangerous as water levels rise. Therefore, all workers should be especially careful when working during a CSO. As a CSO develops, workers should first put on safety clothes. They must keep safety equipment on them until the CSO ends.

The manager will decide how to handle the CSO to avoid contaminated spills. The emergency overflow tanks will be opened and put into operation. Once they are full, overflow water will be channeled into holding tanks. Technicians will open the holding tanks upon orders from the manager. The goal is to prevent spillage of untreated water into waterways.

Only after the facility's tanks are full will technicians begin the process of testing the water for contaminants. All test results must be reported to the manager. The manager will determine what steps are necessary to decontaminate the water in each holding tank. Only then can the water be discharged.

3. You work as a technician at a wastewater treatment facility. According to the instructions above, to what part of the facility should you channel the excess water at the start of a CSO?

    A.   to a waterway

    B.   to a treatment tank

    C.   to a sewer overflow

    D.   to an emergency overflow tank

    E.   to a spillage treatment facility

4. Based on the above instructions, when should you begin to test the water for contaminants?

    F.   when the storm first arrives

    G.   when the water begins to overflow

    H.   when all the facility tanks are full

    J.   when the supervisor gives the order

    K.   when the storm passes and the rain stops

MEMO

TO: All Photogrammetry Technicians

RE: Wildfires

All photogrammetry technicians (PT) must be ready to work as soon as a wildfire alert is reported. They must have all equipment necessary to work until the wildfire is brought under control. The PT will work long hours in the plane. She or he will assist the photogrammatist in taking images of the fire.

The PT will also take images of surrounding areas. The most important images to take are those that show the extent of the fire. The PT must then help take images of the buildings that are possibly in the line of the moving wildfire. These images should be downloaded to headquarters as soon as they are shot. They will be used to determine which residents have to be evacuated to avoid loss of life.

Once these images are sent, the PT should send images of the vegetation surrounding the wildfire. These images help the scientists determine which vegetation will feed the flames and expand the wildfire. Finally, images of soil moisture in areas farther from the site of the fire may be taken. This should be performed only if headquarters requests it.

5. As a photogrammetry technician (PT) working for the U.S. Department of Labor, what are the first and most important images that you help take during a wildfire?

A. the extent of the fire

B. the location of homes near the fire

C. the areas of burned vegetation

D. the rate at which the fire is moving

E. the effect of soil moisture on the fire

6. What image type has the lowest priority in wildfire imaging and will likely be taken only upon request?

F. the extent of vegetation

G. the amount of moisture in the soil

H. buildings potentially endangered by the fire

J. evacuation routes for citizens in the fire zone

K. buildings already burned down by the wildfire

Employee Handbook

One of your most important jobs is to schedule appointments. When a patient calls for an appointment, pull up the patient's chart on the computer. Ask the patient why he or she needs to see the doctor. The patient may have a new problem that is not on the chart. This will affect how long the appointment will take. In most cases, general follow-up visits should be scheduled every 15 minutes. General exams should be scheduled for half-hour appointments. Try to schedule appointments so the doctor always has patients. Do not cancel regular appointments for emergency appointments.

7. You are a medical office administrator for a local family clinic. A patient has just called to try to schedule an appointment. What is the first thing you should do?

    A.   ask if they need a physical exam

    B.   fit them into an open 15-minute slot

    C.   check their medical chart on the computer

    D.   ask if they can come in toward the end of the day

    E.   find out if it is an emergency or a follow-up visit

8. When setting up the doctor's schedule, what is an important thing to avoid?

    F.   cancellations

    G.   too many physical exams

    H.   agreeing to see many new patients

    J.   gaps in the appointment schedule

    K.   leaving too little time for emergencies

Breakdown Procedure

In the event that your vehicle breaks down or can no longer be operated safely, there are several things you should do. First, you should contact the central office immediately. Tell them about the problem. Central office will tell you what options are best for you to follow. If the repair is minor, you may be asked to contact a nearby mechanic. If this is not possible, contact central office to find out if there is an available truck near your location. A new truck may be able to transport the load.

Our company has dispatch hubs in many parts of the country. If there is one near you, they should be able to handle your situation. If a nearby hub has an available truck, contact them. They will arrange to have the load transferred to their truck. If you are licensed for use of the truck that is available, you will haul the load to its destination in their vehicle. If you are not licensed to drive their vehicle, central office will arrange for a new driver. You may then await instructions for returning to your dispatch site.

9. You are a truck driver working for a transportation company. Under what conditions would you seek a new truck?

    A.   if central office cannot be contacted

    B.   if you are unable to contact a nearby mechanic

    C.   if the repair will take a long time

    D.   if there is no dispatching hub nearby

    E.   if you are unlicensed

10. In the event that your truck breaks down, when would you be expected to continue to the final destination?

    F.   when there is no local mechanic

    G.   when there is no local hub

    H.   when the load is put on a new truck

    J.   when returning to your region

    K.   when a major repair on the truck is completed

Weather-related Rules

Most geothermal energy system installations take place outdoors. The company has guidelines to ensure the safety of our outdoor workers. These rules do not apply to days when it is snowing.

In the event of a severe thunderstorm with nearby lightning, all workers are to take shelter in the company's on-site trailer. No worker should be out of doors until the lightning danger has passed.

When it is extremely hot, workers must carry cold water. When the outdoor temperature is over 90°F, workers should drink one cup of cold water an hour. Workers are permitted to take a few minutes to refill their thermos from the water cooler in the trailer. In temperatures exceeding 95°F, workers must take a 10-minute break every hour. This break must be taken in the air-conditioned trailer.

Even with these breaks, workers may start to feel sick or lightheaded while working in very hot weather. If this occurs, they should stop work immediately and go into the trailer to cool off.

11. As part of your work as a geothermal construction worker, you are installing an energy system for a private residence. This morning your supervisor reviewed the company's weather-related rules in anticipation of today's expected weather. According to the above document, for which of the following situations do these rules not apply?

    A. when it is snowing outside

    B. when a thunderstorm strikes

    C. when the temperature is above 95°F

    D. when a worker is feeling lightheaded

    E. when lightning is nearby

12. Today's forecast indicates that the temperature is expected to reach 98°F. How long should each of your outdoor work periods be?

    F. 40 minutes

    G. 50 minutes

    H. 60 minutes

    J. 90 minutes

    K. 120 minutes

Answers are on page 251.

Level 3 Performance Assessment

The following problems will test your ability to answer questions at a Level 3 rating of difficulty. These problems are similar to those that appear on a Career Readiness Certificate test. For each question, you can refer to the answer key for answer justifications. The answer justifications provide an explanation of why each answer option is either correct or incorrect and indicate the skill lesson that should be referred to if further review of a particular skill is needed.

Treating Student Injuries

Most students who visit the school nurse have mild cuts or bruises from falls. Some may have minor injuries from classroom accidents. When treating a cut, stop the bleeding by applying pressure with a clean cotton pad. Then clean the wound with an antiseptic to kill any germs in the cut. Cover the cut with a sterile plastic strip.

Any child brought in with a head injury must be examined immediately. Treat cuts and bruises to the head. Then examine the child's eyes by shining a light into the pupil. If the pupil does not get larger, or dilate, when the light is removed, the child may have a brain injury. The child should be sent to the hospital immediately. Hospitalization is also recommended if the child has a concussion. Double-vision and confusion are symptoms of a concussion.

1. You are the nurse's assistant at a new school. You have been asked to review the employee handbook in order to learn proper procedures. What is the meaning of the word **antiseptic**?

   A. pain killer

   B. germ killer

   C. light

   D. cotton pad

   E. sterile plastic

2. It is important to follow certain steps when a child is brought in for a head injury. What is the meaning of the word **dilate**?

   F. double-vision

   G. concussion

   H. get larger

   J. eye movement

   K. brain injury

Office Supplies Unlimited, Inc.

Date: July 13

Purchase Order: 44281909

INVOICE

Item Number	Description	Quantity	Unit Cost	Total
04677	Lined writing pads (pkg. 12)	10	$8.00	$80.00
15448	Copy paper (10 ream box)	5	46.00	230.00
61119	Dry erase board (36 x 48)	1	38.00	38.00
30021	Dry erase markers, black (box of 10)	2	11.00	22.00
00532	Dry erase erasers (box of 6)	1	5.00	5.00
		Amount Due:		**$375.00**

Please write PO number on your check.

Remit to: Accounts Payable
16 Lowery St.
Danvers, MI 72418

Thank you for your order!

---

3. As an administrative assistant, you are in charge of ordering supplies for your office. You send in an order and receive an invoice from the supply company. What is an **invoice**?

A. a bill

B. a list

C. an amount

D. a purchase

E. an account

4. The supplies company provides you with an address for the Accounts Payable department. Based on the form's information, what does **remit** mean?

F. to owe

G. to remember

H. to bill

J. to pay

K. to order

Planting Bushes and Shrubs

If the bush or shrub you are planting is bare root, soak the roots in water for at least 45 minutes before planting. While the roots are soaking, begin preparing the planting site.

Measure the length and width of the roots. Use a pointed shovel to dig a hole deep enough to hold all the roots in such a way that they are not compressed or folded. The hole should be dug to a depth at which, when filled in, the base of the stem is at the soil line. Dig the hole at least twice as wide as the root system. Remove all large rocks from the dug soil. Place the shovels of soil to the side of the hole.

Mix in organic humus fertilizer at a ratio of 4:1, soil to fertilizer. Mix thoroughly with the soil. Carefully place the shrub or bush into the hole. Spread the roots. If the plant came in a pot, gently remove it by pressing all around the pot. Hold the pot at an angle while you gently shake the plant out of the pot. If the plant is root-bound, carefully use your hands to loosen the soil around the roots. Then spread the most external roots out around the plant.

Place the plant into the hole. Keep it in an upright position as you shovel the soil mixture back into the hole. As each layer of soil is added, use your hands to tamp down the soil. Gaps in the soil will let in air that may harm the plant. Fill the hole until the soil is level with the surrounding soil. The plant should be upright and held solidly by the soil. Water the newly planted shrub thoroughly, for several minutes.

5. As a landscaper working at a state park, how do you prepare a bare root shrub before planting?

    A. You fertilize it.

    B. You soak its roots.

    C. You compress the roots.

    D. You make sure it is upright.

    E. You remove it from its pot.

6. You dig a hole for a new shrub, and are ready to place it into the hole. What should you do if the plant is root-bound?

    F. Water the shrub for several minutes.

    G. Use your hands to tamp down the soil.

    H. Spread out the external roots around the plant.

    J. Remove all large rocks from the soil.

    K. Place shovels of soil to the side of the hole.

Taking an X-Ray

1. Explain the procedure to the patient. Make sure the patient removes all jewelry and other articles that the x-rays cannot pass through.

2. Position the patient on the x-ray table so that the part of the body that needs to be imaged is facing the x-ray apparatus.

3. Lay protective matting over the areas of the patient's body that are not being x-rayed. Leave the part to be imaged exposed.

4. Position the x-ray machine over the part of the body to be imaged. Place the apparatus at the correct height and angle over the body.

5. Use the tape to measure the thickness of the part of the body to be x-rayed. Adjust the controls on the x-ray machine to produce images having the correct density, detail, and contrast.

6. Place the x-ray film under the exposed part of the body to be imaged.

7. Go into the control room, close the door, and activate the control that takes the x-ray image.

8. Remove and develop the film. When it is done, take it to the radiologist.

---

7. As an x-ray technician, what do you do immediately after positioning the patient on the x-ray table?

A. Put film under the body.

B. Put patient jewelry in a safe place.

C. Put protective mats on areas of the body not being x-rayed.

D. Expose the body part to the rays from the x-ray.

E. Make sure the x-ray machine is at an angle.

8. Where are you, as a technician, when the actual x-ray is taken?

F. in a control room

G. with the radiologist

H. adjusting the x-ray controls

J. measuring for density and detail

K. in a darkroom developing x-ray film

Employee Handbook

As a new water quality technician, you will work with a supervisor. Please review the following information about your job.

The technician makes sure that the city's water supply meets set standards for water quality. Technicians are required to test drinking water to make sure it meets these minimum standards of quality. Additionally, all water discharged into bodies of water must be tested to make sure that it meets these standards. Any pollutant that exceeds these standards must be removed from the water.

The water quality technician spends most of his or her time on the job testing water for contaminants and making sure it is clean enough to meet legal standards. Technicians test water at drinking water facilities, wastewater treatment facilities, or at factories.

9. You are a water quality technician, working for a large city. What is the main idea of this passage?

    A. Water discharged into bodies of water must be tested.

    B. Water quality technicians test if water meets standards.

    C. Drinking water must meet contaminants levels.

    D. Pollutants that exceed standards must be removed.

    E. New water quality technicians will work with supervisors.

10. What is a detail that supports the idea that a technician is responsible for checking the quality of the water?

    F. Drinking water must be tested to meet legal standards.

    G. Technicians test water at many factories.

    H. Technicians spend most of their time on the job.

    J. Drinking water must not contain contaminants.

    K. Supervisors work with water quality technicians.

From: Administrative Assistant   **Date:** November 21

    To: All Employees

Subject: Holiday Party

The annual company holiday party will be held on Thursday, December 22 at 2:30 P.M. The party will take place in the company reception room on the 10th floor. As with last year's party, I will be serving as the coordinator responsible for organizing the planning committee.

The planning committee is looking for volunteers to help us get the room ready for the party. We need folks to hang decorations, arrange seating, and so on. We have already hired a caterer who will cook the food, bring it to the reception room, and serve both food and beverages during the party. We have not placed our order yet, so if there's anything you'd like to have at the party, let me know. Also, if you have any ideas regarding music or anything else that will add to the fun, let me know.

Hope to see you all there!

---

11. As an administrative assistant, you are in charge of informing employees about the annual company party. What is the meaning of the word **caterer**?

    A. party planner

    B. restaurant

    C. musician or a band

    D. cooking and serving business

    E. an organization of volunteers

12. You send an e-mail to all employees and announce that you will be in charge of the holiday party committee. What is the meaning of the word **coordinator**?

    F. volunteer

    G. administrator

    H. organizer

    J. receptionist

    K. office monitor

Removing Asbestos

A. Asbestos is extremely hazardous if inhaled. All workers must wear protective suits and masks at all times.

B. In residential asbestos removal, use the vacuum approved for asbestos removal to suck the material out of the walls. The asbestos vacuum has a specially designed trap for asbestos and has highly efficient filters to prevent the leakage or escape of the material.

C. Monitor the gauge on the vacuum. When the inner trap container is almost full, adjust the controls to lock the container. Remove the container and replace it with a new one.

D. Throughout the procedure, consult the air-quality monitor frequently to make sure that asbestos is not becoming airborne, which may be inhaled and damage the lungs.

E. All asbestos containers and other receptacles must be placed in the large, sealed, hazardous waste containers at the site.

F. After the asbestos is cleared, use the vacuum to gather in any remaining particles in the area. Every part of the room and the site from which asbestos was removed must be vacuumed clean after the removal procedure.

13. As a hazardous materials removal technician you are responsible for removing asbestos from a residential building. According to the instructions, what must you do before removing a full container from the vacuum?

A. Use the controls to lock the container.

B. Empty the vacuum's trap.

C. Monitor the amount of airborne asbestos.

D. Seal the vacuum and place it in a waste container.

E. Change the filter on the container.

14. According to the steps listed above, what should be done after the vacuum containers are placed in the sealed hazardous waste container?

F. Put clothing and mask into the waste container.

G. Check to see if there is any airborne asbestos.

H. Vacuum the entire area to remove all asbestos particles.

J. Open the vacuum trap to monitor its level of asbestos.

K. Change the filter on the trap in the vacuum container.

Horizon Surveying Company

Welcome to the project! As one of our surveyor technicians, you will carry out measurements, fieldwork, and other tasks. The surveyor at your job site will supervise your work. You may be assigned to different projects. For example, you might be asked to define property boundaries when people buy land. You might also be assigned to mapping and measuring land for renewable energy projects. These include installations at sites where wind turbines will be set up. Your supervising surveyor will decide what measurements need to be taken on a job. Then you will go into the field to take the measurements and make the map. You will use the tools your supervisor recommends for the job. Tools include laser measuring equipment, three-dimensional laser scanners, steel tapes, and angle measuring equipment. GPS (global positioning system) software is also used.

15. You are a surveyor technician working at an installation site for wind turbines. What is the main idea of this passage?

   A. Surveying is used in fieldwork.

   B. Most surveyors work outdoors.

   C. Surveying involves taking land measurements.

   D. Lasers are the most accurate surveying tools.

   E. Renewable energy often involves land disputes.

16. What is a detail in the orientation document that supports the idea that special software helps technicians work?

   F. All surveyor technicians use laser tools.

   G. Surveyor technicians may use GPS in the field.

   H. Only supervisors are able to use surveying software.

   J. Maps are used to generate land measurements.

   K. Most land is bounded by angles, not straight lines.

Job Description: Head Chef

The head chef determines the evening's menu. The head chef also provides the cooks with the recipes for each dish on the menu. The chef orders the food that is necessary to prepare all the dishes on the menu. When the food is brought into the kitchen, the head chef will tell the cooks how to store each item. The chef will have cooks begin to prepare those food items that can be readied hours in advance. The head chef may also inspect utensils and pots and pans to make sure they are clean. Cooks follow the chef's recipes to make each dish. The head chef usually monitors the cooks' work to make sure the food is prepared properly. Sometimes, the head chef will prepare a dish that is her or his specialty.

17. You have just started working at a new restaurant as head chef and are reviewing your job description. When providing cooks with **recipes** for your menu, what information do you, as head chef, include?

  A. a list of food ingredients

  B. a list of dishes being served that night

  C. the types of food ordered for that night's meals

  D. a description of the desserts

  E. a list of the tasks to be completed before dinner is served

18. As a head chef, when you prepare your specialty dish, what is a **utensil** that might be used on the job?

  F. soup bowl

  G. pie plate

  H. fresh fish

  J. sharp knife

  K. refrigerator containers

Answers are on page 251.

Level 4 Introduction ...

The lesson and practice pages that follow will give you the opportunity to develop and practice the comprehension skills needed to answer work-related questions at a Level 4 rating of difficulty. The *On Your Own* practice problems provide a review of key reading skills along with instruction and practice applying these skills through effective problem-solving strategies. The *Performance Assessment* provides problems similar to those you will encounter on a Career Readiness Certificate test. By completing the Level 4 *On Your Own* and *Performance Assessment* questions, you will gain the ability to confidently approach workplace scenarios that require understanding and application of the reading skills featured in the following lessons:

Lesson 6: Identify Important Details

Lesson 7: Determine Word Meanings from Reading Material

Lesson 8: Apply Multi-Step Instructions

Lesson 9: Choose the Correct Action When Conditions Change

These skills are intended to help you successfully read and understand workplace documents such as procedures, policies, bulletins, and other publications. Such documents are usually straightforward, but sometimes contain longer sentences that include many details. Reading these types of documents often requires the ability to:

- identify details that support the main point,
- understand unfamiliar words that are not defined,
- understand procedures that include several steps,
- paraphrase, or restate, text from the document,
- make decisions based on different conditions.

Through answering document-related questions at this level, you will continue to develop problem-solving approaches and strategies that will help you determine the correct answer in real-world and test-taking situations.

Level 4
Introduction

Lesson 6 ■ ■ ■
Identify Important Details

Skill: Identify important details that may not be clearly stated

Remember!

Recognizing the main idea will help you identify details that support it. The main idea of a document should state the reason why the document is important. The main idea of a longer document usually appears in the first paragraph. In a well-written document, the body paragraphs support and clarify the main idea.

The main idea of a paragraph is usually stated in the first sentence. The sentences that follow should provide details that clarify or explain the main idea of the paragraph.

When reading workplace documents, you may sometimes find that not all important details are clearly stated. Details are often implied, or suggested, because it is assumed that the reader will understand a detail without it being clearly stated. For instance, suppose you weren't sure if you locked your front door. You might ask someone with you to check to be sure that the door is locked. By asking them to do so, you are also likely implying that if the door is not locked, you would like them to lock it.

Skill Examples

Example 1
Identify details in the passage by determining the main idea.

NOTICE
The company does not permit cell phone use in the cafeteria. Additionally, cell phones should be in silent mode at all times within the building during work hours.

Determining the main idea will help you to identify all of the supporting details, even those that may not be clearly stated. The first place to look for a main idea is at the beginning of a passage. The first sentence states the main idea regarding cell phone use in the cafeteria.

Example 2
Identify details that are not clearly stated.

MEMO
To: Support staff
RE: Obtaining supplies
Office supplies are in the closet on the third floor. You may get supplies such as pens, staples, and other supplies used at your desk from the closet.

As you read the details, you see that pens and staples are listed. Although pencils and paperclips are not part of the list, you know they are common desk supplies and are likely to be in the third floor closet.

Lock-Up Procedure

If you are the last employee out of the office, make sure that all machines in the copy room are turned off. In the break room, check to see that the coffee maker is not still turned on. Turn off the fan and all lights in the break room, but leave on the overhead light in the entrance hall. Set the alarm by the front door and leave immediately. Pull the door closed behind you, and use your key to lock the deadbolt.

Skill Practice

Use the document to the left to answer the following questions.

1. What is the main idea in this passage?
   A. Do not be the last one out of the office.
   B. Before you leave, turn down the thermostat.
   C. How to shut down the office if you are the last to leave.
   D. Preventing theft is important.
   E. Wasting energy costs money.

2. What must you do with the coffee maker in the break room if it is turned on?
   F. Be sure the red light is on.
   G. Turn it off.
   H. Wash the pot and put it away.
   J. Leave a note.
   K. Prepare the coffee for the next morning.

Try It Out!

You are on the maintenance staff of a college dormitory. As part of your job, you must inspect the laundry room on each floor of the building. According to the memo, which of the following should you do if a problem is reported with a dryer?

A. Mop the floor before you leave.

B. Check for broken hoses.

C. Repair broken machines, but only on Wednesday.

D. Report the problem to a user.

E. Remove lint from the lint traps.

Memo

To: Maintenance Staff
From: Director of Residential Services
Re: Procedure for inspecting laundry facilities

Maintenance staff must report all problems to the main office. Inspections must be completed on Tuesday.

The problem log is on the bulletin board. If a user reports a problem with a washing machine, run a test cycle on it. Unplug all washers with problems and post out-of-order signs as needed.

Before running a test cycle on a dryer, check to see that the lint trap is clean. Run a test cycle on the highest heat setting and the lowest. Unplug machines that do not heat properly and post signs as needed. Repair experts will be on campus on Wednesdays.

Step 1 Understand the Problem

Complete the *Plan for Successful Solving.*

Plan for Successful Solving				
What am I asked to do?	**What are the facts?**	**How do I find the answer?**	**Is there any unnecessary information?**	**What prior knowledge will help me?**
Identify what should be done if a problem is reported with a dryer.	Problems with washers and dryers must be reported. There are certain steps to take before reporting.	Look for where within the memo dryers are discussed.	Reports are due on Tuesday. The machines will be repaired on Wednesdays.	A lint trap should always be cleared of lint before a dryer is operated.

Step 2 Find and Check Your Answer

- Confirm your understanding of the question and revise your plan as needed.

- Based on your plan, determine your solution approach: *The memo is about how to inspect the laundry facilities. The details of the memo tell how to do that. Although the memo says to check the lint trap, it does not clearly state that lint should be removed. I know that you are supposed to clean the lint trap after each dryer use. Therefore, it is likely that the lint trap should be cleaned before running a test cycle when a problem has been reported.*

- Check your answer. Review all answers to determine if the answer you have selected is the best possible answer.

- **Select the correct answer:** E. Remove lint from the lint traps.
  Even though the memo does not clearly state that lint should be removed from the lint trap, cleaning the trap is likely part of the expected procedure.

Problem Solving Tip

Using prior knowledge can help you understand details that are not clearly stated. In the *Try It Out!* example, it is implied that the lint trap should be cleared of lint every time a dryer is used. Knowing this helps you understand that when inspecting a dryer, if the lint trap is not clean, it should be cleaned before running a test cycle.

Remember!

Details are often implied when it is assumed that the reader understands them without being directly told. When reading workplace documents, knowing this will help you better understand the information that is being communicated.

Sunnie's Café

HOW TO MAKE SUNNIE'S FRUIT SALAD

You will find the fruit for today's salad on the counter beside the refrigerator. Before beginning to put the salad together, wash all fruit.

Peel and section two oranges. Next, peel and slice two kiwi fruit, three bananas, and three peaches (make sure that pits are removed). Put fruit into large mixing bowl. Add one cup of seedless grapes, one pint of strawberries, and one pint of blueberries. Mix fruit thoroughly. Sprinkle with one cup of flaked coconut.

Fill two glass bowls with the mixture. Place a bowl on each end of the buffet. Store all reserve fruit salad until needed.

---

1. Which of the sentences from the instructions on how to make Sunnie's fruit salad tells you that you can expect to make more salad than will fit into two glass bowls?

   A. Before beginning to put the salad together, wash all fruit.

   B. Sprinkle with one cup of flaked coconut.

   C. Mix fruit thoroughly.

   D. Store all reserve fruit salad until needed.

   E. Put fruit into large mixing bowl.

2. Based on your prior knowledge of how food should be stored, where should the reserve fruit salad be stored?

   F. on the counter

   G. in the sink

   H. next to the buffet

   J. in the refrigerator

   K. next to the refrigerator

Golden Cabs

MEMO

To: All dispatchers

Subject: Required information for pickup requests

Dispatchers should get the following information from each person requesting a pickup:

- **Pickup:** Ask for the town and street address, including the number. If there is no building number, ask for the nearest cross street.

- **Phone number:** Ask the customer for a phone number where he or she can be reached.

- **Destination:** Ask for the town and street.

- **Time:** Ask when the customer would like to be picked up. If the caller asks for immediate pickup, tell him or her what the wait time is.

While it is important to take calls as quickly as possible, it is more important to get the correct information.

---

3. You are a dispatcher for Golden Cabs. A customer calls to arrange a pickup. She tells you that she needs to be picked up in 30 minutes to go to the airport. Her pickup location is at 15 North Washington in the town of Greenview. According to the memo, what additional information do you need to get from the caller?

   A. the name of the nearest cross street

   B. a phone number where she can be reached

   C. the town in which she lives

   D. her name

   E. an approximate wait time

4. What sentence tells the dispatcher to be prepared for callers who might not have a specific street address?

   F. Ask when the customer would like to be picked up.

   G. Ask for the town and street.

   H. Ask the customer for a phone number where he or she can be reached.

   J. If there is no building number, ask for the nearest cross street.

   K. If the caller asks for immediate pickup, tell him or her what the wait time is.

Employee Handbook
Vacation Policy

Smith's Hardware gives every employee vacation time. Employees get five days of vacation each of the first two years of employment. After two years of employment, an employee gets ten days of vacation. An employee who has worked ten or more years gets 15 days each year.

Vacation request forms should be sent to the store manager. Requests should be sent at least four weeks ahead of time.

5. You work as an assistant at a hardware store. You check the company policy on vacation time. How many days of vacation can you take after working at the store for three years?

A. 5 days

B. 10 days

C. 15 days

D. 3 weeks

E. unlimited

6. You need to have your time off request approved for an upcoming vacation. Who is in charge of approving vacation time requests?

F. the head installer

G. the company president

H. the store manager

J. your supervisor

K. Mr. Smith

C & G Landscapers

Using the correct method of placing shrubs and trees in the ground is important. Please study the following procedure.

How to Plant Shrubs and Trees

Dig a hole that is the same depth as the root ball and 2 to 3 times as wide. Place the tree or shrub into the hole. Be sure that only the roots, not the trunk, will be covered with soil. Correct the hole if necessary. Fill the hole with prepared soil to cover the roots. Then tamp down the soil around the roots to get rid of air pockets. Water and feed the plant with the nursery's approved mixture.

7. As a landscaper, you are responsible for planting a variety of shrubs and trees. According to the instructions above, how should you dig the hole for the tree or shrub?

    A. as deep as possible

    B. just deep enough to hold the root ball

    C. a little at a time

    D. with an approved shovel

    E. under the head landscaper's supervision

8. While working as an assistant landscaper, you realize that the lower branches of the plant will be covered with soil when you refill the hole. What should you do?

    F. Make the hole wider.

    G. Add soil underneath the root ball to raise the plant.

    H. Feed the plant with the approved mixture.

    J. Water the plant.

    K. Make the hole deeper to lower the plant.

How to Assemble a Nebulizer with a Compressor

As a home health aide, you will sometimes need to set up a nebulizer. This machine is used to make breathing easier for patients with respiratory problems. It does this by dispensing medication in the form of a mist that is inhaled into the lungs of the patient. Proper assembly of the nebulizer is crucial in order for it to function correctly.

Instructions:

Place the compressor close to its power source. Wash your hands before handling the clean nebulizer.

Add the prescribed medication. Put the tubing in the nebulizer. Make sure the parts are tight before adding the mouthpiece. When you turn on the compressor, make sure the nebulizer runs properly.

9. You are a home health aide who is assembling a nebulizer. Why is it necessary to wash your hands?

    A. to keep the nebulizer clean

    B. to clean off the oil from the compressor

    C. to make the patient feel better

    D. to be polite

    E. to avoid getting shocked

10. You are at a patient's home setting up a nebulizer. How will you know how much medication to add?

    F. Follow the directions on the nebulizer.

    G. Ask the client how much to use.

    H. Look at the directions for the prescribed medicine.

    J. Use the measuring spoon.

    K. Check for the mist.

SSJ CONSTRUCTION CO.

Safety Bulletin

Welders must always keep safety in mind. Remember that using your safety gear correctly is important for the safety and protection of all workers. It has been brought to our attention that some welders have been taking shortcuts with their gear. Shortcuts lead to accidents and injuries.

No matter how small the task, you must wear a welding helmet. The helmet protects you from sparks, harmful light, and hot spatter. Remember to adjust your helmet so that it fits securely. Loose helmets can block your vision and cause accidents. Because of the high noise levels, all welders are strongly advised to wear ear plugs.

11. You work as a welder and have just received this safety bulletin. According to the bulletin, which of the following conditions should you prepare for?

    A. loud noise

    B. extreme heat

    C. darkness

    D. extreme cold

    E. long workdays

12. As a welder, safety is very important to you. According to the latest safety bulletin, what should you check for when wearing the helmet?

    F. that no harmful material gets on the surface

    G. that it fits securely

    H. that no earplugs are worn

    J. that a helmet is required

    K. that you cannot hear loud noises

Answers are on page 253.

Remember!

When reading work documents, you may read a word that is familiar in a non-work context but whose workplace meaning you do not know. In *Skill Example 1*, the word *confidential* is commonly used when describing any information considered private. Thinking about other situations in which you have seen a word may help you understand its meaning within workplace documents.

You may also be familiar with words that are related to a term you read in a workplace document. In *Skill Example 2*, the word *acquisition* is used. This word is related to the word *acquire*. Knowing that an unfamiliar word is related to a word you know can often help you understand the new word's meaning.

Lesson 7 ■ ■ ■
Determine Word Meanings from Reading Material

Skill: Use the reading material to figure out the meaning of words that are not defined

Key words that appear in memos, policies, procedures, and announcements are not always easy to understand. When you read such words, look for other words nearby that you know. You can use familiar words to help you understand the meaning of unfamiliar words. Understanding key words in a document can help you to understand its meaning, purpose, and importance.

Skill Examples

Example 1
Determine a word's meaning using clues within the reading material.

> Answer every question on this application form. If you are hired, the form will be part of your confidential employee file. Only you and the human resources department will be able to see your file. If you leave the company, the form will be destroyed to protect your privacy.

The directions above appear on a job application form. The word *confidential* describes a file that only certain people will be able to see. The text also mentions protecting the employee's privacy. Based on these clues, you can determine that confidential refers to keeping information private.

Example 2
Determine a word's meaning using the main idea of the passage.

> **MEMO**
> **To:** All employees
> **RE:** New acquisition
> We are pleased to announce our company's purchase of L & C, Inc. The L & C line of products will improve service to customers. Please see the attached list for an overview of the L & C product line.

The main idea of the memo above is that the company just purchased, or bought, another company. Using this understanding, you can determine that the word *acquisition* in the subject line refers to something that has been bought.

Recording Tool Inventory

List the tools stored in the warehouse on the inventory form. Divide the tools into two categories. In the column headed "Agricultural Tools," list things such as plow blades, hoes, or other tools used on a farm. In the column headed "Other," list tools used in other settings. These might include hammers, sweepers, or other tools that are used but not directly related to farming. Record the number of each kind of tool.

Skill Practice

Use the document to the left to answer the following questions.

1. What is the meaning of the word **categories** as used in the second sentence?

   A. boxes

   B. types

   C. shelves

   D. choices

   E. warehouses

2. **Agricultural** tools are tools used for work in what kind of setting?

   F. store

   G. school

   H. factory

   J. farm

   K. highway

Try It Out! ■ ■ ■

You are a claims clerk for an auto insurance company. You answer phone calls from customers who wish to file claims after having been in an accident. What is the meaning of **competent** in this company memo?

A. worried   D. complete

B. in a hurry   E. able to do the job

C. polite

Memo

To: Claims Clerks
From: Human Resources
Subject: Professionalism

Valley View Insurance wants to be first in customer service. As an insurance claims clerk, you are the voice of Valley View. Often, you are the first person a customer talks to after a car accident. That customer must be made to feel that you can solve his or her problem. Keep the following principles in mind each time you answer a call.

Use a confident voice when you answer the phone. You must not sound rushed. The customer may be upset and confused. You must sound calm and competent. Your tone of voice should make the customer feel that you know exactly what to do to help.

Throughout the call, keep your tone friendly, but professional. End the call by reassuring the customer that you are willing and able to help him or her.

 Step 1 ## Understand the Problem ■ ■ ■

Complete the *Plan for Successful Solving.*

Plan for Successful Solving

What am I asked to do?	What are the facts?	How do I find the answer?	Is there any unnecessary information?	What prior knowledge will help me?
Find the meaning of the word *competent* based on its use in the document.	The term *competent* is used to explain how to sound professional and reassuring to the customer.	Think about the document's main idea. Determine how the word is used to identify its meaning.	The sentences around *competent* help you understand its meaning. Other sentences may not be necessary.	A professional should know how to do his or her job.

 Step 2 ## Find and Check Your Answer ■ ■ ■

- Confirm your understanding of the question and revise your plan as needed.

- Based on your plan, determine your solution approach: *The subject line of the memo uses the word* professionalism, *and the word* professional *appears in the last paragraph, too. Being professional means knowing how to do a job. This may have something to do with* competent. *The memo is about talking to customers in a way that makes them feel better in a difficult situation. A customer wants to feel that he or she will get good service.* Competent *seems to mean being able to help the customer and give the customer good service.*

- Check your answer. Review all answers to determine if the answer you have selected is the best possible answer.

- **Select the correct answer:** E. able to do the job
  The main idea of the memo is that the clerk should sound professional. Being professional means knowing how to do a job well. Based on this understanding, if someone is competent, it means he or she is able to do a job well.

Remember!

The subject line of a memo tells you something about its main idea. This may help you to determine the meaning of an unfamiliar word.

Problem Solving Tip

Eliminating the incorrect answer options can help you more easily determine the correct answer. In the *Try It Out!* example, if you substitute the word *competent* for the possible meanings given as answer options, you can narrow down the correct answer to two possible options: C. polite, and E. able to do the job. By using this problem solving approach, you can more easily and confidently determine the correct answer.

Procedures Manual

Cleaning your Workstation

Every stylist must clean his or her workstation. The following steps should be taken at the end of every shift.

1. Collect all of the equipment used during the day.

2. In the workroom, find the sterilizing solution marked "All-Clean."

3. Pour the "All-Clean" into the sterilizer jar with your name.

4. Immerse non-electrical tools in the solution. Add more solution to cover tools, if needed.

5. Wipe electrical tools with a dry cloth.

6. Put all tools in their proper place inside the cabinet.

7. Remove all other objects from your workstation.

8. Use the disinfectant in the yellow spray bottles to clean all surfaces. Wipe with a cloth.

9. Sweep the floor around your station.

---

1. At the end of your first day as a hair stylist at a new salon, you find the above information in the procedures manual. The first step in the procedure tells you to gather equipment. Which of the following words from the document seems to mean the same thing as **equipment**?

- A. bottle
- B. jar
- C. tools
- D. cabinet
- E. solution

2. After reading step 4, you want to be sure that you understand what should be done. Which sentence in the instructions best helps you to figure out the meaning of **immerse**?

- F. Pour the 'All-Clean' into the sterilizer jar with your name.
- G. Wipe electrical tools with a dry cloth.
- H. Add more solution to cover tools, if needed.
- J. Use the disinfectant in the yellow spray bottles to clean all surfaces.
- K. Sweep the floor around your station.

Meet the Sterling Standard

Job Description: Menswear Department Manager

The Department Manager runs the operations of the department. She or he works to meet sales goals.

The Department Manager's duties include:

- Create schedule for clerks
- Train clerks to perform transactions
- Manage department stock
- Be aware of menswear trends
- Create weekly reports for sales
- Help security on inventory
- Complete sales as needed
- Attend weekly managers' meetings
- Attend regional sales seminars

3. You are applying for a department manager's position at a large department store. Based on the description of duties for this position, what does it mean to **run the operations** of the department?

A. check signatures

B. oversee activity

C. put shirts in bags

D. thank the customer

E. total the sales

4. A department manager is responsible for meeting sales goals for menswear. She or he must know what products will sell. What must you know about in order to be aware of menswear **trends**?

F. discounts on items

G. the latest styles

H. orders for new sweaters

J. sales tax collected

K. the amount of money taken in

Efficiency Appliances, Inc.

Welcome to the Home Repair Division of Efficiency Appliances, Inc. Our Home Repair technicians service and repair all types of gas and electrical appliances, including refrigerators, washers, dryers, and ovens.

The following is a brief summary of the steps we expect technicians to take when servicing most standard appliances. These steps may vary depending on the appliance or issue.

To begin, take apart the appliance carefully to diagnose the exact nature of the problem. Explain to the customer what is wrong with the appliance and provide cost estimates for needed repairs.

Replace any worn or defective parts, including switches, bearings, belts, gears, and defective wiring.

Reassemble the appliance carefully, adjusting, cleaning, and lubricating parts as needed.

---

5. You are a home repair technician for an appliance company, and you have received a memo explaining the responsibilities of your job. According to the memo, what is the meaning of the word **diagnose** in the second paragraph?

A. to take something apart

B. to find out what the problem is

C. to explain to the customer what is wrong

D. to find a new part for

E. to estimate the cost for

6. What is the meaning of the word **reassemble** in the last paragraph of the memo?

F. to take apart

G. to inspect for problems

H. to estimate a cost for

J. to put back together

K. to ship back to the factory

From: Springdale Public Library: Circulation Director
Date: September 22
To: SPL—Library Assistants**ALL
Subject: Shelving checked-in books

We have recently had problems with assistants incorrectly re-shelving books. Please review the following procedure before you begin your next shift.

Standard re-shelving procedure for books:

1. Pick up a blue cart at circulation. Books that have been checked in are placed on blue carts. Do not take books from red bins. These have not been processed for re-shelving.

2. Adjust the books so that all the spines are visible. If any spine is missing its label, return the book to the circulation department.

3. Sort the books on the cart according to the call number on the white label on the book spine. First, use the letters in the call numbers to put the books in alphabetical order. Then sort the books by the numbers that follow the letters.

4. Read the labels of the books on the shelves to find the correct location for the book you are re-shelving.

7. As a library assistant, you are responsible for re-shelving books that have been returned by library patrons. Based on its use in step 1 above, what does it mean for books to be **processed** by the circulation department?

A. sorted

B. numbered

C. labeled

D. alphabetized

E. checked in

8. When you make the spines of the books **visible** as instructed in step 2, what are you doing?

F. dusting them

G. making them able to be seen

H. counting the spines

J. checking in the books

K. making the books available

City Cycles Employee Handbook

Dress Code and Personal Appearance Policy

As an employee of City Cycles, you need to follow the company dress code and personal appearance policy.

Formal clothing is not required, but you are expected to arrive at the shop clean and appropriately dressed.

Store staff

Hair, hands, and fingernails: Any hairstyle is acceptable as long as the hair is neat and clean. The same applies to facial hair. Fingernails must be clean.

Dress: Employees are allowed to wear casual pants, skirts, shorts, or jeans. Casual t-shirts are also permitted. Sales clerks are discouraged from wearing sandals and other open-toed shoes.

Repair shop staff

Hair, hands, and fingernails: For safety, long hair must be secured while in the shop. A hat or cap may be worn. Facial hair must be neat and clean. Fingernails must be clean.

Dress: Staff is expected to arrive at the shop in clean work clothes. Wearing work boots is encouraged.

---

9. You are a clerk at City Cycles. The section describing appropriate dress for store staff tells you that t-shirts are **permitted**. What other word in the handbook means the same thing as **permitted**?

    A.   discouraged

    B.   allowed

    C.   encouraged

    D.   applies

    E.   secured

10. You are reviewing the policy as you get ready to go to work in the bicycle store. You are not sure what the word **sandals** means. Which detail from the policy helps you to understand the term?

    F.   long hair must be secured

    G.   Wearing work boots is encouraged.

    H.   Casual t-shirts are also permitted.

    J.   and other open-toed shoes

    K.   clean work clothes

NOTICE TO ALL HORIZON OFFICE PARK EMPLOYEES

NEW EMPLOYEE SHUTTLE

On May 15, Horizon Office Park will have a direct shuttle available to the employees of all companies within the park. The shuttle will go between the garage on First Avenue and each of the office park zone entrances.

In the morning, the bus will pick up employees at the garage at 7:00. Pickups will take place at 30-minute periods until 10:00. The trip takes 12 minutes.

At the end of the day, the bus will take employees to the garage. The first bus will leave zone E of our facility at 4:00. The last bus will leave at 7:00.

Employees must show their facility ID cards in order to board the bus. The driver will check the cards. Each company will determine if employees benefit from this convenience.

11. You work as an engineer with a firm located in Horizon Office Park. You read the notice that the facility is providing a shuttle for employees. Which word or phrase in the notice best helps you understand what a **shuttle** is?

    A. bus

    B. driver

    C. garage

    D. ID cards

    E. employees

12. The facility manager thinks that the new shuttle service will be a convenience for employees. What is a **convenience**?

    F. something with unreliable service

    G. a very small bus

    H. something that makes life easier

    J. a 30-minute interval

    K. something unexpected

Answers are on page 255.

Remember!

Documents that contain instructions with several steps usually provide clues that help you follow those instructions. Look at the format in which the steps are structured:

- **Numbered lists** make it easy to follow the order of the instructions.
- **Bulleted lists** help to distinguish each step.
- **Flow charts** are a graphic way of showing the order of steps.

When multi-step instructions remain as part of the text, look for words that signal the order of steps. Signal words include: *first, next, following, before, after, then,* and *finally.*

Lesson 8 ▪ ▪ ▪
Apply Multi-Step Instructions

Skill: Apply instructions with several steps to a situation that is the same as the situation in the reading materials

Many workplace documents contain steps that outline the order of a job or procedure. You must be able to understand and apply the steps described in a process that you are expected to follow. It is important to notice the order in which each step is done, as well as how one step logically leads to the next. Practicing this way of thinking about following directions or the steps in workplace documents will help you to do your job correctly and efficiently.

Skill Examples

Office workers who need supplies should first fill out a "Request for Supplies" form. List the supplies you need. Once the form is completed, have your boss initial it. Then give the form to the receptionist in the Supply Department. If you are a warehouse worker, follow the same instructions. Give your form to the receptionist in the Stocking Department.

Example 1
Determine the steps in a procedure.

The instructions explain how to order supplies when needed. Although none of the steps within this procedure is numbered, they are written in the order that they should occur, making the procedure easy to follow. Signal words and phrases such as *first, once,* and *then* reinforce the order of the steps for ordering supplies.

Example 2
Apply instructions to a related workplace situation.

Suppose you work as the supervisor of packaging and shipping in this company's warehouse. You realize that you will soon need packaging tape. By reading the above instructions, you can follow the steps required to order more tape for your department.

Skill Practice

One of your most important duties as a flight attendant is to explain safety procedures to passengers. First, point out the emergency exits on the plane. Get verbal confirmation that people sitting by the emergency exit doors can open them in case of an emergency. Change people's seats if those seated by the emergency exits do not want to sit there. Then explain the situations in which oxygen masks will fall. Explain how to use the mask. Finally, explain how to use the seat as a flotation device.

Use the document to the left to answer the following questions.

1. As a flight attendant, when would you change passengers' seats?

   A. when passengers are exiting the plane

   B. when demonstrating the use of the oxygen mask

   C. when passengers do not want to sit by the emergency exit

   D. when practicing for an emergency water landing

   E. when there is an emergency by the exit door

2. When do you explain how to use the seat as a flotation device?

   F. at the beginning

   G. when the masks fall

   H. when you change seats

   J. at the end of the explanation

   K. before you explain safety procedures

Try It Out! ■ ■ ■

You are a 911 emergency operator. What do you do after the caller first gives you his or her address?

   A. Call the EMT team.

   B. Advise on first aid measures.

   C. Get the caller's name.

   D. Repeat the caller's address.

   E. Ask about the nature of the emergency.

> **911 Emergency Phone Operator**
>
> The first question you should ask when you receive a call is: "What is the emergency?" Encourage the caller to speak slowly. Ask about the nature of the emergency. Determine which agency (police, fire, or medical) to contact. If it is a medical emergency, write down the symptoms the caller tells you. Ask the caller to give the address of the emergency and write this address down. Repeat the address to make sure you wrote it correctly. Contact an ambulance. Announce over the dispatch line the location and nature of the emergency. Assure the caller that help is on the way.

Step 1   Understand the Problem ■ ■ ■

Complete the *Plan for Successful Solving.*

Plan for Successful Solving

What am I asked to do?	What are the facts?	How do I find the answer?	Is there any unnecessary information?	What prior knowledge will help me?
Determine which step comes after being given the caller's address.	You must get the address when a caller reports a medical emergency.	Focus on the step in the procedure that comes after asking for the person's address.	Any steps that come before asking the caller for the address where help is needed.	In an emergency, having the correct address is vital.

Step 2   Find and Check Your Answer ■ ■ ■

- Confirm your understanding of the question and revise your plan as needed.

- Based on your plan, determine your solution approach: *The paragraph describes the steps a 911 emergency operator takes when answering a call. I should look for the sentence that tells about first asking for the address where the emergency has taken place. Once I've found this, I will look at the sentence that follows. This sentence states that then the operator should repeat the address the caller gave.*

- Check your answer. Review all answers to determine if the answer you have selected is the best possible answer.

- **Select the correct answer:**   D. Repeat the caller's address.
  The passage indicates that after the caller states the address of the emergency, the operator should repeat the address to make sure she or he wrote it correctly and sends help to the right place.

Problem Solving Tip

Look for words that give you clues about the answer. For example, look for words such as *before, after, during, first, second, last,* or *finally* in the question. These words give you a hint about the order of steps within a procedure.

Remember!

Steps tell you the order in which things are done to complete a task effectively.

MEMO

To: All New LPNs

RE: Welcome

Welcome to our clinic! As a licensed practical nurse (LPN), you will have specific tasks to perform when greeting a patient for his or her scheduled appointment. First, walk the patient into the exam room. Measure the patient's weight and height. Take the patient's blood pressure and temperature. Take the patient's pulse. Write all of this information in the patient's chart.

Ask the patient about any medication he or she is taking and write down the name of each medication in the patient's chart. For most appointments, you will then exit the exam room and inform the patient that the doctor will be there shortly. However, depending on the nature of the appointment, the doctor may ask you to draw blood for a blood test. You may even be responsible for giving certain injections.

---

1. As a licensed practical nurse, what is the first thing you should do with a patient after you have taken him or her to the exam room?

   A. Take a pulse.

   B. Measure weight and height.

   C. Ask about medications.

   D. Give an injection.

   E. Update the chart.

2. According to the procedures, when would you give a patient an injection?

   F. when the patient has the flu

   G. when the patient has high blood pressure

   H. when the doctor requests it

   J. when the LPN gets a license

   K. when the chart indicates it

Employee Handbook

Welcome to the Forest Service. As a forest conservation technician in Midlands National Forest, your job will usually include the diagnosis and removal of diseased trees.

1. Check for symptoms of tree disease. These symptoms include:
   - dead or hanging branches
   - major splits
   - rotten wood or cavities in the trunk
   - conks or fungus growth at the base
   - insects
2. Chop down the tree as close to the ground as possible.
3. Spray the remaining part of the tree with a weed killer.
4. Later, remove the dead stump and roots to reduce fungus spread.
5. Test the soil for conditions favorable for spread of disease.
6. If soil conditions are favorable for spread of disease, sterilize the soil with weed killer.

3. You are a forest conservation technician and you are looking at a tree that has overhanging branches, cavities in the trunk, and fungus growth at the base. What is the first thing you do?

   A. Chop down the tree as close to the ground as possible.

   B. Test the soil for conditions favorable for spread of tree disease.

   C. Spray the soil with weed-killer.

   D. Remove the dead stump.

   E. Spray the remaining tree parts with weed killer.

4. At what point in the process would you spray the tree with weed killer?

   F. before you check for symptoms of tree disease

   G. before you chop down a diseased tree

   H. before you have removed dead roots of the tree

   J. after the disease has spread

   K. after you have sterilized the soil

Smithfield Air Conditioning Co., Inc.

When installing an air conditioning system, you must:

A. Always follow the blueprints for the building provided by the architect or designer.

B. Always follow the instructions provided by the manufacturer of the air conditioner.

C. Install (a) the motor, (b) the compressor, (c) the condensing unit, (d) the evaporators, (e) the piping, and (f) other necessary components or parts.

D. Connect the installed air conditioning unit to the building's ductwork.

E. Connect the unit to the refrigerant lines.
NOTE: Do this carefully! Do not let any refrigerant chemical escape from the system. It is an air pollutant.

F. Connect the unit to the building electrical system.

G. After installation, run the air conditioning unit to make sure it works properly. Make any adjustments that may be needed.

H. If the unit can be programmed, set the program to control the time the unit is in operation.

---

5. You are working as an HVAC (heating, ventilation, and air conditioning) technician. According to the rules for installing an air conditioning system, what is the second part of the air conditioning unit that you install?

A. the refrigerant

B. the evaporator

C. the building's pipes

D. the compressor

E. the condensing unit

6. Once you have installed the unit, what is the first thing that you hook it up to in the building?

F. the ductwork

G. the motor

H. the electrical system

J. the compressor

K. the programmer

Job Description: Farm Manager

Farm managers are involved in decision-making at the planting, harvesting, and sales stages of crop production. Before planting the crop, the manager reviews data compiled of weather and soil conditions. The manager must first determine whether or not to increase or decrease the amount of irrigation water for the crop, depending on rainfall. The manager must then determine the types and quantities of fertilizer needed for maximum crop production. Based upon this information, the manager directs workers to plant crops, followed as needed by activities such as irrigation and fertilizing.

The manager also must inspect fields to estimate dates for harvesting. Based upon these dates, the manager then assigns workers for harvesting and grading. Finally, the manager confers with buyers to coordinate sale of crops.

7. At your orientation as farm manager, you are given a job description. What is one thing you must do before planting a crop?

   A. Assign workers for harvesting.

   B. Confer with buyers.

   C. Review weather and soil condition data.

   D. Inspect fields to estimate dates for harvesting.

   E. Assign workers for grading.

8. According to your farm manager job description, when do you assign workers to harvest the crop?

   F. before planting

   G. before fertilizing

   H. before checking the soil

   J. after inspecting the fields

   K. after conferring with buyers

Police Patrol Officer Task List

Every police patrol officer covers a neighborhood. During daily patrols, officers may encounter traffic accidents. When at the scene of an accident, remember to do the following:

- Officers should first determine if anyone is seriously injured. First aid may be necessary. Call for an ambulance immediately if someone is injured.
- Unless the accident does not impact the normal flow of traffic, call for more police support to help direct traffic.
- Take down the license plate numbers of all vehicles involved in the accident.
- Perform a field sobriety test. If it is deemed appropriate, test the drivers' blood-alcohol content levels.
- Take into custody anyone who is impaired.
- Call for additional support if any vehicles need to be towed.
- Keep a record of all information at the scene and submit report at police station.

9. As a police patrol officer, what is the first thing you must determine at the scene of a car accident?

- A. when it was phoned in
- B. how many ambulances are needed
- C. if other police officers are present
- D. if traffic flow is impacted
- E. if anyone is seriously injured

10. Under what conditions at the scene of an accident might you take someone involved into custody?

- F. they do not have registration
- G. they are not seriously injured
- H. they are under the influence of alcohol
- J. they do not need to be hospitalized
- K. they have had previous accidents

Procedures Manual

When analyzing bacteria in an infected tissue specimen, the microbiology laboratory technician should do the following:

1. Make sure the specimen is in good condition.

2. Prepare the specimen for analysis.

   a. Prepare a microscope slide.

   b. Place a thin section of tissue on the slide.

   c. Use the correct stain.

3. Place the prepared slide into the microscope. Activate the automatic focus control.

4. Then, observe the specimen as needed.

5. Increase magnification until the presence of bacteria is confirmed.

6. Take a picture of the specimen. Then, fill out a lab report.

7. Give your report to your department head.

---

11. You are a microbiology lab technician. What do you do to prepare a slide just before you put it under the microscope?

    A. Obtain a clean slide.

    B. Cut a thin section of tissue.

    C. Stain it appropriately.

    D. Determine the magnification.

    E. Identify the bacteria present.

12. According to the procedures, under what circumstances would you increase the microscope's magnification?

    F. if you cannot identify what you see

    G. if the bacteria are not yet visible

    H. if the tissue contains too many bacteria

    J. if the bacteria cannot be identified

    K. if there are very few bacteria in the sample

Answers are on page 254.

Lesson 9 ▪ ▪ ▪
Choose the Correct Action When Conditions Change

Skill: Choose what to do when changing conditions call for a different action

Sometimes workplace documents such as project instructions require you to be able to choose what actions to take depending on the conditions of a situation. To be prepared for a variety of situations, such as changing weather conditions, shifting staff or work hours, or revised client demands, it is important to pay attention to the specific instructions that exist for different situations.

Remember!

Documents often contain words and phrases that can help you understand the meaning of the document and what you should do. When reading instructions or procedures documents, *"if-then"* statements often provide clues to signal that, in a certain situation ("if"), you should take a certain course of action ("then"). Being able to identify and use these kinds of clues can help you better understand how to make the correct decisions in the workplace when changing conditions require different actions.

Skill Examples

MEMORANDUM

We have begun replacing our older washing machines with new, high-efficiency (HE) machines. These machines require a special HE detergent. When using the new machines, you must not use the existing detergent. You must also follow new guidelines for how much HE detergent should be used. For loads of linens up to 20 pounds, use two cups of detergent. For loads larger than 20 pounds, an additional cup of detergent should be added for every ten pounds of linens. For instance, if you wash a load of linens that weighs between 21 and 30 pounds, use three cups of detergent. For loads that weigh between 31 and 40 pounds, use four cups, and so on. If using an older machine, please continue to use the regular detergent.

Example 1
Choose what to do when two possible conditions exist.

The memo explains that there are new HE machines being used at this facility. There are also older machines still being used. The two conditions in this scenario—using either a new machine or an old machine—determine which detergent should be used.

Example 2
Identify a rule for determining what to do when conditions may vary.

The changing condition that is described in the memo is the weight of the linens. By reading carefully, you can identify that for each additional 10 pounds of linens, an extra cup of detergent should be added.

New Inventory Form

There is a new inventory form. This form is for equipment in the lab. The new form will not list equipment that is no longer used in the lab. Because of this, all equipment that is no longer used in the lab has been marked with a red label. *Do not list equipment with a red label on the inventory form.* In the column headed "Equipment," list only that equipment without red labels.

Skill Practice

Use the document to the left to answer the following questions.

1. Which condition indicates that you should list equipment on the inventory form?

    A. equipment with red labels

    B. all equipment in inventory

    C. forms with red labels

    D. equipment without red labels

    E. equipment with blue labels

2. What does it mean if equipment is marked with a red label?

    F. It is inventory.

    G. It is new.

    H. It is stored in the lab.

    J. It is no longer used.

    K. It is a new form.

Try It Out! ■ ■ ■

You are an administrative services manager for an accounting firm. You are responsible for updating the client database using new software. According to the memo, which of the following client's data should be transferred into the new database?

A. client whose account has been active within the past 7 years

B. client whose account has been archived within the past 5 years

C. client whose software has been updated recently

D. client whose account has not been active within the past 7 years

E. client whose account has been active within the past 5 years

 Step 1 **Understand the Problem** ■ ■ ■

Complete the *Plan for Successful Solving.*

Plan for Successful Solving

What am I asked to do?	What are the facts?	How do I find the answer?	Is there any unnecessary information?	What prior knowledge will help me?
Decide which client's data should be transferred into the new system.	The memo explains how clients' data should be filed based on account activity.	Locate the condition under which clients' data should be transferred into the new system.	The fact that the software is new is not needed to find the answer.	Companies can improve efficiency by updating their records. To do this, they may choose not to transfer older client data.

Step 2 **Find and Check Your Answer** ■ ■ ■

■ Confirm your understanding of the question and revise your plan as needed.

■ Based on your plan, determine your solution approach: *The memo explains that I must decide whether to enter clients in the database or list their names and archive their files. I will look within the memo to identify what conditions are used to determine that a client's data should be added to the database.*

■ Check your answer. Review all answers to determine if the answer you have selected is the best possible answer.

■ **Select the correct answer:** E. client whose account has been active within the past 5 years
Only certain clients should be transferred into the new database. If clients have been active within the past 5 years, you should transfer their data into the new database. If not, you should list their names and archive their files.

MEMORANDUM

In our effort to update the client database, we will be upgrading to new software. Along with entering new clients into the system, we must also transfer data for clients who have had an active account within the past 5 years into the new database. Keep a list of clients whose accounts have had no activity during the past 5 years. If a client's name is on this list, their files should be archived.

Remember!
You can identify existing conditions and how they change by looking for *"if-then"* statements. As with the memo on this page, sometimes *"if-then"* statements do not include the word *then.*

Problem Solving Tip
The *Try It Out!* example requires you to take different actions depending on different conditions. When you read documents that contain conditional instructions, first identify and list the different conditions that might apply. In this example, there are three different conditions: new clients, clients whose accounts have been active within the last five years, and clients whose accounts have not been active within the last five years. By identifying and listing all conditions, you can better determine which procedures should be followed for each condition.

Cleaning Examining Table and Tools

You must clean the examining table and tools following every examination. Please follow the guidelines below.

1. Remove all tools from the examining table and counter.
2. Put tools with sterilization wrappers back on the shelf.
3. Place tools without sterilization wrappers in the sterilizer tub.
4. Spray the examining table and the counter with disinfectant.
5. Wipe the examining table with a clean cloth.
6. Drain the sterilizer tub, let the tools air dry, and put tools in sterilization wrappers.
7. Place sterilized tools on the shelf.

1. You are a veterinary technologist. You must use the guidelines card above to determine how to sanitize the exam table and tools. The second step requires you to put tools with sterilization wrappers back on the shelf. What step do you take if tools do not have sterilization wrappers?

    A. Place tools on a clean cloth.

    B. Place tools in the sterilizer tub.

    C. Place tools in disinfectant.

    D. Place tools on the shelf.

    E. Place tools on the examining table.

2. As a veterinary technologist, you are preparing to clean the examining table and counter. Under what condition should you spray the surface of the examining table and the counter with disinfectant?

    F. when the tools have wrappers

    G. if there are tools on the examining table

    H. when the sterilizer tub is drained

    J. only if the tools are sterilized

    K. under all conditions

On the Go!
Bicycle Shop

Identifying and Repairing Noise Issues

Experience has proven that one of the most common complaints brought into *On the Go!* is that the customer hears noise such as clicks or grinding sounds while riding. Check to see where on the bicycle the noise occurs, then use the following procedure.

If the noise occurs in the front or rear wheels, then check the brake pads, tire seating, or spoke intersection.

If the noise occurs for each revolution of the pedals, then check to see if the crank arm is loose.

If the noise occurs for each revolution of the chain, check to see if the chain is stiff, bent, or otherwise damaged.

If the customer reports noise when the bicycle hits bumps, then check to see if bolts need tightening or lubricating.

If the customer reports random noises, then check to see if any bolts need tightening.

Obtain customer approval to fix or replace broken parts. All bicycle mechanics must complete a repair ticket and give it to a cashier once the work is completed. Then clean all tools needed for the job and put the tools away.

---

3. You work as a bicycle mechanic at *On the Go!* bicycle shop. A customer has brought in a bicycle with the complaint that she hears a clicking sound coming from the rear wheel. What should you do next?

    A. Check the chain for damage.

    B. Check to see if any bolts need tightening.

    C. Check the brake pads.

    D. Check to see if the chain is stiff.

    E. Check the crank arm.

4. As a bicycle mechanic, you have successfully repaired the bicycle. What should you do next?

    F. Obtain customer approval.

    G. Complete a repair ticket.

    H. Give a repair ticket to the cashier.

    J. Clean all tools needed for the job.

    K. Put the tools away.

From: Green Forest Management   Date: May 5
To: Land Management Professionals
Subject: Tree thinning

Last week, Green Forest Management began the Ridge Trail tree-thinning project. Land management specialists will assist in this effort starting Monday of next week.

On the morning of Monday, May 10, go to your usual check-in point in the morning. If your help is needed on the west end of the trail, there will be a notice in your mailbox. If you do not receive a notice in your mailbox, then you should report to the east end of the trail. Be sure to bring your department log sheet with you.

---

5. You are a land management professional called in to help with the Ridge Trail tree-thinning project. When you report to work on Monday, what will indicate that you should report to the west end of the trail?

  A. a notice in your mailbox

  B. a memo in your department log

  C. a department log in your mailbox

  D. no notice in your mailbox

  E. a notice in your department log

6. Where should you go if you do not receive a notice in your mailbox?

  F. the west end of the trail

  G. the department log

  H. the usual check-in point

  J. the east end of the trail

  K. Ridge Trail check-in

LIBRARY TIP SHEET

Research Inquiries

When patrons come to the library with research inquiries, use the following tips in order to locate the desired information:

- Ask patrons to state the topic of their search.
- Use the library database to locate the information.
- If the topic does not appear, help them restate the topic and enter the information again.
- If their topic appears, tell them the reference titles on your screen. Then use the code in the upper right hand corner of the screen to refer them to the section of the library where the material can be found.

If the above steps do not help patrons find the reference materials they are looking for, start the search again using different search entries.

---

7. As a library assistant, you are responsible for answering routine reference inquiries. If the topic of a patron's search does not appear in the library database, what should you do?

    A.   refer patron to another department

    B.   have patron change the topic

    C.   re-enter a similar topic

    D.   give patron the code on screen

    E.   turn off the database search

8. According to the document, while helping patrons with research, in what situation would you refer the patron to a specific section of the library?

    F.   if their topic appears

    G.   if the database appears

    H.   if they change their topic

    J.   if their topic doesn't appear

    K.   if they re-start their search

Sanitation Policy Daily Procedures

As head chef at *The Ripe Tomato*, it is your responsibility to make sure that employees follow regulations.

- Make sure kitchen staff follow safety regulations when using all equipment and utensils. If standard procedures are not followed, schedule a policy review for staff.

- Make sure cleaning schedules have been initialed by the staff member in charge. If initials are not on the form, fill out a sanitation report for the restaurant manager.

- If food temperatures are not maintained, fill out a sanitation report for the restaurant manager.

9. As the head chef at *The Ripe Tomato*, you are in charge of monitoring employees' compliance to the sanitation policy. What kind of situation would require you to have staff attend a policy review session?

    A.   safe operation of equipment

    B.   use of equipment and utensils

    C.   unsafe operation of equipment

    D.   unsafe cleaning schedules

    E.   use of sanitation policy

10. As head chef, if you find a cleaning schedule that is not initialed by the staff member on duty, what should you do?

    F.   write a new policy

    G.   clean the equipment

    H.   initial the schedule

    J.   fill out a sanitation report

    K.   sign restaurant manager's initial

BUS SCHEDULE CHANGE
for Happy Valley Day Care Center

Some schools will have half days next week. The after-school buses will be on different schedules.

- Children who attend Grover Elementary School will leave their school at 12:15 and arrive at the day care center at 12:45.

- Children who attend the Daily Charter School will leave their school at 12:30 and arrive at the day care center at 12:50.

St. Mary's Elementary School does not have half days next week. Those children will have a normal bus schedule.

11. You are a child care worker at Happy Valley Day Care Center. You are responsible for writing up individual schedules to notify parents of modified bus schedules for the upcoming week. What schedules will you write for parents who have one child attending Grover Elementary School and another attending Daily Charter School?

    A.   arrivals at 12:15 P.M. and 12:50 P.M.

    B.   arrivals at 12: 30 P.M. and 12:50 P.M.

    C.   arrivals at 12:30 P.M. and 12:45 P.M.

    D.   arrivals at 12:45 P.M.

    E.   arrivals at 12:45 P.M. and 12:50 P.M.

12. As a child care worker, you are in charge of notifying parents of any important information. You have just received a call from the parent of a student at St. Mary's asking how many half days are scheduled for her child next week. What do you tell her?

    F.   No half days are scheduled for next week.

    G.   Only one half day is scheduled.

    H.   Two half days are scheduled.

    J.   Three half days are scheduled.

    K.   Half days are scheduled for every day next week.

Answers are on page 256.

Level 4 Performance Assessment

The following problems will test your ability to answer questions at a Level 4 rating of difficulty. These problems are similar to those that appear on a Career Readiness Certificate test. For each question, you can refer to the answer key for answer justifications. The answer justifications provide an explanation of why each answer option is either correct or incorrect and indicate the skill lesson that should be referred to if further review of a particular skill is needed.

Pop's Bakery: Vegan Chocolate Cake

Sometimes customers ask us to make a small vegan cake for one or two of their guests at a party. To make a chocolate cake without animal products, follow these directions. Preheat the oven to 350°F. Lightly grease a 9 x 9 inch cake pan. Dust the pan with the same kind of flour you will use for the cake. You may use wheat or rice flour. In a large mixing bowl, combine 1-1/2 cups of flour with 3/4 cup of sugar, 1/2 teaspoon of salt, 1 teaspoon of baking soda, and 3 tablespoons of unsweetened cocoa powder. Make a well in the center of the dry ingredients. In a separate bowl, mix 1 teaspoon of vanilla, 1/3 cup vegetable oil, and 1 tablespoon of vinegar with 1 cup of cold water. Pour this mixture into the well. Combine the wet and dry ingredients by mixing with a fork. Pour the mixture into the cake pan and bake for 30 minutes.

1. In your work as a baker at Pop's Bakery, you are making a vegan cake for the first time. Which of the following should you *not* use to grease the cake pan?

   A. canola oil

   B. sunflower seed oil

   C. corn oil

   D. vegetable oil

   E. butter or lard

2. How many bowls will it take to prepare this recipe?

   F. one; mix everything at the same time

   G. two; divide the batter in half

   H. two; one for the dry ingredients and one for the wet

   J. three; beat the eggs in a separate bowl

   K. three; put the flour in a separate bowl

— Valley Veterinary Clinic —

Pilling a Cat

As a veterinary technician, you will often be called upon to give a cat oral medication in pill form. Cats are typically less cooperative than dogs when it comes to accepting oral medication. The first step is to restrain the cat. Place the cat on a table. Wrap the cat in a towel, leaving only the head exposed. Stand behind the cat so that the cat cannot move backward. If you are right-handed, use your left arm to keep the cat from moving sideways. Hold the pill between your thumb and index finger of your right hand. Tilt the cat's head back. The lower jaw should drop open. If it does not you will need to gently pry it open with your middle finger. Hold the jaw open and drop the pill as far back as possible in the cat's mouth. Then hold the mouth closed and gently stroke the throat. Blowing on its nose may also encourage the cat to swallow.

3. You are working as a veterinary technician and you are asked to give a cat oral medication in pill form. What purpose does it serve to tilt the cat's head back?

   A.   It helps the cat to breathe.

   B.   It relaxes the cat.

   C.   It keeps the cat from seeing what you are doing.

   D.   It opens the cat's mouth.

   E.   It restrains the cat.

4. Why should you stroke the cat's throat after putting the pill in its mouth?

   F.   to soothe it

   G.   to make it hungry

   H.   to make it swallow

   J.   to make it purr

   K.   to keep from getting bitten

FROM: Joyce Samuels
TO: File Clerks—ALL
SUBJECT: Preparing files for storage

DATE: October 2

Next week all file clerks will prepare files in their department for the company archive. Please be advised of the following procedures for archiving files:

- All files that have not been active for 3 or more years will be deposited in the archive. To decide whether a file is active or not, you must review the contents. Do not rely on any dates that might be on the outside of the folder. You must always look for the latest addition to the file to determine the most recent date.

- Any file that has not been added to in 3 or more years is inactive. Replace the file folder if it is torn or fragile.

- Replace incorrect labels and add labels to any folders that have been replaced.

- Place all inactive files in a box. These will be removed and stored in the archive at the end of each day.

5. You are working as a file clerk. You receive an e-mail about preparing files for the archive. What is an **archive?**

A. a shredding center

B. a copying center

C. a place where old records are stored

D. the company's headquarters

E. the company mail room

6. The e-mail instructs you to be on the lookout for fragile folders. What would a folder that is **fragile** look like?

F. unlabeled

G. about to fall apart

H. plastic

J. covered with writing

K. stiff and sturdy

LEE'S MARKET & SUPERSTORE

Setting up the Sales Drawer

At the start of your shift, pick up your drawer from the customer service department. You should always count the contents of your drawer before opening your register. The drawer should contain the following cash amounts: four $20 bills, one $10 bill, three $5 bills, 50 $1 bills, and one roll each of quarters, dimes, nickels, and pennies. If your drawer is below or over any of these amounts, you should report the discrepancy to your manager immediately. Always secure your drawer before you leave the register.

7. As a sales clerk in a large store, you are responsible for a drawer of cash. Based on the directions, which of the following describes a **discrepancy** you may find when setting up your drawer?

   A. Some bills are damaged.

   B. The drawer is secure.

   C. You have three $5 bills.

   D. You have three $20 bills.

   E. All of the cash amounts are correct.

8. You have worked half of your shift and are ready to leave your register for your lunch break. What does it mean to **secure** the drawer?

   F. Balance the receipts.

   G. Lock the drawer.

   H. Remove the cash.

   J. Open the drawer.

   K. Sort the bills and coins.

Lenny's Locksmiths

Date: June 12
To: All Locksmiths
Re: Proper Identification Reminder

At Lenny's Locksmiths, it is our number one goal to provide all of our customers with the highest sense of security. In order to do this, please review the following simple reminders regarding identification requirements for house calls.

When you go out on a call to assist customers who have been locked out of their home, take your professional identification. Present the customer with your ID. Give them time to examine it. Doing so will help the customer know that you are reputable. You must then ask the customer for his or her picture ID before beginning to work on the lock. Customers want to know that you would not let a person without the proper ID enter their homes. Have the customer sign the work order form. Inform the customer that by signing the form, he or she is granting you permission to begin work on the lock.

9. You are a locksmith reading the above memo. If you are a **reputable** locksmith, what do people believe about you?

    A.   that you are honest and respected

    B.   that you are happy in your work

    C.   that you work quickly

    D.   that you are in training

    E.   that you have a degree

10. Which of the following words means the same thing as the word **security**, as it is used in the memo?

    F.   good will

    G.   humor

    H.   anxiety

    J.   superiority

    K.   safety

Quality Care Consultants

To: Victor Sullivan, President Sullivan Manufacturing Company

From: Quality Care Consultants

Date: January 20

To maximize the productivity of your company, I will be analyzing the following:

1. The materials needed to make your products. I will determine if you are making the best use of the materials used. I will find ways to make material use more efficient.

2. The work-hours needed to make your products. Then I will analyze how efficiently your labor force is used to produce these products.

3. Once these systems are analyzed and improvements recommended, I will evaluate the computerized information systems. These systems control the production process.

4. Finally, I will do an in-depth analysis of your company's financial health and recommend a new system of financial planning.

---

11. As a consultant you have been called in to review the productivity level of a manufacturing company. Why do you analyze the efficiency of the labor force?

    A. to determine if the company is making the best use of materials

    B. to determine if the company is making the best use of work hours

    C. to evaluate the computerized information systems

    D. to analyze the company's financial health

    E. to recommend a new system of financial planning

12. In your work as a consultant, when do you evaluate the computerized information systems?

    F. before evaluating the labor force

    G. after analyzing the company's financial health

    H. before reviewing the use of materials

    J. after recommending new financial planning

    K. after analyzing and improving systems

Smith Avenue Clinic

As the administrative manager of the medical records department at this clinic, make sure that these procedures are followed when updating patient records after clinic visits:

☐ Every record has the name of the patient, the name of the doctor, the date of the last appointment, and the diagnosis codes. If the record contains a diagnosis but no code, look up the code(s) in our Master Code file and insert it in the patient record.

☐ Compare the latest visit with the previous visit. Mark in red any changes in diagnosis. Mark in blue all changes in medication.

☐ Transfer the written patient record to the medical records technician. Have the technician input all the information for the current visit into the patient's computerized file. All color codes should be included.

☐ At the end of the day, check a few written records with their computerized record. Find and correct any mistakes. The next day, inform the technician of any additional corrections you have made.

13. You are working as a manager of the medical records department. What do you do if the written record contains no diagnosis codes?

   A. Input the record without codes.

   B. Mark the omission in red ink.

   C. Refer the omission to the technician.

   D. Look up the code and insert it in the patient record.

   E. Use the diagnosis codes from previous visits.

14. Before giving the written file to the technician, how must you mark changes in the record?

   F. Put them in the computer file.

   G. Mark medication changes in red.

   H. Mark diagnosis changes in red.

   J. Mark new medication by code.

   K. Mark the date of the appointment in blue.

• Better Smile Dental Clinic •

One of the tasks of the dental assistant is to assist the dentist during teeth whitening procedures. It is important that you understand the procedure to be prepared to hand the dentist what is needed. The tools needed for the procedure are

- Industrial strength hydrogen peroxide gel

- Protective mouthpiece

- Clamps

- Laser light

The first step is to apply the protective mouthpiece over the gums to protect them from the hydrogen peroxide gel. If the patient has difficulty keeping his or her mouth open, clamps may be used to better access gums and teeth.

The dentist then applies the hydrogen peroxide gel, covering the teeth. If the teeth are badly stained, a laser light is used to increase the whitening power of the gel.

The clamps are then removed and the patient rinses until the hydrogen peroxide gel has been removed. If stains remain, the process is repeated.

15. You are a dental assistant helping with a teeth whitening procedure. During the procedure, why might the dentist ask you to hand him clamps?

A. to remove bridges

B. to examine loose fillings

C. to protect gums from whitening gel

D. to better access gums and teeth

E. to increase the power of the whitening gel

16. Why might a laser light be used?

F. The patient has loose fillings.

G. The teeth are badly stained.

H. The gums are inflamed or infected.

J. The dentist has difficulty seeing the teeth.

K. The roots require an X-ray.

Date: August 28

From: District Supervisor, Department of Inspection Services
To: Air Quality Technicians
Re: Procedures update

Healthy indoor air quality depends on the lack of contaminants in the air. Industrial buildings' air quality must meet the recently revised standards set by the Environmental Protection Agency (EPA). You should follow these steps in order to meet the new requirements.

- Run the initial air quality test. If the initial results show that air contaminants in the form of gases exist, run a follow-up test for toxic chemicals. Recommend any needed remedies for problems detected during testing.

- If the initial results do not show that air contaminants in the form of gases exist, then continue with the standard test. Check for dust, asbestos, and particles from building materials.

Once all tests have been completed, submit the final report to your supervisor.

17. As an air quality technician working for a state agency, what is the first thing you should do if you find that air contaminants in the form of gases are present?

   A.   Recommend remedies for problems.

   B.   Test for toxic chemicals.

   C.   Check for dust and asbestos.

   D.   Run the initial air quality test.

   E.   Recommend a final report.

18. According to the memo, during the air quality testing procedure, when should you check for dust and asbestos?

   F.   when no gas contaminants exist

   G.   when you run a toxic chemical test

   H.   when you find air contaminants

   J.   when you find gases exist

   K.   when dust and asbestos exist

Answers are on page 254.

Level 5 Introduction

The lesson and practice pages that follow will give you the opportunity to develop and practice the comprehension skills needed to answer work-related questions at a Level 5 rating of difficulty. The *On Your Own* practice problems provide a review of key reading skills along with instruction and practice applying these skills through effective problem-solving strategies. The *Performance Assessment* provides problems similar to those you will encounter on a Career Readiness Certificate test. By completing the Level 5 *On Your Own* and *Performance Assessment* questions, you will gain the ability to confidently approach workplace scenarios that require understanding and application of the reading skills featured in the following lessons:

Lesson 10: Identify Word Meanings

Lesson 11: Identify Meanings of Acronyms

Lesson 12: Define Technical Workplace Words

Lesson 13: Apply Technical Words in Various Situations

Lesson 14: Apply Instructions to New Situations

Lesson 15: Apply Instructions to Similar Situations

These skills are intended to help you successfully read and understand workplace documents such as procedures, policies, bulletins, and other publications. Reading these types of documents often requires the ability to:

- comprehend jargon, acronyms, and words that have several meanings as they are used in context,
- fully comprehend texts that include many details,
- apply technical terms and jargon to specific workplace situations,
- measure several considerations before choosing an action,
- apply information given in a document to situations that are not specifically described.

Through answering document-related questions at this level, you will continue to develop problem-solving approaches and strategies that will help you determine the correct answer in real-world and test-taking situations.

Remember!

Familiarity with other words, as well as with the structure of words, can help you determine the meaning of new or unfamiliar words.

Related Words are words that share the same base word but are used in different ways. For instance, if you know that the word *refer* means "to submit for information or consideration," this understanding might help you determine the meaning of related words such as *referral, reference,* or *referendum.*

Word Structure can be used to help determine a word's meaning if you understand the Greek and Latin roots of words. For example, the root word *hydra* means "water." Knowing this, you can figure out the meaning of a word that uses this root, such as *hydrant* or *hydraulics.*

Lesson 10 ■ ■ ■
Identify Word Meanings

Skill: Figure out the correct meaning of a word based on how the word is used

Identifying the correct meaning of words used in workplace manuals, procedural documents, and e-mail communications is key to understanding workplace communications. Oftentimes you can use the context and other clues within a document to help you understand the correct meanings of unfamiliar words. By understanding how to determine the correct meanings of unfamiliar words, you can better understand the workplace communications that will help you perform successfully in your job.

Skill Examples

School counselors help students who need emotional or psychological support. The counselor talks privately with the student to evaluate what problems he or she is experiencing. By determining what is wrong, the counselor can often help the student solve the problem without further help. Sometimes, however, the problem is serious enough to require a referral for professional help. The counselor has a list of approved specialists from whom the student can receive additional support.

Example 1
Determine the meaning of a word based on the context in which it is used.

The term *evaluate* is used in the second sentence in reference to something done while talking with the student about his or her problems. The next sentence begins, "By determining what is wrong...." This context clue relates to *evaluate,* and can help you determine that to *evaluate* something means to assess or review it for understanding.

Example 2
Use related words to determine the meaning of new words.

In the fourth sentence, the term *referral* is used. You may be familiar with the related word "refer." Using this prior knowledge, along with the context of the next sentence, you can determine that a *referral* is made when referring or recommending that the student see someone else about the problem.

Flight Safety Announcement Guidelines

Demonstrate how, in the event of an emergency water landing, each seat cushion is removable and can be used as a flotation device. Show passengers how to use the oxygen masks in the event of aircraft depressurization. Explain that if the aircraft loses air pressure, the mask will provide passengers with the oxygen they need to breathe.

Skill Practice

Use the document to the left to answer the following questions.

1. What is the meaning of the word **flotation** in the fourth sentence?

   A. lightweight

   B. easily removed

   C. containing a mask

   D. able to float on water

   E. able to float in the air

2. What is the meaning of **depressurization**?

   F. loss of altitude

   G. loss of normal pressure

   H. increase in air pressure

   J. air loss due to turbulence

   K. removal of oxygen from the air

Try It Out! ▪ ▪ ▪

You are a pharmacy technician working at ABC Pharmacy. What do you do when you track **inventory**?

A. Learn about new drugs.

B. Keep records of drug trials.

C. Record the amount of drugs in stock.

D. Determine which drugs are insured.

E. Separate name-brand drugs from generic drugs.

Step 1 Understand the Problem ▪ ▪ ▪

Complete the *Plan for Successful Solving.*

Plan for Successful Solving

What am I asked to do?	What are the facts?	How do I find the answer?	Is there any unnecessary information?	What prior knowledge will help me?
Determine the meaning of the term *inventory*.	Inventory is something for which you must keep accurate records. It is used in reference to medications.	Use context clues provided both in the sentence in which the term is used and in the sentences that follow.	The first and last sentences do not refer to the term *inventory*.	I have taken an inventory of things on the job and even in my home.

Step 2 Find and Check Your Answer ▪ ▪ ▪

- Confirm your understanding of the question and revise your plan as needed.

- Based on your plan, determine your solution approach: *The paragraph states that record keeping is the main part of what a pharmacy technician does. It also states that if the technician sees that the inventory of different drugs is low, he or she must inform the pharmacist, who should order more. This means that an inventory involves determining how much product is in stock. Among the answer choices, option C best describes this task.*

- Check your answer. Review all answers to determine if the answer you have selected is the best possible answer.

- **Select the correct answer:** C. Record the amount of drugs in stock.
  The passage states that if the pharmacy technician finds that drug inventory is low, he or she will order more drugs. Therefore, tracking inventory means determining how much of each drug the pharmacy has in stock.

ABC Pharmacy

As a pharmacy technician, you will be handling medical insurance forms for customers whose insurance covers prescription drugs. You will also maintain accurate records of the pharmaceuticals kept in the pharmacy, including tracking the inventory of both prescription and nonprescription medications. You must inform the pharmacist if inventory is running low for a particular drug. Then the pharmacist will order more. It is illegal for technicians to handle the drugs themselves or to give advice to patients on drug use.

Problem Solving Tip

Find the sentence that contains the word. Read it carefully to see if it provides hints about the word's meaning. Look for other words or phrases in the passage that give you additional clues about the meaning of the word.

Remember!

By understanding how context clues, related words, and word structure can all be used to determine a word's meaning, you can learn to make logical guesses when reading documents that contain new or unfamiliar words.

On Your Own ▪ ▪ ▪

Style Guide

Our copyeditors edit manuscripts that are written mainly by academics. Though these professors are experts in their field, they are not always the clearest of writers. Many academics tend to overuse jargon. Copyeditors must understand when it is acceptable to use jargon. Sometimes commonly used jargon is appropriate. Sometimes it is not. Copyeditors get a feel for the writer's use of jargon when they skim the manuscript before they begin editing.

If a copyeditor still feels that there is too much jargon, making the writing unclear, they should change it to more understandable, everyday English. Remember that our books are specialized and sometimes technical, but they should always be readable. Adjust grammar and wording, as necessary, to make the text easy to read without sacrificing factual information.

1. You are a copyeditor for a major university press. You edit books written mainly by academics. Based on the passage, what is an **academic**?

   A. a textbook

   B. a college professor

   C. a technical book

   D. a type of jargon

   E. a style of writing

2. A copyeditor should change the author's writing if there is too much jargon. Based on the passage, what is the meaning of **jargon**?

   F. factual information that is easy to understand

   G. understandable, everyday English

   H. specialized books that are readable

   J. specialized terminology, often hard to understand

   K. manuscripts written by academics

E-Energy, Inc.
TRAINING MANUAL

As a heating, ventilation, and air conditioning (HVAC) technician for E-Energy, Inc., you will be installing and maintaining HVAC equipment. You will work for both commercial and residential customers. All the equipment we install is highly energy-efficient.

There are skills you must master before you become a supervisor within our company. You must read blueprints. You must read technical specifications related to the equipment being installed and the building it will be installed in. You must understand the technical details for installation of natural gas, electric, and air conditioning systems.

Installation involves more than simply putting the equipment in place. It requires you to safely run feeder lines from water and fuel sources to the equipment. You must also know how to connect air ducts, vents, pumps, and other system components. You may also learn to conduct combustion tests.

3. As an HVAC technician, what information do you know if you understand the **specifications**?

    A.   energy efficiency

    B.   blueprints of the equipment and the building

    C.   technical details about the equipment

    D.   the types of fuel used in heating systems

    E.   alternative, renewable types of energy

4. When installing HVAC equipment, what do you do when you run **feeder lines**?

    F.   Seal pipes containing fuel.

    G.   Run electrical wires to the furnace.

    H.   Test the system for efficient combustion.

    J.   Make sure there are no gas leaks.

    K.   Connect the fuel source to the equipment.

Paper Earth, Inc.
PROCEDURES MANUAL

Remote sensing specialists at Paper Earth, Inc., work with our proprietary software to make maps for our customers. The software we have designed and that only we can use has simplified analyzing information retrieved from satellite data. All of our specialists must become familiar with all of our software's capabilities so they choose which program produces the best image for the customer.

Topographical Mapping

Paper Earth, Inc., makes the clearest topographical maps in the industry. Our state-of-the-art imaging software makes changes in elevation come to life on easy-to-read maps that can easily be customized to suit the needs of our customers.

---

5. You are a remote sensing specialist at Paper Earth, Inc. What is the **proprietary** software that you will use on the job?

    A. topographical maps

    B. satellite data

    C. software available on the Internet

    D. software used only by its inventor

    E. software that is highly sensitive to wavelengths

6. What does a **topographical** map show?

    F. areas of vegetation

    G. wavelengths of chlorophyll

    H. land height and formations

    J. a large expanse of land or ocean

    K. light emitted by different objects on Earth

Dear Staff,

I'm delighted to begin working with you as the new principal at Washington Elementary School. As the administrator of this school, I will listen to and be open to all your ideas for improving our school and the learning experience of our students. In working with you, the teachers, I hope to both expand and deepen the curriculum of all subjects that you teach. Whether it be reading, math, social studies, or science, I believe that learning is more than simply passing tests and meeting standards. Through a school-wide focus on a curriculum based in hands-on learning and critical thinking, I think that together we can enrich our students' learning experiences while making your job more enjoyable and challenging.

It is my main objective to raise the educational standards at our school. I am eager to work with all of you to achieve this aim. My office is always open to you. Please seek me out regarding any issues or ideas you may have. I'm certain that we can make ours one of the best schools in the state.

Sincerely,

R. Edwards

Principal

7. As a teacher at a middle school, you have been asked by your principal to help create the school curriculum. What is one component of a **curriculum**?

    A.   science

    B.   parent-teacher meetings

    C.   teacher training

    D.   standardized tests

    E.   recess

8. Based on the passage, what is the meaning of the word **objective**?

    F.   goal

    G.   subject

    H.   protest

    J.   position

    K.   responsibilities

State Employment Board

To: All Secondary School Vocational Counselors

Subject: New Opportunities

We are happy to announce that our state was one of six states selected by the federal government to receive $100 million in vocational education funding over the next five years.

Most of this new funding is earmarked for training in specific fields. Over half of the funds must be spent on vocational training in the field of renewable/alternative energy and energy conservation. The board asks you to suggest careers in these fields to students. Students who are interested in construction careers should try weatherization programs. This is about making older housing more energy efficient.

You will continue to evaluate students using the usual testing and interview methods. Students who want to follow other career paths should continue to be encouraged and informed about them.

---

9. You are a vocational education counselor who advises students on careers and training. You read that new funds are earmarked for certain careers. Based on the passage, what is the meaning of the word **earmarked**?

    A.   health care

    B.   available

    C.   designated

    D.   competing

    E.   already spent

10. What is one task done by a **weatherization** specialist?

    F.   forecasting

    G.   demolition

    H.   landscaping

    J.   insulating

    K.   painting

From: Ashlee Varishus

Date: April 19

To: All Department Heads

Subject: Quarterly Update

Our quarterly meeting will be held at 9:00 A.M. on Monday, April 27. All Department Heads are expected to attend. Each Department Head will give a presentation about progress and programs in his or her department.

The meeting agenda will focus on the rollout of our latest product, the Talkee™ mobile phone. As the new phone has been scheduled for release within six months, we are all especially eager to hear from the Communications Department about strategies for launching the advertising campaign three months prior to the product release date. The department will present ad campaigns to promote our new speak-text technology. As you all know, competition is fierce in this field, so we have to come on strong and positive to get a huge boost after the initial unveiling.

We are also waiting for the numbers from the Finance Department. Although we are concerned that our share price has been dipping lately, we are confident that a positive public response to the Talkee™ will help our company's stock reach new heights by the end of the year.

I look forward to seeing you all on Monday.

A. Varishus, CEO

11. As a department head in this company, you are helping to develop their new product. What will occur during the product **rollout** mentioned in the e-mail?

   A. The product will be designed.

   B. The product will be publicly sold.

   C. Share prices will go down.

   D. The product will be priced.

   E. The product will be rushed forward.

12. Based on the e-mail, what is a **share**?

   F. a type of profit

   G. new product cost

   H. a part of a product

   J. one company department

   K. a unit of company stock

Answers are on page 256.

Lesson 11
Identify Meanings of Acronyms

Skill: Identify the correct meaning of an acronym that is defined in the document

When reading business documents, you may encounter abbreviations known as acronyms that are used to replace long phrases. An acronym is a word that is formed with the first letters of a commonly used term or phrase. For example, **NASA** is the acronym for the **N**ational **A**eronautics and **S**pace **A**dministration. When you read about **NASA** in a document, you know that it is referring to this government agency. Often, the meaning of an acronym is stated in the document before the acronym is used to replace it. Recognizing acronyms will help you understand how the acronym contributes to the document's meaning.

Remember!

Though acronyms are technically words formed from abbreviations, there are many common workplace abbreviations that don't form words but are often referred to as acronyms as well. They include

ASAP As Soon As Possible

FYI For Your Information

CEO Chief Executive Officer

Other common business abbreviations include *profit and loss (P&L)*, *point of sale (POS)*, *limited liability company (LLC)*, and *business to business (B2B)*. By understanding the meanings of common acronyms and other workplace abbreviations, it is easier to read and comprehend workplace documents.

Skill Examples

The Environmental Protection Agency has recently reviewed the safety of the chemicals used in our plant. In June, we stopped all use of perfluorinated acid (PFOA) in our nonstick products in response to current research on PFOA and replaced it with EPA-approved chemicals. Because of this, we are confident that the EPA will publish a positive report of our company's commitment to public safety. The EPA report is due to come out on Monday.

Example 1
Determine the meaning of an acronym or abbreviation whose meaning is clearly stated.

Immediately following the first use of the term *perfluorinated acid,* the acronym *PFOA* is introduced in parenthesis. By identifying this acronym, *PFOA* can be used to replace *perfluorinated acid* each time this chemical is referred to in the text.

Example 2
Determine the meaning of an acronym or abbreviation whose meaning is not clearly stated.

Though the meaning of the acronym *EPA* is not clearly stated, the reader can look back and find the term that the acronym abbreviates by looking for the series of words that begin with the same letters *(Environmental Protection Agency).*

City Board of Health: Air Pollutant Tracking

Pollutants that must be tracked by air-quality technicians include polycyclic aromatic hydrocarbons (PAHs), nitrogen oxides (NOs), and ethylene dibromide (EDB). Levels of ground-level ozone must also be closely monitored. If the amounts of these hazardous air pollutants (HAPs) exceed health department limits, an air quality warning must be issued to the public.

Skill Practice

Use the document to the left to answer the following questions.

1. What are you looking for when you test for levels of PAHs in the air?
   A. EDB and NOs
   B. ground-level ozone
   C. nitrogen gases
   D. ethylene dibromide
   E. polycyclic aromatic hydrocarbons

2. In the past month, you have had to issue an air quality warning to the public. What does that indicate about the city's air quality?
   F. It contains no NOs.
   G. It has EDB.
   H. It has too many HAPs.
   J. It has few PAHs.
   K. It contains no HAPs.

Try It Out! ▪ ▪ ▪

As a water quality technician, you have received the procedures document to the right. According to the document, all of the contaminants being tested for are VOCs, an acronym that stands for what group of chemicals?

A. benzenes

B. trichloroethylene

C. volatile organic compounds

D. versatile organic contaminants

E. very carcinogenic chemicals

Procedures for Collecting Water Samples
All technicians working on the Mile Creek Site #2 are to obtain sterile samples of surface water. In the lab, they are to test the samples for the presence of one or more chemical contaminants. These include trichloroethylene (TCE), benzene, toluene, trichlorobenzene (TCB), vinyl chloride, and related volatile organic compounds (VOCs) to be determined by the lab supervisor. The results of these tests are to be completed no later than one month after the samples are taken.

Step 1 Understand the Problem ▪ ▪ ▪

Complete the *Plan for Successful Solving.*

Plan for Successful Solving

What am I asked to do?	What are the facts?	How do I find the answer?	Is there any unnecessary information?	What prior knowledge will help me?
Find the meaning of the acronym *VOC.*	*VOC* is used to describe a group of pollutants from the passage.	The third sentence uses the acronym *VOC* and explains what it means.	The first and last sentences do not refer to the acronym *VOC.*	Certain chemicals and classes of chemicals are referred to by an acronym.

Step 2 Find and Check Your Answer ▪ ▪ ▪

- Confirm your understanding of the question and revise your plan as needed.

- Based on your plan, determine your solution approach: *The paragraph describes a list of chemicals for which to test. After listing the names of some chemicals, it refers to other related volatile organic compounds, followed by the acronym VOC in parentheses. I will select option C as the meaning of the acronym.*

- Check your answer. Review all answers to determine if the answer you have selected is the best possible answer.

- **Select the correct answer:**   C. volatile organic compounds
  The passage states that all the specific chemicals listed are related because they are in the group of chemicals called volatile organic compounds (VOCs).

Problem Solving Tip

Look for the phrases and names whose words begin with the letters in the acronym and are in the same order as they are in the acronym.

Remember!

Acronyms are a type of abbreviation that are almost always made up of the first letter of each word in the phrase or name to which they refer. By using acronyms, writers avoid having to write out commonly used phrases and names every time they are used.

> ### Calibration Procedures for CAT Scan Technicians
>
> A computerized axial tomography (CAT) scan technician makes sure that the machine is calibrated, or accurately set up, for each use. The technician must provide vital information for the radiologist. This includes information about the correct scan field of view (SFOV), display field of view (DFOV), alignment, angle, and slice thickness. This information should be on the patient chart. Window width (WW) and window level (WL) must also be listed correctly. Technicians must explain these settings based on the part of the body imaged, its thickness, etc.
>
> In addition to the above, the technician should list the required imaging planes, the matrix size, and the name of the filming format to be used for the patient.

1. You are a technician who operates a CAT scan machine. Part of your job is to calibrate the machine, using an instruction booklet for technicians. The booklet states that you must provide the radiologist with information about the display field of view, which is represented by what acronym?

   A. CAT

   B. WW

   C. SFOV

   D. DFOV

   E. WL

2. WL and WW are set based on which criterion?

   F. temperature

   G. type of CAT scan machine

   H. part of the body imaged

   J. matrix size and plane

   K. field of view angle

U.S. Geological Survey

MEMO
To: Photogrammetrists
RE: Procedures update

As you know, the U.S. Geological Survey (USGS) is undertaking a program to completely revamp and upgrade its topographical maps of the United States. You will be working with a cartographer to create topographic maps of the Sierra Nevada mountain region.

Procedures

Information gathered by satellites operated by the U.S. government will provide initial data. Your global positioning system (GPS) receivers have been upgraded to improve collection of data received from these satellites. This will enhance the accuracy and detail of the new maps.

In addition, you will be using data gathered by planes carrying light-imaging detection and ranging laser technology equipment. The LIDAR laser technology provides the most accurate and detailed topographical information currently available. The laser data is stored on computer disks on the plane and is then downloaded to your computer. An innovative new program allows you to integrate the LIDAR data into the geographic information system (GIS) to create state-of-the art topographic maps.

If you or the cartographer on your team have any questions or concerns, please contact the station supervisor. Thanks for your enthusiasm and great work!

---

3. As a photogrammetrist with the U.S. Geological Survey, you have started using the new LIDAR technology to record topographical information. What is *LIDAR*?

    A. light-imaging detection and ranging technology

    B. laser-directed infrared radiometry technology

    C. laser-information direct analysis and remote sensing technology

    D. longitude decoding axial-laser recording technology

    E. laser-light distant assessment receiver technology

4. What information does GPS equipment provide?

    F. rotation of the earth

    G. position of the earth in space

    H. geological data on topography

    J. position of an object on the earth

    K. global weather system movement

National Oceanic and Atmospheric Administration

The following is a preliminary and very general overview of how NOAA and its constituent agencies are likely to fare in the upcoming federal budget.

CONSTITUENT AGENCY	BUDGET CHANGE	EFFECT ON PROGRAMS
National Marine Fisheries Service (NMFS)	− 2%	None, if efficiencies are improved
National Ocean Service (NOS)	+ 5 %	Funds provided for new program to monitor ocean acidification due to climate change
National Weather Service (NWS)	+ 2%	Funds increase monitoring of climate change-related weather
National Environmental Satellite, Data, and Information Service (NESDIS)	+ 2%	Funds for improving research on climate change and its effects
Office of Oceanic and Atmospheric Research (OAR)	+ 4%	Expand climate change research
Office of Program Planning and Integration (OPPI)	No change	None

5. You are a government service administrator in one of the agencies with NOAA. As noted in the budget overview above, only the NMFS will have cuts made to its budget. Without improved efficiency, what would these cuts affect?

    A. weather data collection

    B. monitoring of sea level

    C. oversight of marine fisheries

    D. research on ocean acidification

    E. provision of satellite data

6. What constituent agency within NOAA conducts research into atmosphere-ocean interactions?

    F. OAR

    G. NOS

    H. NWS

    J. OPPI

    K. NESDIS

A Technologies
EMPLOYEE MANUAL

As a programmer with A Technologies, you will be involved with a group that is creating customized software and programs for our clients. Many of our programmers use common business oriented language (COBOL), one of the oldest business-oriented languages used for creating programs. Most firms use this software to track corporate operations.

Another group of programmers develops application program interfaces for today's most popular operating systems. We currently have programmers who specialize in all major operating systems.

A third group is developing reduced instruction set computing (RISC). RISC recognizes a limited number of instructions, creating a field without boundaries, where the programmer can use her or his creative muscle.

7. As a computer programmer with A Technologies, you work with COBOL. The programming language used in COBOL is best suited to what type of computer environment?

    A. school

    B. library

    C. video game arcade

    D. cell phone application

    E. business and corporate

8. Why is RISC appealing to programmers?

    F. it is generally a type of computer environment

    G. because it eliminates bugs and other computer errors

    H. because programmers can use their creativity

    J. it does not recognize a limited number of instructions

    K. because it is the oldest business-oriented language

To: All HotSolar, Inc. Employees   Date: January 11

From: President and CEO

Subject: New Funding

_____

As you know, HotSolar, Inc. recently received a $150 million investment to develop high-efficiency, low-cost solar thermal technology. The new funding will help us improve our new concentrated solar power technology. Our first prototype CSP installation is almost done. The new funds will allow us to push forward the date for our trial run of the system.

This investment has attracted the interest of Southwest Electric Corp. They will partner with us to create high-voltage direct current capabilities. This will use electricity generated by our CSP installation. Once the HVDC lines are run, then the utility company will connect us into the network. We hope to show that CSP in the desert can provide the HVDC network with enough electricity to power the entire region. There is no loss of power during long-distance transmissions with HVDC.

9. You work as a solar energy engineer for HotSolar, Inc. What is the CSP system you are working on?

    A. a system that manages investments

    B. a system that uses concentrated solar power technology

    C. a system that promotes solar energy research and development

    D. a prototype for an electrical grid

    E. a very efficient type of rooftop solar panel

10. How does CSP improve electrical transmission?

    F. It is a high-voltage direct current with low-cost thermal technology.

    G It loses power during long-distance transmissions with HVDC.

    H. It provides a half-voltage distribution channel for a trial run.

    J. It does not lose power during long-distance transmissions with HVDC.

    K. It provides the network with electricity to power part of the region.

Training Manual: Physician's Assistant (PA)

The following is a brief overview of the training that you will complete as a new member of the team of physician's assistants (PAs) at our multi-disciplinary medical practice.

- As part of your training with cardiologists, you will learn to administer an electrocardiogram (EKG). You may also be trained to do preliminary evaluations of EKGs.

- During your assignment with the neurology staff, you will learn how to prepare patients for EEG tests. While you will not be required to interpret the electroencephalogram tests, you will assist in preparing and administering them.

- You will also be primarily responsible for venipuncture. Most physicians request a complete blood count test for patients who visit for their yearly physical. You will draw the blood for the CBC and will prepare it to be sent to the lab for analysis.

11. In your training to become a physician's assistant, you are currently learning how to give an EEG. What is an EEG, and in what medical specialty is it used?

   A. electroencephalogram; it is used in neurology

   B. electrocardiogram; it is used in heart disease

   C. electro endoscopy; it is used in family practice

   D. electro elevation; it is used in neurology

   E. electric encephalitis; it is used in neurology

12. What is a CBC?

   F. a cardiac background test

   G. a type of EKG

   H. a complete blood count

   J. a complete basal cardiograph

   K. a cardiovascular computer scan

Answers are on page 256.

Remember!

Since computers and software are such a key part of business and society today, much of the jargon used in the computer industry has become commonplace in everyday language. In *Skill Example 2*, you see two examples of jargon from the computer industry—*suite* and *mobile app*. Other jargon from or related to the computer industry includes:

firewall	wiki
e-mail	PDF
download	spam
upload	surfing
browser	blog
cookie	Wi-Fi
desktop	URL

Lesson 12
Define Technical Workplace Words

Skill: Identify the paraphrased definition of a technical term or jargon that is defined in the document

Within the workplace, jargon is specialized language that is specific to a certain industry or field. The restaurant term *86* is a jargon term meaning that an item has been cut ("86-ed") from the menu because the kitchen is out of that item. Technical terms are more formal and may be specific to a certain field or used across many industries. In many workplaces, the term *protocol* is a common technical term used to describe a procedure or code of behavior that employees are expected to follow. By learning the meaning of jargon and technical terms used within the field you work, it is easier to understand workplace communications and respond to them appropriately.

Skill Examples

At XYZ Software, we are proud of the programs our expert computer programmers design. You will be amazed at what a creative computer programmer can develop for your business using a binary code. Using just two digits, our expert staff can create customized software—be it a full software suite or smaller-scale mobile apps—designed to meet your company's needs. Contact us today.

Example 1

Determine the meaning of a technical term that is defined within a document.

In the second sentence, the technical term *binary code* is used. The third sentence informs you that the code the computer programmer uses contains just two digits, or numbers. From this you can conclude that the term *binary code* refers to a code that uses only two digits.

Example 2

Determine the meaning of jargon that is defined within a document.

Two jargon terms are used within the passage to describe the company's range of software products—*suite* and *mobile apps*. Since "full" is used to describe *suite* and "smaller-scale" is used to describe *mobile apps,* you can determine that each product requires different amounts of programming and has different levels of capabilities.

Electrical Repair Procedures

Before beginning work, first shut off the electrical current. After the problem is diagnosed, assemble the tools and parts needed for the repair. Before making the repair, the electrical wires must be grounded. Wires not attached to an object connected to the earth may conduct a current and cause problems. Sometimes, an Ohm meter is used to determine if there is too much resistance in the flow of the electrical current. If there is, new wires should be installed. When the repair is done, the electrical current should be turned back on to make sure everything works.

Skill Practice

Use the document to the left to answer the following questions.

1. As an electrician making an electrical repair, how do you know if a wire is **grounded**?

   A. It is damaged.

   B. It is broken.

   C. It is connected to a circuit.

   D. It is connected to the earth.

   E. It is short-circuited.

2. If you use an **Ohm meter**, you are trying to determine

   F. if there is a short circuit.

   G. if there is a grounded wire.

   H. if there is resistance to electricity flow.

   J. if there are broken wires.

   K. if the problem is fixed.

Reading for Information

Try It Out! ▪ ▫ ▫

You are an employee at a publicly owned company and have received the memo to the right. In the fourth sentence of the memo, to what does **fiduciary duty** refer?

A. trust

B. profits

C. investment

D. management

E. productivity

MEMO TO STAFF

Ours is a publicly owned corporation. That means that thousands of people own stock in our firm. They have invested in our firm because they believe that we will grow and increase our profits. As the CEO, I have a fiduciary duty to our investors. That means I must fulfill the trust they put in me to run the company in a sound and profitable way. As our profits have doubled during this year, I am sure investor confidence in our ability to meet their financial goals has been confirmed. I want to thank everyone in the firm for the fine job you have been doing this past year. Well done!

 Step 1 **Understand the Problem** ▪ ▫ ▫

Complete the *Plan for Successful Solving*.

Plan for Successful Solving

What am I asked to do?	What are the facts?	How do I find the answer?	Is there any unnecessary information?	What prior knowledge will help me?
Find the meaning of the term *fiduciary duty*.	The term is stated as a duty of the head of the company toward the investors.	First locate the term. Then use the sentences surrounding it to see if its meaning is defined.	The first three sentences come before the term's use but do not help identify its meaning.	I know that the CEO has an obligation to maintain the confidence of both employees and investors.

Step 2 **Find and Check Your Answer** ▪ ▫ ▫

▪ Confirm your understanding of the question and revise your plan as needed.

▪ Based on your plan, determine your solution approach: *I will locate where the CEO first uses the term* fiduciary duty. *He first uses this term in the fourth sentence. In the next sentence, he explains that this means he works with the confidence of the investors, who trust him to keep the company profitable. The term* fiduciary duty *therefore seems to refer to a responsibility a CEO has to the company's investors. I will select option A as the meaning of the term.*

▪ Check your answer. Review all answers to determine if the answer you have selected is the best possible answer.

▪ **Select the correct answer:**   A. trust
In the memo, the term *fiduciary duty* refers to the relationship between investors and the CEO. It relates to the trust of the investors that the company will be run well and, hopefully, at a profit.

Problem Solving Tip

Look for words, phrases, sentences, or descriptions in the passage and near the technical term that help explain what the term means.

Remember!

Jargon and technical terms are words used to mean something specific to a field of study or in a job or career. Sometimes a technical term is a common word that has a different, technical meaning. Jargon, however, refers to specialized language that consists of terms not used outside of one particular field.

NOTICE TO ALL EMPLOYEES

We have recently discovered that two of the dyes being used for our new line of textiles may be having adverse health effects on some workers. If you start to feel ill either at work or at home, please inform management immediately. We will schedule and pay expenses for a physician to test your exposure to these substances.

Be confident that we are taking all necessary steps to address the chance that these substances may be dangerous. I want to assure you that government regulators studied these substances before we started to use them. Neither substance was listed as poisonous; however, because of recent complaints, we have decided to conduct our own toxicological tests. The materials have been sent to a reliable lab for testing. We should have results in about two weeks.

In the meantime, for safety's sake we are asking all line workers to wear protective clothing. It should cover all exposed skin. You must also wear a facemask at all times in the production area.

We thank you for your patience as we work to quickly resolve this situation. Please feel free to contact me at any point should you have any additional questions or concerns. As always, your feedback is welcome and appreciated.

Regards,

M. Richards, Safety Engineer

1. As a health and safety engineer at this company, you have found that some substances might be having adverse health effects on workers. What is an **adverse** health effect?

   A. opposite

   B. negative

   C. delayed

   D. allergic

   E. neurological

2. What does a **toxicological** test determine?

   F. if something is healthful

   G. if something causes a rash

   H. if something is poisonous

   J. if something is airborne

   K. if something is an acid or a base

From: Randy

Date: **May 7**

To: TS Specs, Inc.

Subject: Writing Specs and Instructional Manual for the Pacer RX

I wanted to take a moment to update you as to the status of the development of our new laptop computer. The prototypes of the new Pacer RX will be complete by early next week. Once these fully functional samples of the new laptop are ready, we will send one over to your office so you can explore using it and get used to its many new features. I'm sure you'll find that working with the "real thing" will give you a far better grasp of how to write the documentation that will help customers understand how to use the new computer.

As we discussed before, you will also be responsible for writing the technical specifications for the laptop, in order to document the details about the computer design. We really like the proposed outline you have submitted so far. Once you receive the prototype, let us know if you have any questions.

Keep up the good work!

Randy

3. You are a technical writer for Tech Specs, Inc. You have been contracted to write user instructions for a new laptop computer. Before you can finish your work, you must use the prototype. What is a **prototype**?

A. a working model

B. an original drawing

C. a technical blueprint

D. a type of documentation

E. a computer operating system

4. What are technical **specifications**?

F. the code and model number

G. details about the design of the computer

H. a notice of why this computer is unique

J. a list of the components inside the computer

K. a list of questions

Draft Wind Energy
Press Release

Draft Wind Energy will soon release a new windmill. Our engineers have improved the efficiency of the Whoosh-5, our current model windmill. The new Whoosh-6 features rotors made from malleable materials. This helps them change their shape while they are rotating. The shape of the rotor, or blade, changes based on wind conditions. This makes sure the greatest amount of energy from the wind is transferred to the turbine.

In addition to the new construction of the rotors, a computer in the control tower monitors wind conditions. It adjusts the shape of the rotors and blades as well. Our new, more efficient, rotors can transmit more rotational energy to the motor. This helps the turbine generate more kilowatts of electricity for every turn of the windmill's rotors.

5. As a wind power engineer with this company, you helped design the new windmill using the advanced malleable material. What is a **malleable** material?

    A.   a hammered material

    B.   a rotating material

    C.   an efficient material

    D.   a flexible material

    E.   an unshaped material

6. What is a windmill **rotor**?

    F.   control

    G.   tower

    H.   turbine

    J.   engine

    K.   blade

READER'S PUBLISHING: Job Announcement

EDITOR—FULL TIME

Experience:

- At least five years of experience overseeing the production of trade books, from manuscript to bound book.

Skills/Responsibilities:

- Ability to maintain strict schedules for each of the steps in the publishing process.

- Evaluate the quality of writing in the manuscript, or draft version, of the book.

- Coordinate manuscript delivery to the copy editor.

- Send copyedited manuscript to the author for corrections and/or revisions.

- Approve the changes made by the author.

- Coordinate delivery of the final manuscript to the production department.

7. You are an editor at Reader's Publishing. You are responsible for evaluating manuscripts. What is a **manuscript**?

    A.   a copyedited book

    B.   a contract for a book

    C.   a draft of a book

    D.   a published book

    E.   a template of a book

8. What does an author do when he or she makes **revisions**?

    F.   changes the manuscript

    G.   sends the book to the printer

    H.   evaluates the schedule

    J.   sends the manuscript to the production department

    K.   sends the manuscript to the copy editor

Trainer's Manual

Most of our stock analysts are trained both on the job and in the classes you teach. Your responsibility is to make sure that the trainee learns all of the needed skills. You also must introduce and explain new concepts the trainee will be using on the job.

Trainees must understand trend lines, which show the general direction of moving averages for various durations. Chart analysis of the overall shift of a stock's price is another important tool analysts use in evaluating a stock.

Trainees must also be able to use technical analysis algorithms. Our company has created these mathematical formulas to help us find the value of a stock. The analyst trainee must understand each part of the algorithm. He or she must know where to get the data that are entered into the formula to give a usable result.

9. As a trainer for stock analysts at a company, you must help trainees understand skills and new concepts. What does a **trend line** show?

   A. different time scales

   B. types of charts

   C. stock features

   D. how to use algorithms

   E. general direction of movement

10. What is an **algorithm**?

   F. a type of stock

   G. a type of investment

   H. a mathematical formula

   J. the value of a stock

   K. movement of stock prices

To: All Employees of ABC Manufacturing

From: Yvette López, Industrial Engineer

As the newest member of the ABC Manufacturing team, I am delighted to be working with you all. As you know, my goal as an industrial engineer is to be what used to be called an "efficiency expert." My main job is to make everyone's job easier, quicker, and more efficient.

In my job I work a lot with computers and complicated mathematical formulas. Yet I feel that it is just as important to communicate with workers. I value the feedback I get from you about how a process can be made better. I have found that the best way to increase productivity is to engage with the employees who are actually producing the goods. Their suggestions for improving output, or our capacity for making more products for less money and in less time, are invaluable.

In my experience, nearly every worker has good ideas about how we can maximize production—and profits. Of course, the more we produce, the more we all benefit in terms of job satisfaction and security.

11. You are an industrial engineer with ABC Manufacturing. Your main job is to increase productivity. What is **productivity**?

   A. product output

   B. cutting costs

   C. factory size

   D. number of employees

   E. product value

12. According to the document, if you improve **output**, you

   F. make more products.

   G. lose fewer employees.

   H. find better tax breaks.

   J. expel less toxic waste.

   K. advertise more effectively.

Answers are on page 256.

Lesson 13 ▪ ▪ ▪
Apply Technical Words in Various Situations

Skill: Apply technical terms and jargon and relate them to stated situations

You must be able to apply technical terms and jargon within the workplace. For example, a meeting may end with the leader stating everyone's *action items* and asking for everyone to *circle back* the following day. By understanding these terms, you know that your action items are the things that you are responsible for completing, and that the leader would like to meet again tomorrow ("circle back") to discuss what progress has been made.

Remember!

Once you have an understanding of key technical terms within your industry or profession, you must then be able to apply them. Within workplace situations, these terms are used as everyday language, and employees within an industry are expected to understand how to carry out instructions that use jargon and technical terms without having to ask what they mean. Such understanding obviously takes time; however, the sign of a good employee is one who, upon reading or hearing unfamiliar jargon, works to learn its meaning and how it is applied.

Skill Examples

Our agency is starting a big ad account for a new soft drink. The creative director is the manager of the team working on this account. The text should be brief and catchy. It should convey the essence of the product we have been hired to sell. Graphic designers should submit their art and illustrations to the creative director. Illustrations must be eye-catching and enhance the copy submitted by copywriters. Please review the client's specs for this project.

Example 1
Understand and apply jargon to stated situations.

The passage provides directions to the creative team at an advertising agency. The last sentence asks the team to review the client's specs for the project. The term *spec*—an abbreviation for *specification*—is a commonly used jargon term.

Example 2
Understand and apply technical terms to stated situations.

As a member of this creative team, you may be asked about guidelines for writing copy. *Copy* is a technical term used in advertising to describe the text written for published materials. People who write copy are copywriters.

Skill Practice

1,000-Mile Checkups

Every truck must be thoroughly checked after trips of 1,000 miles or more. If the distributor is not routing electrical voltage properly, the spark plugs will not fire correctly and the engine may be damaged. If the driver reports that the engine is not running smoothly, the mechanic should check the solenoid, which controls the opening and shutting of the valves. Valves that do not operate smoothly can ruin an engine.

Use the document to the left to answer the following questions.

1. Under what conditions would you suspect that the **distributor** is not working properly?

   A. if fluid levels are low

   B. if the wires are wet

   C. if new spark plugs are needed

   D. if the spark plugs are firing incorrectly

   E. if the valves are loose

2. When would you replace the truck's **solenoid**?

   F. when tire pressure is high

   G. when you replace the spark plugs

   H. when valves do not operate smoothly

   J. when the distributor is malfunctioning

   K. when the valve seals are worn

Try It Out! ▪ ▪ ▪

You are a writer of nonfiction books. You are about to begin writing a new book, for which the publisher has sent you guidelines. When writing a book, what information do you include as part of the **bibliographic material**?

A. figures

B. quotes

C. statistics

D. 100,000 words of text

E. references used

Writer's Guidelines

As in all the titles within our *American History* series, you will provide 100,000 words of text. This does not include the bibliographic material, which lists your references and is set at the back of the book. Note that all dates, facts, figures, quotes, statistics, and other directly cited material must be referenced. You are also required to provide figures, tables, maps, and other illustrations that expand on your topic. A "Further Reading" section must contain both written and online sources that the reader can access for more information.

 Step 1 ## Understand the Problem ▪ ▪ ▪

Complete the *Plan for Successful Solving.*

Plan for Successful Solving

What am I asked to do?	What are the facts?	How do I find the answer?	Is there any unnecessary information?	What prior knowledge will help me?
Identify what information is included in bibliographic material.	*Bibliographic material* is referred to as a listing of the author's references.	Locate where the term is first used, and search for text that helps define the term.	Most of the passage, except sentences 2 and 3, does not help define the term.	I know that bibliographies have to do with research.

 Step 2 ## Find and Check Your Answer ▪ ▪ ▪

- Confirm your understanding of the question and revise your plan as needed.

- Based on your plan, determine your solution approach: *The passage describes guidelines a writer must follow. It states what the writer must submit as part of the book. In the second sentence, the passage explains that the writer must submit bibliographic material with the text. That sentence also defines this material as the reference material the author used to get the information used in the book. I will select option E as the meaning of the term.*

- Check your answer. Review all answers to determine if the answer you have selected is the best possible answer.

- **Select the correct answer:**   E. references used
  The passage states that the bibliographic material includes a list of the references that the author used. What must be listed in the references is further spelled out in the next sentence.

Problem Solving Tip

Look for the situation in which the technical term or jargon is used in the passage. Consider how the term is used in that situation, and see if it makes sense in a new context.

Remember!

Jargon and technical terms mean something specific in a field of study or in a job or career. As specialized terms, they often apply only in certain situations. Notice the description of the situation in the part of the passage that contains the jargon.

Gray Water Installations, Inc.
PROCEDURES BULLETIN

Our company designs and constructs gray water systems. One of our specialists will visit your building site to evaluate it. Then the specialist will recommend the most efficient used-water filtration and recycling system. Most of our gray water systems purify used water. They do this by using an energy-efficient, self-contained underground filtration system. However, where possible, we can design a fully functioning above ground, plant-based gray water installation.

Plant-based systems use no power. They contain wetland plants that slowly remove contaminants, particles, and other materials from the used water piped into the wetland from the home. The plant-based installation is designed so that the water is not recirculated until it is fully filtered. Gray water systems are excellent for saving water, as they permit reuse of water coming from sinks, bathtubs, washing machines, and dishwashers (but not from toilets). Gray water can be recirculated for use in toilets and for watering plants. In general, gray water is not potable, so these units are not recommended for drinking, only for non-potable uses.

1. You are a water-use efficiency expert and an installer of gray water systems. How would you define **gray water** to a prospective customer?

   A. It is a system of low-flow faucets.

   B. It is a system that waters and uses plants.

   C. It is a system that cleans and recycles water.

   D. It is a system that recycles uncontaminated water.

   E. It is a system that functions using no energy.

2. Why is gray water not **potable**?

   F. because it is not pure enough for drinking

   G. because it is recirculated over and over again

   H. because it contains bits of plant material

   J. because it may contain germs from the toilet

   K. because it may absorb underground soil contaminants

Memorial Hospital: Job Announcements

Positions Open: Our hospital has job openings for registered nurses with experience in the following specialties. Please apply only for positions for which you are qualified.

1. **Nephrology Clinic RN**
   Requirements: You must be licensed for the treatment of kidney disease. You must also have at least three years' experience working in a kidney dialysis center or clinic.

2. **Geriatric RN**
   Requirements: You must be a licensed geriatric nurse with at least two years' experience working with the elderly. Experience in treatment and therapy for diabetes, hypertension, or Alzheimer's disease is required.

3. **Trauma Center RN**
   Requirements: At least one year of experience in a trauma center or emergency room setting.

4. **Oncology RN**
   Requirements: You must be licensed in the treatment of cancer. The position that is open in our oncology department requires experience in the administration of chemotherapy treatment for all types of cancer. This position is in the adult treatment center. There are currently no openings in the pediatric clinic.

---

3. As a registered nurse, you are reviewing open positions in your hospital. You are licensed to work in the **nephrology** center. That means you have experience treating what type of diseases?

   A. kidney disease

   B. diabetes and blood disease

   C. Alzheimer's and senility

   D. adult-onset cancer

   E. severe trauma

4. You are also considering working as a geriatric nurse. A **geriatric nurse** works with what population of patients?

   F. men

   G. women

   H. children

   J. infants

   K. elderly

From: Riley Franks, Technology Manager

To: Computer Support Specialists

Subject: System-Wide Upgrade

Date: April 21

As part of the firm's technology review process, I will be evaluating all of the information technology (IT) capabilities. As many of you know, our Internet presence is excellent. Our Web site and the many links to our company have been well managed and are providing positive results for the firm. However, the intranet network that allows company employees and departments to communicate with each other is in serious need of improvement. Within the next two months a new intranet system will be complete. You will be notified when the new intranet system is ready to go live. You will also be trained in its use.

Finally, after reviewing the questionnaires you submitted to me, I realize that some of our computer hardware is also in need of an upgrade. Based on the information you provided, I will be reviewing the technical specifications of every computer in the company. For those of you whose computers are more than five years old, your computers will be replaced. For those of you whose computers are more current, we will first look to see if we can install new hardware, including monitors, hard drives, video drives, DVD drives, and other items that will make your computer-based work easier and more efficient. I assure you that whether you receive a new machine or upgraded hardware, your computer will be state-of-the-art, will run like new, and will work seamlessly with our software and our IT systems.

5. As a computer support specialist at this firm, you have just received the above e-mail. What type of system does your technology manager monitor when she oversees the firm's **intranet**?

    A. its electrical wiring

    B. its web site and links

    C. its use of the Internet

    D. its internal network

    E. its information technology

6. What is involved in a computer or system-wide **upgrade**?

    F. getting better equipment

    G. downgrading the newest software

    H. redesigning DVDs

    J. increasing questionnaires

    K. specifying video monitors

Operating Room Procedures

As a member of the operating room (OR) team, you are responsible for preparing the OR prior to surgeries. The following checklist provides a brief overview of your responsibilities.

- After you scrub up, you must sterilize all the instruments to be used to ensure that they are free of contaminants.
- Once the instruments are disinfected, you must set them out on the surgeon's tray in the order in which they will be used. You may also be asked to make sure instruments with moving parts are working properly.
- You must make sure that surgical drapes and solutions are sterile.
- During surgery, you may be asked to monitor the patient's vital signs and check the patient's chart.
- If a laboratory specimen is taken during surgery, you may be responsible for preparing it and taking it to the lab for analysis.
- You may also be asked to assist the surgeon in holding retractors, helping to count sponges, needles, supplies, and cutting sutures (or stitches) so that they can be removed once a closed incision is healed.
- After the surgery, you may be asked to transfer the patient from the OR to the recovery room.

7. As a surgical technician in a hospital, why is it important for you to make sure instruments are **sterile**?

    A.   because they are not disposable

    B.   because surgeons like cleanliness

    C.   because they must be free of contaminants

    D.   because they have moving parts

    E.   because they have moving parts

8. When might you help in cutting the **sutures**?

    F.   when taking the patient to recovery

    G.   when arranging instruments on a tray

    H.   when cleaning the drapes and solutions

    J.   once a closed incision has healed

    K.   when stitching up the patient after surgery

Good Energy Homes

EMPLOYEE HANDBOOK

As the materials conservation manager at Good Energy Homes, you are responsible for making sure that construction of our environmentally friendly and energy-efficient homes conserves materials as much as possible. Some conservation measures to consider are:

- Encourage designers to use two-foot increments when placing studs, and windows and doors in relation to the studs.
- Wherever possible, use pre-manufactured floor and roof systems. This reduces or eliminates the need for new sawn lumber.
- Use prefinished materials that do not require additional painting or coatings.
- Use sealed concrete floors.
- Use recycled or salvaged building materials where possible. Materials salvaged from other building sites must be tested to make sure they are in excellent condition, free of toxicity, and sturdy enough for use in new construction.
- Where possible, use construction materials made from recycled materials.
- Buy materials from companies that use renewable sources of energy (such as solar or wind) to run their manufacturing processes.
- Use only wood products harvested from certified, sustainable-use sources. Lumber having a Type A Forest Sustainability Certification ensures that the forests are not being destroyed in the process of logging.

9. You are a materials conservation manager with a construction company. Where would you get **salvaged** materials?

   A. at a municipal recycling center

   B. at the site of a demolished house

   C. at a forest certified lumber yard

   D. at a premanufactured materials firm

   E. at a prefinished materials company

10. Why would you buy **sustainable** forest products for the homes your company builds?

   F. because they are certified

   G. because they are made of recycled wood

   H. because they help preserve forests

   J. because they are manufactured

   K. because they are made using solar energy

INSTRUCTION MANUAL: Surveyor Field Work

Before going into the field, the surveyor must do research in libraries or county or municipal records offices. The job may require you to look up old deeds, old survey reports, and other documents that describe the legal boundaries of the land you are to survey. Research may also yield information about hidden construction, such as buried building foundations.

Once you have completed your research, you may begin your field work. Before beginning actual measurements, try to locate landmarks or boundary markers discussed in the older records. Identify and mark surface features that will aid the survey, including surface water, old stone walls, hills, notable trees or vegetation, etc. You must then use your knowledge of the site to choose the instruments needed for the survey. In addition to tapes and scanners, you will also likely need to use theodolites to measure the angles at the boundary corners.

Once all field measurements are taken, the data should be entered into our database, which will create a visual image of the property. If a map is also needed, data can be exported into our cartographic software program, which will enable you to produce a wide variety of maps based on the criteria you enter.

Once you have verified the accuracy of all images and maps, prepare the final report and make three copies. You will need one copy for our files, one for the property owner, and one for the county records office.

---

11. As a surveyor with this company, in what situations would you use **theodolites**?

    A.   when there are no identifiable surface markers

    B.   when the land has surface water

    C.   when the boundaries meet at odd angles

    D.   when the land is hilly

    E.   when you find they were used in old surveys

12. When would you input your data into a **cartographic** software program?

    F.   when the data are sparse

    G.   when the boundaries are unclear

    H.   when you must file a report with the county

    J.   when the land was not previously owned

    K.   when you need to make a map of the land

Answers are on page 256.

Lesson 14 ▪ ▪ ▪
Apply Instructions to New Situations

Skill: Apply straightforward instructions to a new situation that is similar to the one described in the material

It is important to understand what you are expected to do after reading instructions in documents such as e-mails and manuals. Managers often communicate instructions in writing, and employees are expected to apply them to new situations. For example, retail stores and restaurants often have detailed written instructions for how to open and close each day. It is expected that everyone completes the tasks that are listed within the instructions.

Remember!

Certain key words are commonly found in a variety of instructions. Some words you might find include:

do   push
open   turn
record   remove
prepare   explain

These kinds of words can help you identify what action you should take. They are often found at the beginning of a sentence.

Other words tell you how or when something should be done. These words, called *signal words,* include:

always   on
before   off
first   after
next   finally

Skill Examples

When recruiting personnel for our company, first explain what our company does and what positions are open. Ask candidates what skills they will bring to the job and how they will benefit the company. Be candid in informing them if you feel that their skills match the jobs we have available. If the applicants seem promising, ask them for a résumé. Ask them if they have any questions about the company or about careers with the firm.

Example 1

Apply instructions to a situation that is the same as the one described.

The instructions explain how a personnel recruiter should conduct an interview with job applicants. The recruiter may wonder what to do if an applicant is a good candidate for one of the open positions. The instructions explain that the recruiter should ask for a résumé and list follow-up questions that might be asked.

Example 2

Apply instructions to a situation that is similar to the one described.

An applicant may have skills that do not match a current open position but might match other positions that are currently filled. Though the instructions do not explain what to do in this case, the applicant's information should still be gathered in case a position better suited for his or her skills becomes available.

Skill Practice

When taking an inventory, always carry a clipboard with the list of products we sell and the recommended amount of each item we like to have on hand. First, get an order form from the supply supervisor. In the storeroom, check each item in the order in which it is listed on the form. If an item has been completely sold out, write "Full Order" next to that item. Widgets are our best sellers, and we like to have 1,000 on hand. If there are two boxes of widgets, and each box holds 100, then write 200 in the "In Stock" column next to the item name.

Use the document to the left to answer the following questions.

1. You are taking inventory at this company. What is the first thing you do after you obtain the list of products the company sells?
   A. count items
   B. get an order form
   C. write "Full Order"
   D. open boxes and count contents
   E. count items one by one

2. Your inventory shows that you have only one box of widgets in the storeroom. Based on the information in the passage, how many boxes of widgets must you order?
   F. one
   G. six
   H. nine
   J. ten
   K. one thousand

Try It Out! ▪ ■ ▪

You are an executive secretary at a large auto parts manufacturer. To whom would you write using an *external memo* template?

A. a department head

B. a company vice president

C. all the company's employees

D. a company you do business with

E. the president of the company

Memo-writing Protocol

Our company uses several different kinds of memos, depending on the purpose and the recipient. As an executive secretary, you must know when to use each one. An informal note from one employee to another should be created with the *employee memo* template. An informal or formal memo from an executive or manager to a group of employees should be created with the *administrative memo* template. When using these templates, be sure to fill in the "To:" and the "Subject:" lines above the body of the memo. All correspondence sent to clients or others outside the company must be created with the *external memo* template, which contains the company's logo.

 Step 1 ## Understand the Problem ▪ ■ ▪

Complete the *Plan for Successful Solving.*

Plan for Successful Solving

What am I asked to do?	What are the facts?	How do I find the answer?	Is there any unnecessary information?	What prior knowledge will help me?
Determine when an *external memo* template is used.	The passage explains when each type of memo template should be used.	Locate where it is explained when the *external memo* template should be used.	The first five sentences do not refer to the *external memo* template.	I know that the word *external* means "outside."

Step 2 ## Find and Check Your Answer ▪ ■ ▪

- Confirm your understanding of the question and revise your plan as needed.

- Based on your plan, determine your solution approach: *The paragraph describes when to use each type of template, depending on who is to receive the memo. The last sentence mentions the* external memo *template, and explains that this template should be used when writing to clients or others outside the company. I will select option D as the answer because it refers to a recipient outside the company.*

- Check your answer. Review all answers to determine if the answer you have selected is the best possible answer.

- **Select the correct answer:** D. a company you do business with
  The passage states that the template is used for correspondence outside the company. A company that this firm does business with is a company outside the firm. Because of this, you would use the *external memo* template to communicate with them.

Problem Solving Tip

Look for words, phrases, sentences, or descriptions in the passage that explain in what situation a certain action should be done. Then apply that information to answering the question.

Remember!

The instructions given within a passage are often general and can be applied to multiple situations. To answer questions such as the one in the *Try It Out!* example, you must first note what situation the question is asking about. Then find where within the passage the situation is mentioned and what you are expected to do when in that situation.

Unemployment Insurance Eligibility Verification

Determining Eligibility

You must determine the eligibility of applicants for unemployment insurance provided by the government. To do your job properly and to prevent fraud, you must verify that an applicant's situation merits benefits. To this end, you must:

A. See that the application is completely filled out. Obtain and record the information on the applicant's identification card (driver's license, passport, etc.). The applicant must also provide proof of address (a utility bill, etc.).

B. Record proof that the applicant's job has been terminated. Proof consists of a bona fide document from the company stating that the applicant was not terminated for cause. Photocopy this document and send it to the Verification Section, where they will contact the employer to confirm termination.

C. Record proof of the applicant's wages from the previous job. Photocopy one or more pay stubs and place it in the applicant's file.

D. Obtain proof from the applicant that he or she worked a minimum of nine months in the last year. If not, applicants are ineligible for benefits.

E. Verify the date of job loss.

F. Explain to the applicant how benefits are calculated and that it will take up to two weeks to receive the first check. If the applicant is in immediate need of funds, send her or him to the emergency social services department for evaluation and help.

1. As part of your job as a social services interviewer, you screen applicants' eligibility for unemployment benefits. The applicant at your desk worked 3 months in the last year. What do you do?

    A.   See that the application is filled out.

    B.   Inform her that she is ineligible for benefits.

    C.   Send her to the Verification Section.

    D.   Take a photo of the applicant for an ID.

    E.   Contact her previous employer for verification.

2. An applicant cannot wait two weeks for his first unemployment check. What do you do?

    F.   Ask for documentation from a bank.

    G.   Obtain proof from his employer.

    H.   Refer him to emergency social services.

    J.   Make sure the applicant was not fired for cause.

    K.   Refer the applicant to the Eligibility Appeal Board.

Standard Procedures in Response to a 911 Medical Emergency

The emergency medical technician (EMT) needs to be able to quickly react and assess the situation in order to provide competent, accurate care to patients. To do so, the following procedures should be followed at all times:

1. Upon arrival at the scene, assess the patient's condition.

2. If the condition is life-threatening, conduct appropriate procedures. These include, but are not limited to, techniques to open the airway if the patient is not breathing. If a tracheotomy is needed, only a licensed EMT may perform it. Restart the heartbeat if it is absent, either manually or with paddles (the latter only by a licensed EMT). Stop severe bleeding using appropriate procedures and materials. Suspected heart attack or stroke requires immediate hospitalization.

3. If the patient is not critical, get a medical history, including medications taken and the circumstances of the emergency. Treat minor injuries.

4. If the injury is minor, the patient may be treated and may remain in the home. If the patient's condition is critical, prepare the patient for transport to the hospital. Immobilize the head if there is a suspected brain injury.

5. Prior to transport, immobilize the patient on a backboard. Place this on a stretcher, and make sure the patient is well secured. Carry the patient to the ambulance. If the patient's condition is life-threatening, the EMT with the most advanced license should remain with and monitor the patient, while the other EMT drives to the hospital.

6. At the hospital, transfer the patient to the emergency room and provide the ER doctors with the written record they have made of the patient's condition and their treatment so far. Speak with the doctor to convey important details not on the written record.

7. Check ambulance supplies and restock those supplies that are running low.

---

3. You are an EMT whose current patient has collapsed with severe chest pain. What do you do?

   A. Manually restart his heart.

   B. Use paddles to restart the heartbeat.

   C. Ask if the patient's situation is critical and if he needs hospitalization.

   D. Prepare the patient for transport to the hospital.

   E. Administer heart medication if the patient wants to remain at home.

4. Your next patient is at home with a minor cut from a steak knife. You determine the patient is not critical. What do you do?

   F. Take the patient to the hospital immediately.

   G. Stop the bleeding and prepare the stretcher.

   H. Check that the patient's heartbeat is normal.

   J. Offer the patient a blood transfusion.

   K. Get a medical history and treat minor injuries.

LDO Consulting Inc.   December 13
122 S. Windsor
Frisco, CO 80443

Dear Sunbright Solutions:

It is a pleasure to be working with your firm as a consultant management analyst. By thoroughly analyzing the firm's presence on the Internet, I will be making recommendations for improving the effectiveness of that presence. Before I begin my analysis next week, however, I wanted to give you a bit more detail as to the steps that I will take and what it is I am looking to accomplish.

My first order of business is to evaluate the firm's Web site to determine if it presents an interesting and inviting face to the web-surfing public. If the company's Web site needs to be redesigned to make it more effective, I will submit my recommendations for the redesign. I will also submit a procedure the firm can follow for future Web site updates.

Once I have completed my analysis of the design and functionality of the Web site, I will analyze the Web sites and search engines that link to the firm's Web site and/or to the firm's products. If I determine that there are too few links to your Web site or products, I will prepare a plan of action for increasing the firm's Internet visibility. There are methods available, such as submitting your Web site URL to search engines, that I will recommend to ensure that the most popular Internet search engines display your firm's name and/or its products when various relevant search terms are entered.

Finally, I will also make sure that news coming out of your firm is included in industry and other news blogs and e-mail newsletters. This is an excellent way to keep the industry and the public informed about your company and its products.

Sincerely,

Stella Thomas

5. You are an analyst working with an outside consultant. What do you do if the firm's Web site is cluttered or boring?

   A.   Increase links to it.

   B.   Add online sales of products.

   C.   Increase its visibility.

   D.   List it in newsletters.

   E.   Redesign it.

6. You find that an Internet search for the firm's products does not yield results for the firm. As a consultant, what is one thing you can do for the firm?

   F.   Create a blog for the firm.

   G.   Hire a graphic designer to update the Web site.

   H.   Submit the Web site URL to search engines for the firm.

   J.   Pay to have other Web sites provide links for the firm.

   K.   Have the firm rename its products so they appear in searches.

From: Ackerman, Tanya

Sent: Fri Oct 30 08:43:46

Subject: URGENT

Good morning,
I need 35 color copies, double-sided, printed in the 3-slides per page with notes format of the following presentation files:

market_analysis_2007thru2010
5year_MasterPlan
new_mrkts_growth_forecast

I have put these files in my transfer folder. After printing, please staple all of these files.
I also need 35 copies of the Quarter 1 Sales document that is also located in that folder.
They need to be delivered no later than first thing Monday AM to:

Tanya Ackerman (Guest)
Oasis Gardens Hotel
714 Seventh Avenue
Crescent Canyon, AZ 62579

Sorry for the short notice, but I just received confirmation that this presentation is happening.
Please confirm that you will be able to have these printed and shipped in time.

Thanks,
Tanya

---

7. You are an administrative assistant for a marketing consulting group, and you have just received this e-mail from your boss, requesting that specific files be printed, stapled and shipped to her at a conference in Arizona. According to the e-mail, how should you prepare the Quarter 1 sales document?

    A.   You should place it in the boss's transfer folder.

    B.   You should make 35 color copies, double-sided, and staple them.

    C.   You should transfer the information to a CD.

    D.   You should transfer the information to a spreadsheet.

    E.   You should send one hard copy to the boss's hotel room.

8. Your boss has just called you and said that she is going to give the exact same presentation next week in New York. What question do you need to ask her in order to get started?

    F.   What is the presentation going to be about?

    G.   How many people will be at the presentation?

    H.   What is the hotel address?

    J.   Where can I find the material that you need?

    K.   What is the file name for the presentation?

Guidelines: Trench Excavation

When creating a trench for a residential geothermal heating/cooling system, follow these guidelines:

1. Prepare a flat area to stockpile excavated material.

2. Excavate a trench whose walls are not less than 6 inches or more than 8 inches below either side of the pipe to be installed.

3. Have a pump worker remove all water from the bottom of the trench. Dig side drainage ditches along the trench for water runoff.

4. Grade the bottom of the trench to provide uniform bearing and support for the pipe.

5. Remove all spongy or unstable materials from the trench that will undermine a firm foundation for the pipe. Replace with approved material as instructed by the construction supervisor.

6. Backfill the excavation with the stockpiled material. Compact until firm.

   Note: Do not backfill until the site has been inspected and approved by the appropriate official.

7. Backfill by depositing material in 6-inch-deep layers. Carefully tamp down each layer before adding the next. If during backfill sharp rocks or other sharp objects are found, remove them, as they may pierce the pipe.

---

9. You are a geothermal construction worker preparing a trench. What should you do if you find unstable material in the trench?

   A. Replace it from the stockpile.

   B. Remove it with water.

   C. Tamp it down until it is compact.

   D. Replace it with approved material.

   E. Have it approved by an official.

10. While you are backfilling the trench, you notice a rock in the stockpiled material that has a sharp edge. What should you do?

   F. Place it at the outer edge of the trench.

   G. Surround it with softer, spongy material.

   H. Compact it within looser, softer soil.

   J. Use it to create the firm base for the pipe.

   K. Remove it because it may damage the pipe.

From: Ann Li, Government Accountability Office (GAO) **Date:** April 19

To: Financial Service Institutions

Subject: Report Overview

Our team has been asked to evaluate the federal government's oversight options regarding the financial services sectors. This includes banks, investment banks, brokerages, hedge funds, and similar institutions.

As a primary research team at the GAO, we will be writing the part of the report that describes the background of this sector of the economy. We will describe how it functioned in the past and how it has functioned recently. We will offer our analyses of why it has run into such serious problems lately. All of you are researchers, and some of you are economists. We will use your expertise to illuminate this problem for Congress. We will meet periodically to discuss strategy and share progress reports.

All of you have access to the Library of Congress and the Congressional Record. You can also access reports from the various divisions of the federal government. As per GAO guidelines, if you find it necessary to interview or obtain records from private individuals or from the states, please contact me. As head of the department, I will make arrangements for you. Also, we anticipate that we will discover a certain amount of complex mathematical or accounting data, which no one on our team may be able to interpret. In that case, I have obtained authorization for you to pass these data on to the GAO's accounting specialists for analysis. You may seek their assistance on your own.

Feel free to let me know if you need further assistance, referrals, or expertise from another part of our agency, or from outside the agency. I will make the necessary arrangements so you can get the information you need.

---

11. As a researcher working for the GAO, you have been asked to move from the financial services research team to a new team researching the automobile industry. Your first task is to analyze how the automobile industry functions. To do so, you need information from the state of Michigan. What should you do?

   A. Find it in the Congressional Record.

   B. Find it in the Library of Congress.

   C. Have your department head arrange for you to get it.

   D. Have the head of the department bring in someone from Michigan.

   E. Have someone from Michigan who works at the GAO provide the information.

12. During your research, you have found what you believe may be irregularities in the account books of one automaker. You do not have a strong understanding of accounting. What should you do?

   F. Arrange an interview with the automaker's accountant.

   G. Pass the information on to the Department of Commerce.

   H. Have your department head analyze the information for you.

   J. Have an accounting expert at the GAO analyze the information.

   K. Refer all irregularities to the Securities and Exchange Commission.

Answers are on page 256.

Lesson 15 ■ ■ ■
Apply Instructions to Similar Situations

Remember!

When reading instructions, specific conditions that help you decide what to do are often indicated in the text by "if-then" statements.

In such statements, the word *if* indicates the condition, and the word *then* indicates the action that should be taken.

If you receive an approved order form, *then* you should complete the order for processing within 24 hours.

Sometimes "if-then" statements do not include the word *then*.

If you need time off, you must submit a request at least one week in advance.

Skill: Apply complex instructions that include conditionals to situations described in the materials

Many workplace instructions include steps during which more than one result could occur. In these instances, there are often different "next steps" that must be taken. For example, when counting the money in a cash register drawer at the beginning of a shift, a cashier knows how much money should be in the drawer. If the amount of money is correct, the cashier may begin his or her shift. If the amount of money is incorrect, the cashier needs to notify the appropriate supervisor of the error. A situation in which the appropriate next action depends on the result of a previous action or event is called a *conditional*.

Skill Examples

The construction manager must make sure materials are available on-site when they are needed. Lack of necessary materials at a particular time can result in worker downtime and schedule delays. This may result in financial costs to the builder. Construction managers should phone suppliers one week prior to the date materials are needed. If there is any doubt that the materials will be ready, the manager should hire other suppliers.

Example 1

Apply complex instructions to a conditional situation.

The passage describes a construction manager's main duties. The manager needs to know what should be done if a supplier cannot deliver materials on time. The last sentence explains that the manager should hire another supplier if the materials cannot be delivered on schedule.

Example 2

Apply complex instructions to a similar situation.

A situation may arise where the supplier notifies the manager just days before the delivery date that they will no longer be able to deliver the materials on time. In this situation, the supplier should again try to hire another supplier that can deliver the necessary materials on schedule.

Testing Lung Capacity

Perform the first spirometer test with the patient in a sitting position. Note the test results. Help the patient on the treadmill and ask the patient to begin walking at a slow pace for two minutes. Immediately perform another spirometer test. Listen again to the lungs. If the patient complains of extreme fatigue or shortness of breath, discontinue the test immediately. If the patient does not complain of extreme fatigue or shortness of breath and the results of the first walking exercise are at or near normal, repeat the walking exercise at an increased rate of walking speed.

Skill Practice

Use the document to the left to answer the following questions.

1. Under what circumstance should a patient exercise at a greater speed?

   A. before the first spirometer test

   B. after the first spirometer test

   C. if the results are normal after slow walking

   D. if lungs are strained after slow walking

   E. when sitting tests are normal

2. Under what conditions should you stop testing a patient?

   F. if you note the test results

   G. if the patient is sitting

   H. if the patient needs help getting on the treadmill

   J. if the patient becomes short of breath

   K. if the patient walks slowly

Try It Out!

You are a loan counselor at a bank. Based on the information in the passage, under what conditions might a client whose income cannot cover any loan still get the loan from the bank?

A. The client gets another job.

B. The client expects to get a raise.

C. The client pays no income taxes.

D. The client has no outstanding debt.

E. The client has a qualified co-signer.

Loan Screening Procedures

In order to accurately screen a client, you must obtain all current bills and credit records. Review the materials the client brings in, making sure that all utility and credit card bills are included. The client should also bring in rent, mortgage, or loan payment statements. Review the client's income by looking at tax returns or pay stubs from the past three years. Based on this information, calculate the client's income and expenses. Explain to the client the amount of any loan that his or her income can cover. If the client's income cannot cover any loan, explain why that is the case. If the client is in dire need of a loan, you may determine if they have a relative who will co-sign for the requested loan. In this case, you must obtain the same financial information from the co-signer as you did from the client.

Step 1 — Understand the Problem

Complete the *Plan for Successful Solving.*

Plan for Successful Solving

What am I asked to do?	What are the facts?	How do I find the answer?	Is there any unnecessary information?	What prior knowledge will help me?
Determine under what condition a loan can be given to someone whose income cannot cover it.	The client lacks income to cover a loan. There are conditional procedures for allowing a loan to be given to the client.	Look for *"if-then"* statements that refer to the client lacking sufficient income to cover a loan.	Everything prior to the last two sentences describe the screening process, not the approval process.	I know that a parent may co-sign a student loan for a child.

Step 2 — Find and Check Your Answer

- Confirm your understanding of the question and revise your plan as needed.

- Based on your plan, determine your solution approach: *The procedures describe what information must be obtained before determining if a client can be approved for a loan. The question asks when a loan may be approved even if the client does not have enough income to cover the loan. The last two sentences describe conditions by which a co-signer can help the client get the loan. I will select option E because it best matches this condition.*

- Check your answer. Review all answers to determine if the answer you have selected is the best possible answer.

- **Select the correct answer:** E. The client has a qualified co-signer.
  The passage states that an emergency loan can be granted to a client with insufficient income if a relative who can prove he or she can qualify for a loan is willing to co-sign for the loan.

Problem Solving Tip

Look for sentences or descriptions in the passage that explain the conditions under which a certain action can be taken. Such explanations can often be found within *"if-then"* statements. Then apply that information to the question or problem being posed.

Remember!

Not all *"if-then"* statements contain the word *then*. In the *Try It Out!* example, both the seventh and eighth sentences contain *"if-then"* statements that do not include the word *then*.

Credit Solutions Inc.
233 Record Blvd.
Laurel, MD

June 11

Dear Mr. Duran,

I am sorry to have to inform you that your request for a loan has been denied. I did extensive research into your credit history. I found that you are a homeowner and that you have consistently paid your mortgage on time and in full. That is a very positive part of your credit history. Your credit history also reveals that, in general and with only a few exceptions, you pay your credit card bills on time.

However, your credit history also shows that about 10 years ago, an automobile you owned was repossessed because you were behind on your car loan payments. Everything else in your credit history would lead us to offer you the loan you seek. Unfortunately, the default on your car loan is too serious a matter for our firm to ignore.

It is therefore with regret that our company must reject your request for a loan.

Sincerely,

M. Johnson
Credit Analyst

1. As a credit analyst supervisor with Credit Solutions Inc., you are required to review denial letters sent out to loan applicants. Based on this letter, what might convince your company to lend money to an applicant?

   A.   The applicant is a homeowner.

   B.   The applicant has no credit cards.

   C.   The applicant pays a low mortgage interest rate.

   D.   The applicant pays the mortgage on time.

   E.   The applicant has a short credit history.

2. In which situation, as communicated in the analyst's letter, would your company be inclined to refuse an applicant a loan?

   F.   if the applicant failed to pay a loan

   G.   if the applicant rented an apartment

   H.   if the applicant did not own a car

   J.   if the applicant had too many credit cards

   K.   if the applicant had no credit history

Checklist: Truck Servicing

Follow our company checklist when checking or servicing our firm's trucks. Make a notation on the checklist next to each item you have looked at and found to be in good working order. Basic systems to be checked during routine maintenance include inspections of the braking system, the steering mechanisms, the wheel bearings, compression, and other engine parts and systems. If you find that any of these systems needs repair, schedule a repair and have the truck taken to the service department to be fixed.

Most new trucks will require you to analyze the information in the microprocessors, or computer chips, that control engine function. You must hook your laptop computer to the microprocessor and use our software to obtain a reading from the computer. The computer output will indicate if all systems are functioning well. It will also indicate which, if any, systems need repair or adjustment.

All trucks must be tested to ensure that they meet current emissions standards. New trucks have emissions controls that, if working properly, reduce emissions to within government standards. Older trucks may have to be retrofitted with emission-control devices to reduce harmful exhaust gases. If you find any trucks that do not meet these standards, schedule a retrofit with the service department.

3. You are a diesel service technician with a large trucking company. When do you need to use a computer to do your job?

  A. when making a repair

  B. when analyzing exhaust emissions

  C. when testing emissions

  D. when retrofitting an older truck

  E. when a truck has a microprocessor

4. When would you order a retrofit on a truck?

  F. when it is too old

  G. when it emits too many harmful gases

  H. when its computer chip indicates a faulty exhaust system

  J. when it needs a complete replacement of the muffler system

  K. whenever government emissions standards change

PROCEDURES MANUAL

Monitoring Integrated Control Systems

Every wind turbine has integrated control systems. It is your job to monitor these systems to make sure they work properly.

Monitoring Computer Controls

The computer controls should be monitored. You should make sure they align the physical conditions with rotor performance. Other conditions monitored include vibration and temperature. All measurements should fall within the strict guidelines for performance. Any measurement outside these guidelines means there might be a problem.

Circumstances for Physical Inspection

A physical inspection should be performed when monitoring reports indicate measurements outside the guidelines. This may include unbalanced or misaligned blades, looseness or weakness in the gears, weakness in the turbine foundation, or excess vibration. Technicians should make all necessary repairs as soon as possible.

Monitoring Lubrication System

The wind turbine's centralized, automated lubrication system is especially important. If the lubrication control grease is abnormal, the technician should do a manual check and lubrication of all parts. Be aware that this can introduce contaminants into the lubrication system. We ask managers to make every effort to fix this system via the computer. It is necessary to shut down a turbine to replace the lubrication control device rather than lubricate the parts by hand.

---

5. You are a technical manager at a wind energy company. Under what conditions would you have to do a hands-on inspection of the wind turbine and its various parts?

    A. if the turbine is underperforming

    B. if the computer controls are not working

    C. if the measurements are too high or too low

    D. if a repair cannot be made in a timely manner

    E. if wind speed is low enough to permit a physical inspection

6. In what situation might it be necessary to shut down the wind turbine for a vital repair?

    F. to replace lubrication controls

    G. to remove contaminants from the gears

    H. to locate the source of excess vibration

    J. to replace a misaligned blade or rotor

    K. to tighten any loose or weak gears

From: Christopher Kant

Date: August 21

To: Drafting Department—All

Subject: Design Protocol

Management has been informed that the client wants changes in the design of the new aircraft. Once the client approves our sketches, drafters can finalize amending the current design using the recently upgraded computer aided design and drafting (CAD) software.

Once a revised design is approved, you will have to recalibrate the technical details of the aircraft. Aerodynamics should not be affected by the design changes. However, the technical specifications of the design will require a recalculation of most design elements. CAD should calculate all changes in the number and type of fasteners and other structural elements needed to accommodate the new design. Also, pay special attention to any changes that might have to be made to the electrical system or to any safety systems in the aircraft. Alterations of this type could substantially increase the cost of production, so the client may again rethink the plane's design.

Sorry for this last-minute e-mail. We look forward to seeing your designs.

Thank you,
Chris

7. As a technical drafter for a company that builds airplanes, in what situation might you be asked to resubmit design sketches?

    A. when the CAD system is too detailed

    B. when a design change is requested by a client

    C. when the aerodynamics is not affected by the change

    D. when the aircraft has aerodynamics

    E. when the cost of the aircraft may change

8. Which system would a drafter attempt to keep unchanged in order to hold down costs?

    F. the safety system

    G. the CAD system

    H. the structural system

    J. the fastening system

    K. the aerodynamic system

COST ESTIMATE CHECKLIST

The sales department management team needs a cost estimate for our new vehicle. Please include:

1. **The cost of any new machinery needed for production.** First, an exhaustive attempt must be carried out to adapt current machinery to the new project. Consult with engineering to determine the feasibility of adaptation.

2. **The cost of labor.** This is particularly important if new hires are needed to work with the proposed new materials.

3. **The cost of materials.** The selling point of the new vehicle is the incorporation of carbon fiber into the body. This will provide greater strength and safety, with far less weight. We are aware that carbon fiber costs much more than steel. We need you to determine if that extra cost can be absorbed through higher sales. Greater sales are anticipated because of the excellent gas mileage carbon fiber will give the car. Consult our sales departments for more data.

4. **The cost of subcontracting.** Can our current subcontractors provide parts at current or lower prices? Determine the minimum number of units we must produce to keep subcontracting costs at their current level. Please provide a complete list of all carbon fiber contractors and the bid from each.

5. **Total cost of production.** After factoring in all the costs, provide a break-even point for the number of vehicles we need to produce and sell at or below the price. This is our target price. In your estimate, emphasize those factors, aside from materials, that will allow us to meet our cost target.

---

9. You are a cost estimator for an auto company. Under what conditions is the cost of machinery kept low when manufacturing a new vehicle?

   A.   when no new workers must be hired

   B.   when new materials are not introduced

   C.   when existing machinery can be adapted

   D.   when new equipment can be bought cheaply

   E.   when the new vehicle is identical to current models

10. Why must the cost estimator calculate the minimum number of vehicles produced?

   F.   because most people don't buy new model cars

   G.   because labor costs are lower when more cars are made

   H.   because there is very little carbon fiber produced

   J.   because higher production reduces subcontractor costs

   K.   because the target price depends on the car's fuel efficiency

Consultant Responsibilities: Legal Registered Nurse

A legal registered nurse consultant at our law firm has the following responsibilities:

- Interview potential clients. Use your medical expertise to evaluate their claims. Based on the interview, determine if this is a case the firm might accept.

- Obtain a copy of all relevant medical records. Evaluate these records and write a summary report. Submit this report to the attorneys. Your report should explain why the medical records do or do not support the potential client's case.

- If you determine that the case warrants further investigation, contact witnesses and others involved in or related to the claim. Initially, written notes based on interviews or letters will be sufficient to help us determine if we will take the case. Your notes should include a summary of your evaluation of the case's viability. Later, if we take the case, these witnesses will be asked to come into the office to give depositions, or statements.

- If a case seems to have merit, collect more evidence, as needed, to support it.

- Determine the dollar amount of damages the client is likely to be awarded.

- When all materials have been assembled, provide the attorneys with a comprehensive written evaluation of the case. Attach all of the above noted materials for our review.

- If our firm decides to take the case, you must be available to consult with the legal team on all relevant medical issues.

11. As a legal registered nurse consultant, you evaluate potential clients. At what point in the process of evaluation do you submit an initial report to the lawyers?

    A. after getting the medical records

    B. after conducting all interviews

    C. after the firm has decided to take the case

    D. after determining the cost of the case

    E. before meeting the potential client

12. In what situation do witnesses make official statements to the lawyers?

    F. during your investigations

    G. when the case goes to court

    H. when the medical records are incomplete

    J. before the lawyers decide to take the case

    K. after the law firm decides to take the case

Answers are on page 256.

Level 5 Performance Assessment

The following problems will test your ability to answer questions at a Level 5 rating of difficulty. These problems are similar to those that appear on a Career Readiness Certificate test. For each question, you can refer to the answer key for answer justifications. The answer justifications provide an explanation of why each answer option is either correct or incorrect and indicate the skill lesson that should be referred to if further review of a particular skill is needed.

EPA Job Description:

Data Technician

Data technicians in the climate change division of the Environmental Protection Agency (EPA) will gather, organize, and input data received from research scientists at agencies, institutions, and universities. The majority of the data you will gather as part of our ongoing monitoring of greenhouse gases (GHGs) must be entered into the appropriate data file. In addition to GHGs, you must be able to identify, separate out, and input data about long-lived GHGs (LLGHGs), such as carbon dioxide and methane, into the database dedicated to tracking them. Additionally, you must identify and maintain the database of trace gases, such as chlorofluorocarbons (CFCs), that contribute to greenhouse warming. A separate database tracks trends in atmospheric water vapor (AWV).

Accuracy of data input is vital. The accumulated data will become part of the report sent by the United States to the Intergovernmental Panel on Climate Change (IPCC) for inclusion in their next comprehensive report on the global climate. These data help inform the panel in developing recommendations for international climate change policy.

1. The above passage is part of your job description as a new data technician with the Environmental Protection Agency. You receive a report containing measurements of carbon dioxide in the Midwest. What acronym do you look for in the database into which you must input this information?

   A. CO_2

   B. GHG

   C. AWV

   D. EPA

   E. LLGHG

2. You input data about the amount of trace gases in the atmosphere. Which greenhouse gas amounts do you input in the column labeled CFC?

   F. water vapor

   G. methane

   H. IPCC

   J. LLGHG

   K. chlorofluorocarbons

Medical Examiner's Office
Technician Manual

As a technician at the Medical Examiner's Office, you must maintain the strictest procedures regarding non-contamination of evidence. When aiding in the investigation of a homicide, all forensic evidence must be obtained with sterile tongs and stored in sterile containers. Evidence may be disallowed in the legal case if it is contaminated in any way. For this reason, the technician must wear surgical gloves, protective clothing, and a hair covering when retrieving evidence. Small evidentiary items, such as bits of fiber, glass, soil, etc., must be placed in an appropriate container. Samples of body substances, such as fluids, hair, and tissue are kept in sterile laboratory receptacles for further analysis.

It is vital that all samples be labeled with the case number and the contents. All case samples must also be stored together. If the medical examiner discovers a bullet in the victim, you are responsible for sealing the container and transferring it to the police department for ballistics tests. These tests are intended to yield information about the gun, the bullet, and the conditions under which it was fired. You are to keep a record of all samples that are transferred out of the Medical Examiner's Office, including when they are sent out and when they are returned. All reports and analyses must be kept with the other case materials.

3. As a Grade II technician in the County Medical Examiner's Office, why is it important to keep **forensic** evidence uncontaminated?

    A. because it reveals the cause of death

    B. because it forms the legal basis of the case

    C. because it reveals fingerprints that identify the criminal

    D. because it always contains traces of the perpetrator

    E. because it is first sterilized for storage in contaminant-free containers

4. What information is revealed during a **ballistics** test?

    F. fingerprints

    G. identification of body fluids

    H. the type of firearm used

    J. whether the bullet caused the death

    K. the police interpretation of the crime

Before getting a permanent assignment at our hospital, all operating room registered nurses will have the opportunity to serve in various capacities before, during, and after surgeries are performed. After you have completed training and had experience in each aspect of OR nursing, we hope to be able to offer you a more permanent position in the area of your choice, depending on current staffing needs at that time.

As part of your training, you will have the opportunity to work in the following areas over the coming months:

- **Perioperative Nurse:** You will spend several weeks as a perioperative nurse in the OR. Here, you will gain experience in all the functions of an OR and act as one of the surgeon's assistants. You will handle surgical instruments, control bleeding, and perform postsurgical suturing of the wound.

- **Perianesthesia Nurse:** You will also get a chance to work as a perianesthesia nurse. In this capacity, you will deliver both pre- and post-operative care to patients who have been given general anesthesia during surgery. You will monitor their vital signs after surgery and make sure they revive completely and without complications from the anesthetic.

- **Postoperative Nurse:** As a postoperative nurse, you will monitor patients who are brought into the recovery room after surgery. Again, you will observe and record their vital signs and make sure no post-surgical complications set in. In consultation with the surgeon, you will help determine when post-surgical patients can be moved from recovery to their rooms.

5. You are a new operating room nurse. According to the e-mail above, what is one task a perianesthesia nurse performs?

   A.   assisting the surgeon

   B.   administering anesthesia

   C.   injecting pain killing drugs

   D.   monitoring patients' vital signs

   E.   moving patients out of recovery

6. The prefix *peri-* means "all around." What does this tell you about what a perioperative nurse does?

   F.   arranges surgeries

   G.   assists before, during, and after surgery

   H.   treats patient complications after surgery

   J.   monitors the effects of general anesthesia

   K.   consults with the surgeon about the patient

Employee Handbook

In preparing a design for a client's advertising campaign, there are several steps that should be followed. Most important, the graphic designer must determine the needs and wants of the client. The designer must get to know the client so as to fully understand what the client wants the design to convey, how it should appeal to customers, and so on. It is crucial that the designer know who the targeted audience is for the design.

After the graphic designer understands what the client wants, he or she must do the necessary research into the cultural and social aspects of the target audience. Knowing your audience is an invaluable tool in creating an effective graphic design. Once these factors are known, the designer can begin working on the graphic design.

The design must have images that are relevant and attractive to the target audience. The initial design idea is then presented to the client. The client's comments and suggestions for changes must be taken into account when the graphic designer works on the second draft of the graphic. Changes may include a rearrangement of graphic elements on the page, reworking the colors used in the graphic, altering the style of the visual elements, or other changes that the designer believes will achieve the client's goals. The final design is then presented to the client for approval.

At this point, if the graphic designer has done the job well and truly understood the needs of the client, only minor changes should be necessary. The final design is then submitted to the creative director for approval. Finally, the design is readied for public distribution in whatever format or venue the client has chosen.

---

7. As a graphic designer with this advertising agency, which of these steps should be taken before working on an initial graphic design for a client?

   A. Research the target audience.

   B. Present your ideas to the client.

   C. Rearrange graphic elements.

   D. Get approval from the creative director.

   E. Rework the colors used in the graphic.

8. Based on the steps outlined in the passage, which of the following is a design element that might be changed in the second draft of the graphic design?

   F. the size of the ad

   G. the ad's distribution venue

   H. the ad's target audience

   J. the colors used in the ad

   K. the ideas inserted by the creative director

Patient Treatment Manual

Carpal Tunnel Syndrome Treatments

Occupational therapist (OT) assistants whose clients have carpal tunnel syndrome have several options in carrying out the therapist's prescribed treatment. The assistant should recognize that the extreme pain the patient experiences comes from the stress on the nerve that runs through a sheath in the wrist. The syndrome arises from maintaining the wrist in an unnatural or unsupported position for a long time over a long period. Symptoms may include painful tingling in the affected hand, a weakening in the hand and fingers, and an inability to squeeze the hand shut. Many patients cannot sleep because of hand pain. They may experience referred pain to the nerves of the forearm and shoulder.

The OT assistant may be asked to work with the patient on simple hand-strengthening exercises. These may include clenching and stretching the arms, hands, and fingers, then relaxing them. An important part of the assistant's job is to determine the equipment the patient works with on the job. It is the physical set-up at work that most often leads to carpal tunnel syndrome. Using pictures or equipment in the therapist's office, the assistant should have the patient identify the position of the hands during work. The assistant should recommend ergonomic equipment that the patient can use to do the same job without straining the damaged nerve. Ergonomically designed equipment supports the body in a natural position that prevents stress and damage. Sometimes, something as simple as an ergonomic wrist support can go a long way toward relieving the pain of carpal tunnel syndrome in patients who work long hours at a computer keyboard.

9. You are an occupational therapy assistant treating a patient with carpal tunnel syndrome. What is the **carpal tunnel**?

  A. the fingers

  B. hand muscles

  C. a nerve sheath in the wrist

  D. bones in the forearm

  E. shoulder to wrist nerves

10. What characterizes an object that has an **ergonomic** design?

  F. It is only used in offices.

  G. It relieves stress on the body.

  H. It keeps the body immobile.

  J. It can be used for many hours.

  K. It must accompany proper exercise.

From: Don Trinelli, Industrial Production Manager

Date: February 22

To: Manufacturing Managers—All Locations

Subject: Planning Phase

During the planning phase of our proposed new product, we expect you to adhere to the following guidelines to determine cost and efficiency of production:

1. Meet with designers and engineers developing the product. Evaluate blueprints and technical drawings. Determine machinery, tools, and materials needed for manufacturing the new product.

2. Prepare a complete list of parts needed. Determine if it is more cost-effective for our firm to make these new parts or to buy them from suppliers. Get an estimate for supplies from each parts supplier. Compare that cost with the cost of in-house manufacturing of each part.

3. If the cost of in-house manufacturing depends largely on developing new software, refer the matter to our software department. If it is more dependent on recalibrating current equipment, engineers or factory supervisors can provide you with accurate estimates.

4. Prepare a time-phase chart that indicates how long it will take to design and make the tools needed to manufacture the product. Include in the chart the estimated time needed to "debug" the tools and to solve all problems.

5. Prepare learning-curve charts to show how long it is expected to take our workforce to master the new equipment to make the new product with the greatest efficiency and at the lowest cost. If costs do not diminish over a reasonable time period, we may have to rethink processes.

6. Using all the above information, calculate the standard labor hours needed to produce a specified number of the new product. Convert this value to dollar amounts. Factor in waste, overhead, and profit to yield a unit cost figure in dollars.

Please feel free to come to me if you have any questions. Keep me posted as your analysis proceeds.

Thanks,
Don

---

11. As a manufacturing manager, you are reading the above letter from the industrial production manager at the factory for which you work. What would you advise the directors to do if manufacturing parts for a new product is more expensive than buying them?

    A. Redesign the new product.

    B. Use fewer parts in the product.

    C. Train workers to make the parts more quickly.

    D. Purchase the parts from the suppliers.

    E. Deduct overhead from the cost of the parts.

12. You are preparing learning-curve charts. When would a learning-curve chart have to be re-created?

    F. when costs do not decrease in time

    G. when "debugging" the process is too difficult

    H. when standard labor hours are too great

    J. when factory machinery cannot be recalibrated

    K. when no suppliers have the parts you need

Kapowski Construction Company Handbook

An energy-efficient building must not only use energy efficiently while it is occupied, it must be constructed in accordance with the highest standards of sustainable resource use.

- **Use regional materials.** Select materials that are found or manufactured within the region. This yields energy savings in transport.

  - Regional materials shall make up at least 10 percent of all construction materials.

  - Regional materials making up only part of a construction product are calculated as a percentage based on weight.

  - Use of regional materials must be documented.

- **Biobased materials.** These materials have plant or animal materials as the main ingredient. At least 50 percent of materials should be documented as biobased.

- **Reused material.** At least 5 percent of materials should be refurbished or reused. Documentation of the amount of reused materials must be provided.

- **Recycled content.** Both postconsumer and preconsumer materials should make up at least 10 percent of material content by weight.

  - Calculate the recycled content value based on the estimated cost of materials. Documentation is required.

  - If only part of the product uses recycled material, determine recycled content value of a material assembly by weight, with the fractional value of the weight multiplied by the total estimated cost of the material assembly.

---

13. You are a construction manager in charge of purchasing energy-efficient materials for a construction company. What material would you buy for the construction of a house in order to meet the requirements for using biobased material?

    A. granite countertops

    B. soy-based insulation

    C. flagstone walkways

    D. solar roofing tiles

    E. polyvinyl chloride pipes

14. In what circumstances would you need to calculate the fractional value of recycled content in an assembled product?

    F. if only part of the product uses recycled material

    G. if none of the product components has been refurbished

    H. if the product is made only of preconsumer material

    J. if you cannot get documentation regarding recycled content

    K. if the materials are not obtained within the region

Technician Manual

Troubleshooting Computer Problems

If the computer is working but no programs are functioning, there are several things to investigate. You might first want to examine the computer motherboard, which is the central printed circuit board (PCB) of the computer. The PCB controls all the circuits that run the central processing unit (CPU), the brains of the computer that allow it to function. The motherboard also controls computer peripherals, such as the keyboard, mouse, monitor, etc. If any of these peripherals are not functioning, check to see if they work when connected to a functioning computer. If they do, the motherboard may need replacement.

Sometimes, programs on a computer do not work properly because the computer does not have enough random access memory (RAM). Check the amount of RAM in the computer against the amount required by the program the client cannot run. If the program needs more RAM in order to run properly, tell the client that additional RAM must be purchased and installed. Occasionally, a program does not work because of problems with the DVD/CD-ROM, or optical drive. If the program disk opens and works on a functioning computer, the client's computer needs a new optical drive.

15. As a computer repair technician, the computer you are working on seems not to be working at all. You suspect a problem with the computer processing unit. Where do you find the circuits that enable the CPU to function?

   A. on the PCB

   B. on the CPU

   C. on the RAM

   D. on the monitor

   E. on the DVD/CD-ROM

16. You find that a client does not have enough memory on his computer to run a program. What do you suggest the client do to correct the problem?

   F. Get a new CPU.

   G. Buy another mouse.

   H. Install a new DVD/CD-ROM.

   J. Buy more RAM.

   K. Buy a new motherboard.

SOL ELECTRIC COMPANY
Employee Handbook

Power plant dispatchers at our utility company control the flow of electricity through our transmission lines. They must constantly monitor control systems to make sure electricity is flowing properly, and in the correct amount, to where it is needed. They must monitor current converters, voltage transformers, and circuit breakers. The dispatcher must also monitor the pilot board. The pilot board is a map of the grid system that shows the status of the transmission circuits and the connections to factories and substations.

One of the most important responsibilities dispatchers have is anticipating changes in the need for electricity. Weather conditions are often a good indicator of potential changes in the need, or demands, for electricity. When a change in the need for electricity is expected due to weather forecasts, dispatchers must contact the control-room operators. Dispatchers instruct the operators to be ready to start or stop boilers and generators.

Dispatchers are also first responders during emergencies such as transmission line failures. In these situations, they are responsible for routing the electrical current around the affected areas. Current is routed away from the down substation to nearby functional substations so the outage is confined to just the one substation and the area it serves.

---

17. You are a power plant dispatcher at a local utility company. Under what condition would you inform the control-room operators to be prepared for an increase in electricity use among your customers?

A. when the dispatchers start the boilers

B. when a current is routed from the substation

C. when a heat wave is forecasted for the area

D. when the grid system is upgraded

E. when substations are added to the grid

18. In what situation would you have to reroute electrical current?

F. when use is low in one area

G. when there are too many substations

H. when the circuit breakers are malfunctioning

J. when transmission lines at a substation fail

K. when the voltage transformers cannot produce usable electricity

Answers are on page 256.

Level 6 Introduction...

The lesson and practice pages that follow will give you the opportunity to develop and practice the comprehension skills needed to answer work-related questions at a Level 6 rating of difficulty. The *On Your Own* practice problems provide a review of key reading skills along with instruction and practice applying these skills through effective problem-solving strategies. The *Performance Assessment* provides problems similar to those you will encounter on a Career Readiness Certificate test. By completing the Level 6 *On Your Own* and *Performance Assessment* questions, you will gain the ability to confidently approach workplace scenarios that require understanding and application of the reading skills featured in the following lessons:

Lesson 16: Recognize Underlying Details

Lesson 17: Use Technical Terms and Jargon in New Situations

Lesson 18: Identify the Less Common Meaning of a Word

Lesson 19: Apply Complicated Instructions to New Situations

Lesson 20: Determine Principles Behind Workplace Directives

Lesson 21: Apply Principles to New Situations

Lesson 22: Explain the Rationale Behind Workplace Documents

These skills are intended to help you successfully read and understand workplace documents such as elaborate procedures, complicated information, and legal regulations. Reading these types of documents often requires the ability to:

- read complicated sentences that include jargon and technical terms,
- identify when key information is not clearly stated,
- recognize the rationale and principles behind workplace policies and procedures.

Through answering document-related questions at this level, you will continue to develop problem-solving approaches and strategies that will help you determine the correct answer in real-world and test-taking situations.

Lesson 16 ■ ■ ■
Recognize Underlying Details

Skill: Identify implied details

People in the workplace imply messages everyday through spoken words, body language, and written documents. A coworker's frown may imply that he or she does not agree with an idea. Similarly, while some facts are stated clearly in workplace documents, others are sometimes implied. In order to understand the entire meaning of a workplace communication, you must be able to recognize and understand messages that are both stated and unstated.

Remember!

An implied detail is a detail that is suggested but not directly stated. Identifying implied details can be thought of as inferring, or "reading between the lines." For example, workplace dress codes sometimes list specific items that should not be worn to work. The guidelines cannot list every possible article of clothing, but by providing samples, workers are expected to infer what type of clothing is or is not appropriate. When an invitation to a corporate event states that attendance is "strongly encouraged," this might imply that management would like everyone to attend.

Skill Examples

Effective immediately, all national salespeople must submit expense reports to the accounts payable department no later than 1:00 P.M. on the fifth day of each month. A receipt must accompany individual expenses over $10, and receipts totaling more than $150 require a detailed written explanation of the expense. Furthermore, it is mandatory that your immediate supervisor authorizes your report; reports not signed by your supervisor will be returned and reimbursement will be delayed.

Example 1
Make assumptions based on related details and clues within the message.

The message directly states when expense reports must be submitted, but does not directly state the consequence of a late report. Despite this, there are two clearly expressed details that serve as clues. The first clue is that there is an absolute deadline. The second clue is that a specific consequence for submission of an unsigned report is explained. From these two clues, you can reasonably assume that reimbursement will likely be delayed.

Example 2
Identify implied details by the tone or feeling of the text.

The way in which a workplace communication is written also provides clues as to the details and meaning of the message. The tone of the above message indicates a strong warning. Words such as *must*, *require*, and *mandatory* indicate that the company expects complete compliance. The lack of words such as *please* or *we would appreciate* further indicates the strength and tone of the message.

MEMORANDUM

The human resources department has a limited number of orchestra-level tickets available for two upcoming theatrical performances. A drawing to win the tickets will be held on Friday. All full-time and part-time employees are eligible. To enter the drawing, please submit your name and phone extension to Patty Henson by Thursday at 5:00 P.M.

Skill Practice

Use the document to the left to answer the following questions.

1. Participation in the drawing is
   A. discouraged.
   B. restricted.
   C. mandatory.
   D. strongly suggested.
   E. optional.

2. The cost of the tickets to employees is
   F. limited.
   G. free.
   H. to be determined.
   J. valuable.
   K. unknown.

Try It Out! ■ ■ ■

You are a registered nurse at a pediatric hospital. Periodically, the nurse manager posts articles to alert patient care providers of current medical trends. Which of the following details are implied in this alert?

A. All humans who contract Lyme disease will develop a rash.

B. Lyme disease is caused by infected ticks.

C. If patients complain of some of the symptoms of Lyme disease, they should be quarantined.

D. Dizziness and heart palpitations are symptoms of Bell's palsy.

E. Doxycycline, amoxicillin, and cefuroxime axetil are names of antibiotics.

LYME DISEASE ALERT

A case of Lyme disease was recently diagnosed and treated by our hospital staff. While this ailment is not typical in our area, please review its symptoms, risks, and treatment. Lyme disease is transmitted when an infected tick bites a human. These ticks, found in wooded and bushy areas, are most active in the early and mid-summer months.

Symptoms and Risks

Initial symptoms of Lyme disease can include fever, headache, fatigue, and erythema migrans—a circular skin rash that begins 3 to 30 days after the patient is bitten and expands over a period of several days. The expanded rash may take on the shape of a bull's eye with a clear center, and the rash may be warm to the touch. If the disease is left untreated, patients can develop Bell's palsy, dizziness, and heart palpitations. Meningitis can develop, causing stiffness of the neck and severe headaches. Untreated infections can lead to joint pain, swelling, and arthritis of the large joints as well as neurological issues. It is important to remember that not all patients experience all of these symptoms.

Treatment

In most cases, antibiotics will cure Lyme disease in its early stages. If the disease has progressed to affect the neurological or cardiac systems, ceftriaxone or penicillin can be administered intravenously. If caught early enough, however, doxycycline, amoxicillin, and cefuroxime axetil are the most commonly used medications.

 Step 1 Understand the Problem ■ ■ ■

Complete the *Plan for Successful Solving.*

Plan for Successful Solving

What am I asked to do?	What are the facts?	How do I find the answer?	Is there any unnecessary information?	What prior knowledge will help me?
Identify an implied detail in the alert.	The alert describes the causes, symptoms, and treatment of Lyme disease.	Identify the stated details. Use clues within the stated details and use previous knowledge.	No. Every section must be read to rule out the incorrect answers.	Names of common antibiotics.

 Step 2 Find and Check Your Answer ■ ■ ■

- Confirm your understanding of the question and revise your plan as needed.

- Based on your plan, determine your solution approach: *I will read each answer and determine whether or not to rule it out as incorrect. Answers A, C, and D are all false. Answer B is true, but it is a stated detail, not implied. To verify Answer E, I reread that antibiotics are used for treatment in the early stages of the disease. The alert later lists three medications used to treat Lyme disease "if caught early enough." It is reasonable to assume that these medications are antibiotics.*

- Check your answer. Review all answers to determine if the answer you have selected is the best possible answer.

- **Select the correct answer:** E. Doxycycline, amoxicillin, and cefuroxime axetil are names of antibiotics.
  The first sentence under the "Treatment" heading explains that antibiotics are used to treat Lyme disease. Later in the paragraph these medications are listed, so it is reasonable to assume that they are antibiotics.

Problem Solving Tip

Do not over-assume when you are trying to identify implied details. You must be fairly certain that the stated details support the implication you are making.

Remember!

Because implied details are not stated directly, you have to make inferences from stated details and information in the passage. Some transition words that can help you find stated details and information include *specifically, in particular, for example,* and *in other words.*

On Your Own ▪ ■ ■

Housing Policies for First-Year Students

All first-year students are required to live in campus dorms. The only exception to this rule applies to students who live within a 20-mile radius of the university. In accordance with affirmative action standards, roommate assignments are made with no consideration to race, religion, or national origin. The university will consider roommate requests for first-year students but strongly discourages two students from the same high school requesting to live together. A residence contract must be read, signed, and submitted by students before they receive dormitory and roommate assignments.

Since the university views community dining as an integral part of the residential campus experience, freshman are encouraged to dine in assigned dining halls; however, students may bring their own mini refrigerators and microwaves to use in their rooms.

As with all campus buildings, smoking and illegal drugs are prohibited in all dormitories. Alcohol is strictly prohibited in all first-year housing.

1. You are the Dean of Student Housing at a university. Per your request, the Assistant Dean has written new policies that will affect first-year students and has submitted them for your approval. One objective of the university is to encourage first-year students to branch out and meet new people. How do the housing policies imply this objective?

    A. by allowing students who live nearby to commute from home

    B. by discouraging students who know each other to live together and by encouraging students to eat at dining halls

    C. by allowing refrigerators and microwaves in dorm rooms and prohibiting alcohol

    D. by requiring students to eat at dining halls and by allowing students who live nearby to commute

    E. by following affirmative action standards and by prohibiting smoking and illegal drugs campus wide

2. First-year students often ask in advance about housing for following years. Using clues within the policy statement, which statement is likely true of returning students?

    F. They are required to live in dormitories.

    G. They are not permitted to live in dormitories.

    H. They must live within a 20-mile radius of the university.

    J. They may live in apartments or other off-campus housing only.

    K. They may live in dormitories or off-campus housing.

Shared Physical Custody Arrangement

I. The parties, after giving due consideration to all relevant factors, have agreed that it is in the children's best interest that the parties have joint care, custody, and control of their minor children. The parties agree to confer with each other and to share decision-making authority as to important decisions affecting the welfare and upbringing of the children with a view towards arriving at decisions that will promote the best interest of the children. Substantial decisions regarding the health, medical, and dental care; religious and secular education; vacations; travel; summer activities such as summer camp; welfare; and upbringing of the children shall be made on a joint decision-making basis.

The parties agree that during the time each of them has physical custody of said children, that parent shall decide all routine matters concerning the children's welfare. The parties further agree to cooperate with one another in establishing a mutually supportive arrangement regarding such routine decisions. The parties further agree, however, that in the event, after due consultation with one another, a disagreement arises as to a particular decision or course of action with reference to the minor children, the Husband shall be the legal custodian and custodial parent of said minor children of the parties, and shall have the final and ultimate decision-making authority as to any and all matters concerning the minor children not in conflict with the provisions of this agreement and upon which the parties cannot or do not agree.

II. The parties agree that it is in the children's best interest to share as much time with each parent as possible. Therefore, the parties have reached an agreement whereby they would share physical custody with said children so that each parent would be sharing approximately the same amount of time with the children. In the event the parties move from their present location to the extent that they live more than fifty (50) miles from each other, then the parties agree that the alternate weekly visitation schedule would not be in the children's best interest.

III. The parties stipulate and agree that, since they will be enjoying a shared physical custody arrangement, neither party will be required to pay child support to the other party.

---

3. A client of the firm where you work as a paralegal has asked for clarification on his divorce settlement. While his children are spending the week at his home, his daughter is invited to a birthday party for his neighbor's daughter. The party will be held in the afternoon at the neighbor's house. Does he need to discuss his daughter's attendance with his ex-wife?

    A. Yes, because it involves travel.

    B. Yes, because the mother might not know the neighbor.

    C. No, because it falls under the category of routine matters.

    D. Yes, because they will need to share the cost of a birthday gift.

    E. No, because he is ultimately the legal custodial parent.

4. Which of the following scenarios would most likely require a joint decision between the children's parents?

    F. Setting a reasonable homework time and routine at their mother's house.

    G. Making an appointment for a yearly physical.

    H. Getting braces on their son's teeth with the parents sharing the cost.

    J. Both children visiting their grandmother on the days that they are at their mother's house.

    K. Attending a baseball game with their father.

PRESS RELEASE

Today the Hoctor Zoo announced its plans to open an outdoor food court near the entrance of the grounds. Due to open next spring, the food court will serve a variety of menu items from several national fast food, pizza, and ice-cream chains. Three new snack bars, spread throughout the zoo, will offer assorted bagels, fruit cups, single-serving packs of raw vegetables and dips, cheese sticks, and other healthy snacks. Community picnic areas will be constructed to accommodate large groups, such as visiting schools. Operating hours of the food court will be the same as those of the zoo, from 9:00 A.M. to 6:00 P.M.

Upon its opening, the food court expects to serve over 2,000 people per day. Hailey Chen, the zoo's director, said, "We are pleased to provide new services to meet the needs of the families, tour groups, students, and other visitors of the zoo. We aim to make their visits as enjoyable as possible and hope to exceed their expectations."

Currently, the zoo's concession stands serve only small snacks and beverages. Feedback from a recent customer survey rated limited dining variety, service, and seating as the zoo's leading weaknesses. Waycross Zoo, about two hours south, is Hoctor's closest competitor. Waycross contains one franchise pizza restaurant, one snack shop, and a dozen vending machines.

Chen also mentioned that additional benefits of the food court include a generation of new jobs in the city and increased revenue to support zoo programs.

---

5. You are the public relations manager for Hoctor Zoo. One of your interns has written this press release for your approval. Which of the following messages is implied in the first paragraph of the press release?

A. The zoo's goal is to promote healthy eating by its patrons.

B. The current concession stands will continue to sell small snacks and beverages.

C. Fast food restaurants will be spread throughout the zoo.

D. A greater selection of food choices will be available when the new food court is open.

E. Some restaurants will offer private seating.

6. Considering both stated and implied details, which of the following best lists the reasons that the zoo is building the food court?

F. The zoo is currently losing money and may have to close.

G. They want to address the negative comments given in the customer survey, make more money, and help small food-service businesses.

H. They want to gain an advantage over their competition, earn more profits, and make customers happy.

J. They want to overcome their weaknesses and open other zoos in other cities.

K. They want to provide healthier food choices to their customers, provide new jobs, and eventually open zoos in other cities.

COMMUNITY INITIATIVES REPORT:

Reducing Violent Crimes Among Youths

A local urban police force has positively impacted violent crime among youths by implementing a new program. Teams of police officers and probation officers work together to make sure that youth gang members and other offenders follow the terms of their probation.

The impact of the program was seen in a single night. Four officers—two police officers and two probation officers—arrived at the crime scene. They found a 15-year-old shooting victim lying on the ground. There was a crowd around him. Some of the people in the crowd had previously been punished for crimes. When the anti-gang police officers from the area got out of the car, the onlookers stayed at the scene. Although the officers were well known and taken seriously, the witnesses stayed, as they felt that there was no harm in watching. When the other two officers stepped out of the car, the crowd began to disperse right away. Many of them recognized the probation officers.

Having police and probation officers working together has made a tremendous impact on the city. In the last several years, there has been an estimated 70 percent decrease in the number of people under the age of 25 who have been killed by guns. Statistics also showed improvement of probation compliance, from an estimated 17 percent to 50 percent complying with the terms of their probation.

The program has earned great support from the community. Grateful parents, grandparents, and guardians of the probationers are among the most enthusiastic supporters. Many community groups, such as clergy members, social workers, youth outreach programs, and school police officers, have also offered their support.

---

7. As the police chief in a major metropolitan area, you are responsible for reducing crime. In order to generate ideas for your own community, your immediate supervisor has sent you this report about another city's program that has reduced youth crime in their area. Reread the situation about the officers responding to a call. It points out that the crowd began to disperse once the onlookers recognized the probation officers. What does this detail imply?

A. Four officers of any kind are more threatening than two.

B. The onlookers did not take the police officers seriously.

C. The onlookers thought the police officers had jurisdiction over another area, so they were not worried that they would question them.

D. The probation officers might recognize some of the onlookers and realize that they were violating their own probation rules.

E. The probation officers, probably dressed in street clothes, were mistaken for detectives.

8. What is implied in the report about the offenders who are on probation?

F. If they comply with curfews, area restrictions, and other terms of their probation, they are less likely to commit other crimes.

G. Their parents, grandparents, or guardians have not raised them well.

H. They likely sell illegal weapons and drugs.

J. They have not met with clergy.

K. There are so many teens on probation that the probation officers cannot recognize most of them in a crowd.

Report Summary: Employee Training

While working for Old Time Sweet Company, 84 percent of employees received some kind of formal training and 96 percent received some kind of informal training. Old Time Sweet Company paid for all training referred to in this survey. During the six-month survey period from May to October, employees received an average of 30.4 hours of training, of which 10.1 hours were spent in formal training and 21.3 hours in informal training. In other words, 70 percent of the training took place through informal instruction.

Age: The youngest and oldest workers were less likely to have received formal training during the last 12 months than were workers ages 25 to 54. Workers 24 years of age or younger and workers 55 years of age or older received about half as many hours of total training as workers 25 to 54 years old.

Full- or part-time: Full-time workers (35 or more hours per week) were more likely to have received formal training in the last 12 months than were part-time workers (72 percent versus 56 percent). Similarly, during the May to October period, full-time workers received an average of 49 hours of training, compared to 13 hours for part-time workers. Full-time workers received about five times as much informal training (34 hours for full-time versus 8 hours for part-time workers) and three times as much formal training (15 hours versus 5 hours).

Earnings groups: Those in the bottom group of the earnings distribution were less likely to receive formal training and received fewer hours of formal training than higher earners. Sixty-two percent of those in the bottom group received formal training in the last 12 months compared with 84 percent of those in the top group. Low earners received 4 hours of formal training during the six-month survey period versus 23 hours for the top group.

9. You have recently been hired as a training and development specialist for Old Time Sweet Company, a company that manufactures and sells candy. You want to determine the current training needs of the company's employees by reading last year's training report summary shown above. What logical inference can you make from the information that relates age and training?

    A. The employees between the ages of 25 to 54 have more personal time in which to attend training.

    B. The company delays training younger, inexperienced workers until they are sure the employment arrangement is likely to last.

    C. Many college graduates fall in the youngest category, and they will demand more on-the-job training.

    D. The company inadvertently discriminates against the older workers and does not want to pay for additional training for them.

    E. Workers ages 25 to 54 earn peak compensation and are better able to afford to pay for training.

10. Based on the data for full- or part-time employee training, what inferences can you make about part-time employees and training?

    F. Part-time employees are looking for more training opportunities.

    G. Training slots are filled by full-time employees, leaving fewer openings for part-time employees.

    H. Part-time employees may have less ability to take time for training because they work fewer hours and have outside commitments.

    J. Part-time employees perform tasks that don't require training.

    K. Part-time employees do not want to learn new skills or improve upon their existing skills.

From: L. Martinez, Family/Child Welfare Supervisor

To: All Family and Child Social Workers

Re: Stress

Please know that the supervisors and administrators of our agency are well aware of the high stress level associated with careers in social work. Many social workers experience stress due to heavy caseloads, long and unpredictable hours, insufficient service resources for your clients, low salary, and other factors. High stress levels can cause fatigue, psychological problems, sleep disorders, and cardiovascular problems.

For that reason, we are happy to offer a complimentary stress-reduction program. The program is run by specialists at Lytle University but will be held at our agency. This eight-week course begins on April 26 at 7:00 P.M. It assures improvement in the well-being of participants. The program teaches coping skills as well as relaxation techniques.

A recent survey conducted by the National Association of Social Workers details several methods of stress reduction. Social workers acknowledge the use of exercise (75%), meditation (35%), therapy (30%), prescription medication (24%), drinking of alcohol (18%), and not reporting to work (8%) to reduce stress. Obviously, not all of these techniques are recommended or acceptable by us. We invite you to join the Lytle program to find the stress-reduction methods that will best meet your overall health needs.

For more information or to enroll in the program, please contact Chris Bedford at x352.

11. As a family social worker for an agency that provides public assistance to those in need, you receive the above memo. Which of the following choices best states the implied meaning of the first paragraph?

A. All social workers develop physical health problems at some point in their careers.

B. You should not worry about what is best for your clients.

C. Most social workers don't work hard enough to obtain service resources for their clients.

D. The social workers at your agency are displaying inappropriate behavior.

E. The management staff of the agency is concerned about your welfare.

12. Which combination of methods of stress relief mentioned are most likely deemed inappropriate?

F. drinking alcohol, attending therapy, and not reporting to work

G. prescription drugs and attending another stress-management program

H. meditation and drinking of alcohol

J. drinking alcohol and not reporting to work

K. not reporting to work, exercise, and prescription drugs

Answers are on page 259.

Lesson 17 ■ ■ ■
Use Technical Terms and Jargon in New Situations

Skill: Apply technical terms and jargon to new circumstances

As you have learned in previous lessons, technical terms and jargon are words and phrases that have certain meanings when used in specific jobs and career fields. Once you understand what a term means, you can use your previous knowledge to apply it to new situations.

Remember!

By identifying the meaning of jargon within the context it is used, you can apply it to a new context.

Below are examples of jargon used in various fields and professions:

Profession	Jargon
Food Services	baste, knead, glaze
Transportation	layover, boarding pass, one-way
Medical	CAT scan, C-section, pulse
Athletics	curveball, batter, basket, dribble

Skill Examples

The Information Technology (IT) staff will be installing a spam filtering service for all e-mail users. This will decrease the amount of spam, or unwanted e-mail, received in employee inboxes. The new service will also help reduce the risk of viruses, which can damage both files and a computer's operations. The goal of the service is to ensure that all employees receive clean mail, free of spam and viruses.

Example 1
Determine the meaning of technical terms or jargon in a message.

The message explains that the new service will decrease the amount of spam received in employee inboxes. You can determine the meaning of the term *spam* because its definition—unwanted e-mail—is given immediately after its first use.

Example 2
Apply technical terms or jargon to a new situation.

A new situation is introduced when the company installs a spam filtering service to the e-mail system that already exists. You can apply your understanding of the goal—to keep e-mail free from spam and viruses—to know that a **virus** is harmful.

As an elementary Special Education teacher, you are responsible for making sure that teachers and staff at your school implement Individual Education Programs (IEP) for students with special needs. An IEP must state when services begin, how often they will be provided, where they will be provided, and how long they will continue. Special accommodations for students will improve their access to learning. For example, a student with a severe hand tremor has trouble taking notes in class. His IEP includes having the teacher provide him with a written set of notes.

Skill Practice

Use the document to the left to answer the following questions.

1. What is the purpose of an **IEP**?
   A. to take notes for students with special needs
   B. to support learning for students with special needs
   C. to support learning for the teachers and staff
   D. to learn more about supporting parents
   E. to learn more about special accommodations

2. Which of the following is information that would most likely be included in an IEP?
   F. a student's grade point average from her previous school
   G. a description of a student's speech therapy routine
   H. a student's physical description
   J. math problems for a student to work on
   K. a student's ethnicity

Try It Out! ■ ■ ■

You are Director of Finance at a large office building. You have been asked to review a memo in which the advantages and disadvantages of outsourcing are presented. In which of the following new situations could **outsourcing** be used?

A. hiring a temporary employee for one day because an assistant is sick

B. starting your own company and asking former co-workers to join you

C. using an outside company to provide technical support to customers who have questions or problems with your product

D. sending your staff to an outside location to lead a focus group that asks consumers about your product

E. mailing surveys to customers to ask for feedback

> **To:** Director of Finance
> **From:** Business Operations
> **Re:** Outsourcing
> One area that has been considered for outsourcing is janitorial services. We now have five employees who clean our offices. They all report to a manager in our facilities department. All five work full-time. Some often work six days a week.
>
> **Advantages of Outsourcing:**
> • Outside janitorial companies are more reliable. If anyone calls in sick, the company provides a replacement for that day.
> • Outside companies provide their own cleaning supplies and equipment.
> • Outside companies recruit, interview, and train their own staff.
> • We would not be responsible for providing outsourced staff with company benefits, workers' compensation, and similar items.
>
> **Disadvantages of Outsourcing:**
> • Our current janitorial staff would lose their jobs.
> • Although the companies require background checks for their employees, they could pose a security risk as they work in our offices.
> • We have less management control over the outsourced staff.

 Step 1 ## Understand the Problem ■ ■ ■

Complete the *Plan for Successful Solving.*

Plan for Successful Solving

What am I asked to do?	What are the facts?	How do I find the answer?	Is there any unnecessary information?	What prior knowledge will help me?
Apply the word *outsourcing* to a new situation.	The details of the memo help clarify the meaning of the word *outsourcing.*	Identify how the word *outsourcing* is used in the current situation. Determine to which answer option the term best applies.	Some of the advantages and disadvantages do not clarify the meaning of *outsourcing.*	Prior work experience where jobs are outsourced.

 Step 2 ## Find and Check Your Answer ■ ■ ■

■ Confirm your understanding of the question and revise your plan as needed.

■ Based on your plan, determine your solution approach: *From the memo, I see that outsourcing is the hiring of an outside company to do a job that could otherwise be done by in-house employees. In this case, cleaning services are being considered for outsourcing. Based on this understanding, I will determine which answers require a company to hire an outside source.*

■ Check your answer. Review all answers to determine if the answer you have selected is the best possible answer.

■ **Select the correct answer:** C. using an outside company to provide technical support to customers who have questions or problems with your product
This answer fits the same criteria as the first situation. Hiring an outside company to provide technical support and staff, as opposed to having this work done by employees within your company, is an example of outsourcing.

Problem Solving Tip

In the *Try It Out!* example, *outsourcing* is described through specific details about the advantages and disadvantages of using it for janitorial services. Once you understand the term within the context of this particular situation, it is possible to apply it to new situations in which a company hires an outside source to help meet their staffing needs.

Remember!

There are many terms such as *outsourcing* that are rarely used in everyday speech but are commonly used in the workplace. Learning the meanings of these commonly used terms is a necessary first step in order to be able to apply them to new situations.

Date: September 7

From: Monica Park, Head Pharmacist

RE: Welcome

Welcome to your new job as a pharmacist in our drug store. Your previous work as a physician's assistant contributed significantly to you being offered this position.

The main duties of your new position include reviewing prescriptions that have been written by doctors and dispensing the medications to patients. You will also counsel patients regarding dosage so that they know exactly when and how much of the medication to take. You'll explain storage methods of the medication. For instance, some medications must be kept at room temperature and others in the refrigerator. You will also need to explain side effects that patients should watch for when they take their medication.

If you have any questions or concerns about your new responsibilities, please do not hesitate to ask. Once again, welcome!

1. As a pharmacist at a drug store, you dispense medication. Which of these other new duties might require **dispensing**?

    A. learning the side effects of new medications

    B. scheduling meetings with employees

    C. handing out pamphlets that describe prevention of common illnesses

    D. reading résumés of those applying for a job at the pharmacy

    E. donating your time to work at a vaccine clinic

2. Which of these new jobs might involve determining a **dosage**?

    F. a financial planner who suggests investments his clients should make

    G. a medical specialist who administers a radiation treatment to a cancer patient

    H. a chemical expert who determines what ingredients should be avoided in production of medications

    J. a public relations specialist who needs to call someone to solve computer problems

    K. an orthopedic specialist who is determining where to send a patient for physical therapy

From:	Eduardo Torres, Art Department Manager	Date: November 15
To:	Art Department—ALL; Editorial Department—ALL	

Subject: Archiving old files

Because of the high volume of electronic files that are currently on our server, you may have noticed that our computer system has recently begun to slow down considerably. For this reason, we are implementing the use of a new archive system. This mass-storage system will allow everyone to store the files that they are no longer using. The files will be removed from our active server and placed into long-term storage. You will still be able to pull these files from the archives when needed, but they will no longer slow down our computers.

Please take some time this week to flag old files that you have saved on the server. These should include any files from previous editions of our magazine that you do not intend to reuse in future versions of the magazine. Compile a list of the file names and locations and send via e-mail to Mitchell Asbury to authorize him to move the files to the archive system. If you should find that later you need to access archived files, please contact Mitchell at x876 and he will retrieve the files for you.

3. You are a production specialist at a local events magazine. Part of your job is placing photographs, text, and other design elements on each page. You must store files from old editions of the magazine. What does the term **edition** mean in terms of the magazine?

    A.   type

    B.   format

    C.   layout

    D.   style

    E.   version

4. Which of the following new situations describes another type of **archive** system?

    F.   A hotel may use an archive system to take inventory of the cleaning supplies used by the maid staff.

    G.   A car dealership may use an archive system to track automobiles on their lot by model, color, and options.

    H.   A library may use an archive system to store rare books, written records, original published papers, and valuable documents.

    J.   A department store may use an archive system to record current sales and returned products.

    K.   A hospital may use an archive system to enter medical information for new patients.

To: All Employees   Date: November 1

From: Sondra Williams, Store Manager

Subject: Seasonal changes

To prepare for the holiday shopping season, Keller's Grocery Store is making the following changes. Please read the changes carefully so that you can better direct customers.

1. The produce section will be rearranged to make room for seasonal items. Apples and pears will be combined into one case. All berries will be combined into another case. Fruit and nut baskets and other seasonal items will be placed to the left of the produce section. This setup will improve the flow of our store. Shoppers will be guided to walk through the holiday section.

2. Consumers' budgets are tight, so we are pushing our private label products. All food and cleaning supplies carrying the Keller name will be marked down 30 percent, making them considerably less expensive than most name brands. Remember to remind customers that our private label products are guaranteed. If they are not happy with our product, we will exchange it for another brand of their choice.

3. Holiday candy, small toys, and stocking stuffers will be placed near the cash registers by the other impulse purchases. Extra gift cards will also be placed on these racks.

5. As a clerk in a grocery store, you receive the above e-mail that informs employees that products carrying the Keller label will be marked down to attract customers. While shopping at Brooke's Stationary, an office supply store, you notice that Brooke's brand products are priced lower than other products. What would Brooke's products also be known as?

    A.   seasonal items

    B.   budget items

    C.   private label

    D.   name brand

    E.   branding

6. Based on the meaning of an impulse purchase in the above context, which scenario below describes an **impulse purchase** in a new situation?

    F.   older toys placed in the discount section of a toy store

    G.   expensive shampoos and hair products at a salon

    H.   watches in a mall kiosk

    J.   bookmarks sold near the checkout counter of a bookstore

    K.   bulk cases of diapers near the front of a warehouse club store

To: All new sales trainees

From: Marissa Torres, VP of Training

Re: Training session #1

Congratulations on your new position as an insurance sales trainee. Your first product training session will be held on October 1. It will begin at 9:00 A.M. The topic of this session is term life insurance.

As you may know, term life insurance is exactly what it sounds like. It is insurance that is not permanent. Instead it covers a specified number of years, or term, that the client elects. The major benefit of term life policies is that they offer maximum coverage for affordable premiums. We offer policies for terms of 15, 20, and 30 years. Although it does not build cash value as other policies may, it is usually easily converted. It can be changed to a permanent whole life or universal life policy that accumulates cash value.

We look forward to helping you learn the details of our term policies.

7. You are a new sales trainee at an insurance company. One of your duties involves computing and deducting premiums for health care plans. At the end of your first product training session about term life insurance, you are informed that your company also handles auto insurance. What does the term **premium** mean in the context of auto insurance?

   A. credit

   B. percentage

   C. fraction

   D. payment

   E. coverage

8. When you are trained in auto insurance, part of what you will learn will be how to convert single driver policies to family policies. In this new situation, what is the meaning of **convert**?

   F. change

   G. purchase

   H. get rid of

   J. evaluate

   K. remove

From: Cecilia Able, Owner of Able Realty   Date: December 12

To: District Managers—ALL

Subject: Commission rates

The ability of our clients to access the Internet has greatly affected our industry. On the one hand, it has enabled our clients to preview photographs and details of homes without leaving their computers. Our sales agents, who used to drive potential buyers from home to home, can now guide their clients to view only the homes that catch their attention. On the other hand, the market has experienced an increase of discount broker firms, who offer limited services to sellers for a lower cost. Some of these firms provide no services other than listing a client's home on the MLS (multiple listing service).

In order to allow our sales agents to thrive in this changing market, Able Realty is announcing a change in our commission rate policy. Under our current policy, the typical commission rate charged by our agents is 6 percent total. Our listing agents receive a 3 percent commission. Listing agents are hired by clients to sell their homes. The commission is based on the total sale price of the home. The buyer's agent, the one who finds a buyer for a home, also receives a 3 percent commission. If an agent finds a buyer for a home where they are also the listing agent, the total 6 percent commission is paid to that agent. For instance, if Agent A is both the listing agent and the buyer's agent for a home that sells for $300,000, Agent A would be paid an $18,000 commission.

As of January 1, Able Realty is allowing all listing agents to lower their commission rates by as much as one percent. This lowering of commission rates is not required. You may choose to lower your commission rate on some sales but not on others. It is entirely up to you if and when you choose to lower your rate.

We hope that this flexibility assists you in selling more homes and allowing home sellers to get better prices for their sales. Please remember that we expect all of our agents to provide quality, full-service care to all of our clients, no matter what commission is charged.

---

9. You are a district manager for Able Realty. A friend of yours wants to put his house up for sale. Whom would you tell him to contact?

    A. a discount broker

    B. an MLS agent

    C. a commissioned agent

    D. a buyer's agent

    E. a listing agent

10. The agent that your friend contacted thanks you because now he is eligible for a 6 percent **commission**. According to the document, what does this mean?

    F. He is also representing a buyer for your friend's house.

    G. He has sold the house within thirty days.

    H. He has sold enough homes to achieve seniority status.

    J. The selling price is over $100,000.

    K. He has represented this client before.

Dangers of Fluoride Toothpaste

The Centers for Disease Control and Prevention (CDC 1999, 2001) has now acknowledged the findings of many leading dental researchers, that the mechanism of fluoride's benefits are mainly topical, not systemic, Thus, you don't have to swallow fluoride to protect teeth. As the benefits of fluoride (if any exist) are topical, and the risks are systemic, it makes more sense for those who want to take the risks to deliver the fluoride directly to the tooth in the form of toothpaste. Since swallowing fluoride is unnecessary, there is no reason to force people (against their will) to drink fluoride in their water supply.

Despite being prescribed by doctors for over 50 years, the US Food and Drug Administration (FDA) has never approved any fluoride product designed for ingestion as safe or effective. Fluoride supplements are designed to deliver the same amount of fluoride as ingested daily from fluoridated water.

11. As a dental assistant, you have just read the above article on the use of fluoride to prevent tooth decay. Your understanding is that the article's use of the word **topical** means that fluoride is

A. controversial

B. of contemporary interest

C. applied to the surface

D. relatively harmless

E. swallowed

12. The dentist you work for says that she has a patient whose tooth infection has become systemic. Based upon your experience, you understand **systemic** to mean

F. occurring at regular intervals

G. presenting obvious symptoms

H. affecting the entire body

J. affecting only the extremities

K. having a long history

Answers are on page 259.

Lesson 18 ▪ ▪ ▪
Identify the Less Common Meaning of a Word

Skill: Use context clues to determine the less common meaning of a word

When reading a business or workplace document, you may find that the way a particular word is used does not match your understanding of the word. There are many words that have a common meaning when used in everyday conversation but a less common meaning when used in the workplace.

Remember!

Common multiple-meaning words used in the workplace include *firm* (which in a business setting could mean "a company or a business" and in a more common setting could mean "secure"), *object* (which in a law firm could mean "to put forth in opposition" and in a more common setting could mean "something that can be seen or felt"), and *note* (which in a business setting could mean "to notice" and in a more common setting could mean "a musical sound"). Some of these words have definitions that are related, such as *quarter (Skill Example 1),* and some that are quite different, such as *page (Skill Example 2).*

Skill Examples

Example 1
Use prior knowledge of a word's common meaning to determine its less common meaning.

> The supplies for the next quarter have been delivered. In an effort to keep costs down, the budget committee has decided that each department will be allotted a limited amount of supplies. If a department uses its allotted supplies before the end of a quarter, it will need to make a special request to order more.

Your department has received a memo about reducing costs. You are familiar with the word *quarter*, but only as a coin whose value is 25 cents. You realize this coin must be called a quarter because its value is one-fourth, or one-quarter, of a dollar. In the memo, the word *quarter* is associated with a period of time, so a quarter in this context must mean one-fourth of a year, or three months.

Example 2
Use context clues to determine a word's less common meaning.

> New procedures have been put into place for those employees who work after hours and need to communicate with a manager who is not on-site. Everyone who has access to a landline phone can place a page if any urgent issues arise after hours. Be aware that a page should only be placed when an immediate response to a question or issue is necessary.

In this passage you see the common word *page*. You know the word *page* as a noun that names a part of a book or other printed material. There is no mention of printed material, and the word *page* refers to an action. The passage is about communicating with the manager who is not on-site after hours. Using this context as a clue, you can determine that a *page* is a kind of communication.

Skill Practice

From: Jill Moore
To: Financial Managers
Subject: Outside Auditor Inquiries
Financial managers will conference next Tuesday to discuss the completion of the audit. The outside auditors have presented us with a list of problems that we need to address. Be ready to present possible approaches to solving these problems.

Use the document to the left to answer the following questions.

1. What is the meaning of the word **conference** as it is used in the e-mail?

   A. travel

   B. gather or meet

   C. attend seminars

   D. conduct trainings

   E. register for trainings

2. Which of the following words or phrases means the same as the word **address** as it is used in the e-mail?

   F. speech

   G. cover up

   H. eliminate

   J. postal location

   K. fix

Try It Out! ■ ■ ■

Your supervisor in the biology laboratory where you are beginning a job as a laboratory assistant has asked you to monitor an experiment. You have just read the procedures to the right from the lab's manual. You think of **culture** as the arts and traditions of a community. What does the word mean in the context of these biology lab procedures?

A. glassware

B. the heating progress

C. cells grown in special conditions

D. temperature of the laboratory

E. density of cells

Step 1 Understand the Problem ■ ■ ■

Complete the *Plan for Successful Solving*.

Plan for Successful Solving

What am I asked to do?	What are the facts?	How do I find the answer?	Is there any unnecessary information?	What prior knowledge will help me?
Determine the meaning of *culture* as it is used in the document.	The text describes how to monitor cells that are being cultivated.	Look closely at the details of the document and think about what meaning makes sense in the context.	The sentence about keeping a log does not help me understand the meaning of the word.	The document is about "cultivating cells." To cultivate something is to help it grow.

Step 2 Find and Check Your Answer ■ ■ ■

■ Confirm your understanding of the question and revise your plan as needed.

■ Based on your plan, determine you solution approach: *There are words in the text that I associate with growing. The procedures describe the things I should be observing as these cells grow. Culture seems to refer to the cells that are being grown. I'll select the option that best expresses that idea.*

■ Check your answer. Review all answers to determine if the answer you have selected in the best possible answer.

■ **Select the correct answer:** C the cells grown in special conditions
This answer makes sense. These directions tell what to check for in the growth of the cells for an experiment.

BIO LAB PROCEDURES FOR CELL CULTURE

When cultivating cells for an experiment, check the culture daily. Observe changes such as the color of the medium in which they are growing and the density of cell growth. Record your observations in your log. Include the name of the cell line and the nature of the medium. Calculate the doubling time of the culture at least once a week. You will harvest the cells when their density prevents further growth.

Problem Solving Tip

To test your answer, try reading the sentence with the word you want to understand by first replacing the word with your answer. If it makes sense in the sentence and in the rest of the text, then the answer you have chosen is likely the correct answer.

Remember!

You can often figure out a less common meaning of a familiar word by thinking about what the rest of the terms in the passage have in common. The term *log* has a more common meaning in everyday life than in the workplace. The term *log* is typically used to describe a section of wood that is cut from a tree. In most workplace communications, however, it refers to a regularly occurring record of events. Clues that help you understand the meaning of *log* are *check*, *observe*, *record*, and *calculate*.

On Your Own ■ ■ ■

Randini's on 9th

NOTICE TO MANAGERS

The Neighborhood Association of Restaurants is sponsoring the second annual "chef swap." This year, six restaurants in the River Village neighborhood are taking part in this exciting event. Each evening, one of our chefs will work in concert with a chef from another restaurant to serve an exciting new dish. If you were on the staff here last year, you probably remember "chef swap" as both rewarding and challenging. With our now seasoned staff, I'm sure that this year's event will run more smoothly. Managers are cautioned to begin preparing staff well in advance of the arrival of a visiting chef.

1. As a manager at Randini's, you have received this announcement about an upcoming event. What is the meaning of the word **concert** as it is used in the third sentence?

    A.   a musical performance

    B.   effort

    C.   a hot kitchen

    D.   formal dress

    E.   combined action

2. What does the word **seasoned** mean in reference to the staff?

    F.   positive

    G.   experienced

    H.   well paid

    J.   inexperienced

    K.   excited

Date: January 11

From: Sonia Baker, Bank Manager

To: Junior Loan Officers

RE: Raising concerns on applications

We've recently been receiving complaints that problems that should be noticed during initial loan application reviews are repeatedly being overlooked. When you review a loan application, you should flag any information given by the applicant that might raise concerns. You are not the sole reviewer of any application, but it is your responsibility as a first reviewer to alert the senior loan officer to potential problems with an application. Before forwarding an application, attach any documentation that the applicant might have provided.

3. You are a junior loan officer who has received this memo about reviewing loan applications. What action does the word **flag** in the second sentence name?

    A. draw attention to

    B. crossing out

    C. erasing

    D. questioning

    E. ignoring

4. You know that the word *sole* can mean the bottom of a foot or shoe, but what does **sole** mean in this memo?

    F. most important

    G. least important

    H. only

    J. last

    K. most powerful

From: VP of Sales   Date: June 17

To: Sales Managers—Southeast Region

Subject: Upcoming Seminar

Many homeowners who are restoring homes will be interested in materials that match the original roofing on their homes. Slate, though expensive, is the choice of many who own homes built 100 years ago or more. Certainly, slate is appropriate for the style and scale of these homes. Depending on the pitch, or angle, of the roof, this material can be challenging for a roofing crew. One of our vendors is offering a seminar on selling and installing slate roofing. You and your staff are encouraged to attend. Your expenses will be covered.

5. As a sales manager who is not familiar with roofing materials, you are interested in attending the announced seminar. What does the word **pitch** mean in the context of the above e-mail?

    A.   state of repair

    B.   sound when tapped

    C.   tar used

    D.   degree of slant

    E.   leakiness

6. You are familiar with the term scale as an instrument that is used to measure weight. What does **scale** mean as it is used in the above e-mail?

    F.   color

    G.   value

    H.   age

    J.   size

    K.   location

From:	Chris Livingston	Date: November 15
To:	All Employees	
Subject:	New Software Apps	

Greetings!.

As all of you know, our creative department has been developing ideas for software applications—or "apps"—to create new mediums by which we reach new and existing customers. We are very pleased to announce that development of our company's new software app has been completed and is now going through a quality assurance phase to debug any issues that might be discovered.

At the same time as the QA is being conducted, we will begin the app rollout to the public through new and exciting ways. Our primary tool will be social networking and video sharing sites to promote the new app. To help in this endeavor we have hired a consultant in video networking to ensure that our video goes viral. Based on our marketing research, by creating a viral video that reaches at least one million potential customers or more, we anticipate that all costs associated with the developing the app will be covered within four months of its release.

We are excited about this new direction for our company and the potential it creates for us to reach current and potential customers in new and innovative ways. Through the growing realm of new technologies such as social networking and mobile apps, we have an abundance of new ways to interface with our customers and to promote and expand our brand.

To learn more, please visit the "New Initiatives" page on our company intranet.

Best!

Chris

---

7. As a software engineer, you receive the above e-mail about new software applications. What does **viral** mean as it is used in the e-mail?

    A.   caused by a virus

    B.   a bug in the computer software that causes it to malfunction

    C.   a harmful or corrupting agency

    D.   sold in a variety of stores

    E.   rapid spread of information online through communication and sharing

8. When you **interface** with customers, what do you do?

    F.   alter their mobile apps

    G.   pitch a sale

    H.   interact with them

    J.   work on a computer with them

    K.   develop an app

Memo

To: Hospital Residents

From: Gary Albin, PA Hospital Coordinator

RE: Advising patients

Please note that the following paragraph from the Resident's Handbook has been revised.

Be sure to review this amended paragraph so that you understand and become familiar with this important update in regard to patient relations procedures:

As a resident, you know that clear communication with patients is important. Often a patient consults a resident for clarification on instructions from an attending physician. It is important to keep in mind that patients may not be familiar with medical terminology. Using too many technical terms can overwhelm patients, making them reluctant to ask other important questions. Think about what you want to say before you speak to a nervous patient. Overwhelming patients with hasty advice is never helpful and can cause harm.

---

9. You are a physician's assistant in a local hospital and have just read this memo that notifies you of an updated paragraph from the Resident's Handbook. What is the meaning of **note** as it is used in the first sentence?

    A. advise

    B. record

    C. revise

    D. quote

    E. ignore

10. As opposed to hospital residents, the **attending** physician is

    F. in charge of overall patient care.

    G. not a licensed physician.

    H. training to become a physician.

    J. not a hospital employee.

    K. responsible for revising the Resident's Handbook.

To: Police Supervisors

From: Dolores Mendez, Police Chief

Re: Budget Cuts

The department is disappointed by the town's decision to cut our budget. Although these cuts smart, they will not keep us from doing our primary job, protecting citizens and their property. We should all be grateful that the issue of staff cuts has been tabled and will not be addressed again in this fiscal year.

   The department will continue working with the city council to demonstrate the fiscal and resource needs of the department in order to prevent future budget or staff cuts. In this way, we hope to be able to continue our dedicated and ongoing work in the community. The department will move forward by focusing on finding resolutions that will prevent any interruption of these services in the future.

11. As a police supervisor, you receive the above memo after a recent meeting of the town budget committee. What does the word **smart** in the second sentence mean?

    A.   make sense

    B.   don't make sense

    C.   are reasonable

    D.   are puzzling

    E.   hurt or sting

12. What does it mean that an issue has been **tabled**?

    F.   considered

    G.   postponed

    H.   recognized

    J.   dismissed

    K.   misunderstood

Answers are on page 259.

Apply Complicated Instructions to New Situations

Skill: Apply complicated instructions to new situations

When reading documents such as company policies and guidelines, you need to be able to understand and apply the instructions that these documents contain. For example, when you start a job, you might receive instructions about how to set up and access voicemail or e-mail. Once you understand how these systems work, you will know what to do when new situations arise, such as having to record a new greeting that alerts people you are out of the office.

Remember!

Employers provide instructions in order to give guidance when questions arise about how to complete workplace tasks. Such instructions are often provided with the expectation that employees will refer to them before asking colleagues or supervisors questions about how to perform specific tasks. Because of this, it is important to read through workplace instructions carefully and make certain that you understand each of the steps described. Learn the meaning of any unfamiliar words and phrases. Review any complex ideas so that you have a thorough understanding of the document and how to apply it to the appropriate situations.

Skill Examples

Example 1
Apply instructions to a similar situation.

Transfer of Credits Policy

Students requesting a transfer of credits for courses taken at another college or university must submit the following:

- an official transcript
- the most recent course catalog from their previous school

Students should note that only credits, not grade point averages, can be transferred.

The passage describes the policy at a university for transferring credits from another college or university. Students may wonder if their grades will transfer. The last sentence of the last paragraph states that only credits, not grade point averages, can be transferred.

Example 2
Apply complicated instructions to a new situation similar to the one described.

Flextime Guidelines

Each unit, in cooperation with its respective director, establishes its own flextime schedules. The immediate supervisor determines if flextime is appropriate for his/her unit and for which positions.

The passage is about the flextime policy of a manufacturing company. An employee may question whether or not he can maintain his current flextime schedule if he transfers to another unit. The information needed to answer his question is in the second sentence. It states that supervisors determine flextime based upon the needs of their particular units.

Skill Practice

The City of Dover Falls is seeking qualified contractors to perform permanent repairs to a number of sites around the city damaged by recent floods. Sealed bids must be received by the Office of the City Clerk by Tuesday, June 2 at 11 A.M. If you wish to bid, please submit your sealed submittal in a mailing container or envelope that is plainly marked "SEALED BID ENCLOSED—JOB NAME." Be sure that your submittal includes a notarized disclosure form. The Office of the City Clerk is located at 6621 Parkview Avenue, Dover Falls, OH. Bids will not be received in any office or department but that of the City Clerk. Please note that bids sent via facsimile will not be accepted.

Use the document to the left to answer the following questions.

1. You wish to submit a bid for wiring a police station. Where should you submit this request?

   A. the Mayor's office
   B. the City Clerk's Office
   C. the police station
   D. to a contractor working at the site
   E. to a union representative

2. All bids are due tomorrow and your supervisor has asked you to fax a bid. You should

   F. fax it directly to the Mayor's office.
   G. fax it directly to the City Clerk's office.
   H. fax it to a union representative first.
   J. fax it to the owner of the property.
   G. inform him that bids cannot be faxed.

Try It Out! ■ ■ ■

You are a phone receptionist for a sunglasses manufacturer. You receive a call that asks for a product with which you are unfamiliar. According to the instructions, what should you do?

   A. Check an office directory.

   B. Ask the caller to call back.

   C. Ask if you can call the caller back.

   D. Consult with another receptionist.

   E. Consult with a supervisor.

Step 1 Understand the Problem ■ ■ ■

Complete the *Plan for Successful Solving.*

Plan for Successful Solving

What am I asked to do?	What are the facts?	How do I find the answer?	Is there any unnecessary information?	What prior knowledge will help me?
Determine what to do when handling a call about an unfamiliar product.	The instructions explain company standards for answering calls.	Look for where information is provided about what to do when uncertain about how to direct a call.	The first four sentences do not refer to what to do when uncertain about directing a call.	I am sometimes put on hold when a call I place to a business needs to be directed to a specific department.

Step 2 Find and Check Your Answer ■ ■ ■

- Confirm your understanding of the question and revise your plan as needed.

- Based on your plan, determine your solution approach: *The instructions indicate the standard procedures for answering phone calls. The last sentence describes what steps to take if you are not sure where to direct a call. As you are unfamiliar with the product referenced, it is likely that you are also uncertain of the person or department to whom the call should be directed. Therefore, the same steps should apply to this new situation.*

- Check your answer. Review all answers to determine if the answer you have selected is the best possible answer.

- **Select the correct answer:** E. Consult with a supervisor.
  If you do not know the product the caller is referring to, then you are in a situation that is similar to being uncertain about the department or extension to whom the caller should be directed. The passage states that, in this situation, the receptionist should put the caller on hold and consult with a supervisor.

Telephone Communication Standards

It is important to be both courteous and professional when answering the phone. Begin by saying, "Good Morning/Good Afternoon," then state the name of our company. Say, "This is," and provide both your first and last name. Then ask, "How may I help you?" Speak slowly and clearly. If you are uncertain about the department or extension to whom the caller should be directed, ask if you can put him or her on hold and then consult with a supervisor.

Problem Solving Tip

Making decisions in real workplace scenarios may require you to think of options other than those that are outlined within instructional documents. In test-taking situations, however, you should always be certain to read all answer options before choosing your answer.

Remember!

The instructions given in workplace documents are often general so that they can be applied to a number of similar, related situations. The scenario presented in the *Try It Out!* example is just one instance in which a receptionist might be unsure as to how a call should be directed. Because it is difficult to list every possible situation, it is important to understand how instructions relate to other situations to which they might be applied.

Department of Health Procedures Manual

The following rules state that pharmacies should deliver prescribed drugs and devices to patients in a timely manner. The pharmacy must meet the patient's need onsite unless one or more of the exceptions described in the rules are present. The pharmacy must assure that patients have access to lawfully prescribed or clinically safe drugs.

The rule provides examples of situations when it may not be appropriate to deliver prescribed drugs, devices, or provide an equivalent:

- National or state emergencies or guidelines affect the availability, usage, or supply;
- Potentially fraudulent prescriptions;
- Unavailability of the drug despite a good faith effort to comply with the Board's rule on adequate stock;
- When a pharmacy is not compensated for its usual and customary or contracted charge.

The rule requires pharmacies to provide patients with an alternative to appropriate therapy in a timely manner. When the drug is not in stock, alternatives include:

- Obtain the drug or device and deliver it to the patient;
- Contact the prescriber and obtain authorization to provide a therapeutically equivalent product;
- Return the unfilled prescription to the patient or the patient's agent if requested by the patient or the patient's agent;
- At the request of the patient, communicate or transmit the prescription information to a pharmacy of the patient's choice that will fill the prescription in a timely manner.

---

1. You are a pharmacist. A customer's medication is out of stock, but he needs to take it in a few hours. You should

- **A.** tell the customer that he must go to another pharmacy

- **B.** inform the customer that he has to wait until the medication is in stock at your pharmacy

- **C.** contact the customer's doctor to see if his medication can be replaced with a generic brand

- **D.** ask your supervisor what to do

- **E.** give the customer a similar medication and offer him a discount

2. In which of the following situations would it not be appropriate to provide a prescription to a customer?

- **F.** a customer is suspected of forging a prescription

- **G.** you have never seen the customer before

- **H.** the customer does not pick up the prescription on time

- **J.** the customer wants to purchase groceries at the pharmacy counter

- **K.** the doctor has authorized the customer's prescription

Road Repair Agreement between the City of Belleville and J. Wadsworth Construction Co.

This agreement outlines that the Operator will fix any damages made to roads that are on any property that is permitted by the City. The Operator is required to make repairs. This is true even if a permit is issued to allow for the drilling of more gas wells. This requirement should continue during the entire term of this Agreement. The Operator is required to make a videotape of all roadways before the start of drilling. The Operator is required to give a copy of the videotape to the Director of Transportation. The Operator shall notify the Director of Transportation when drilling operations are done. The Director of Transportation will decide if repairs to any roadways are required.

3. As an operator of contracting equipment used to drill gas wells for Belleville, you must be aware of the road repair agreement described above. As you complete the job, the owner of a dry cleaning establishment adjacent to the drill site demands that you repair a large crack in the street outside of his establishment that he claims was caused by your drilling. Your defense is that the crack existed prior to drilling. How can you prove this?

    A.   by gathering affidavits from other members of your crew

    B.   by referring to a videotape made prior to drilling

    C.   by gathering affidavits from other business owners adjacent to the dry-cleaning establishment

    D.   by referring to the permit issued by the city prior to drilling

    E.   by referring to conditions described in the application for the permit

4. In the course of the project, one morning you notice a buckle and fairly large pothole on a street adjacent to your drilling site. What, if any, steps should you take?

    F.   No steps are needed.

    G.   Ascertain from property owners whether or not the damage existed prior to drilling.

    H.   Take measurements and photographs only.

    J.   Notify the Director of Transportation immediately.

    K.   Notify your union representative.

State University

Complaint Resolution Procedures

When the Labor Relations Manager receives a written complaint, she or he must follow procedures for forwarding the complaint. The Labor Relations Manager must inform the employee filing a complaint that he or she will receive a response to his or her complaint within fifteen calendar days. The complaint should be forwarded to the university official at the administrative level above that of the employee's immediate supervisor for response. The complaint should be sent with copies to the appropriate administrator. If the appropriate administrator is unavailable to handle the complaint, it should be sent to the administrator one level up. The administrators refer to the Vice Chancellor–supervisor of the Dormitory Director, the Dormitory Director–supervisor of the Dormitory Assistant Director, and the Dormitory Assistant Director–supervisor of the Resident Assistant. The Labor Relations Manager must notify the employee of the date the reply is due.

The university official must send his or her decision to the employee within fifteen days from the date the complaint was received from the Labor Relations Manager. The written decision should be sent on official university stationery. The letter should be delivered through the university mail service to the employee. A copy should also be sent to the Labor Relations Manager.

---

5. You are a Labor Relations Manager at a large university, and you have forwarded a complaint filed by a resident assistant against another resident assistant regarding inappropriate comments to the Dormitory Director. The Director is out on vacation for two weeks. What action should you take?

   A. handle the request on your own

   B. tell the resident assistant to re-submit the complaint in two weeks

   C. forward the complaint to the Dormitory Assistant Director

   D. notify the university president

   E. forward the complaint to the Vice Chancellor

6. A student has filed a complaint against a resident assistant. To whom should you forward the complaint?

   F. the assistant dormitory director

   G. the dormitory director

   H. the vice chancellor

   J. the student's parents

   K. the case does not fall under your jurisdiction

Classifications of Fire

Type of Fire	Source	Means of Extinction
Class A	ordinary combustibles	water
Class B	flammable liquids and gasses	CO_2 (liquids); dry chemical or Halon (both)
Class C	electrical equipment	CO_2, dry chemical or Halon.
Class D	combustible metals	dry powder

7. As a firefighter, called to put out a fire inside a restaurant, you discover that the fire is burning behind a gas stove in the kitchen. Employees and patrons have been evacuated, but pots containing stewed tomatoes, rice pilaf, and poached flounder remain on the stove with the burners still on. How should you extinguish the fire?

    A. Remove the food from the stove.

    B. Extinguish the fire with water.

    C. Extinguish the fire with CO_2.

    D. Extinguish the fire with a heavy cloth.

    E. Disconnect the gas line.

8. A week later, the restaurant owner contacts the fire station and asks you to clarify why the insurance company classified the fire as a Class B. Which of the following explains this change?

    F. The fire occurred in a kitchen.

    G. The fire occurred in a commercial business.

    H. There were no civilians present.

    J. Natural gas caused the fire.

    K. The fire was not allowed to burn for very long.

Residential Elevator/Work by Others

The following preparatory work, which must be performed with the elevator installation, is to be done by others and is part of the work of other sections.

A. Construct a hoistway of the correct size for the new elevator, based on the elevator construction drawings.

B. Connect the telephone in machine room to an outside line, and not to the internal electronic phone system.

C. Provide passageways from elevator hoistway to machine room for electrical lines.

D. Painters must first complete all wall patching and grouting before the installation of hoistway doorframes. Then painters will apply the final gloss on hoistway doorframes.

E. Make padding of inside door satisfy local safety code requirements.

F. Install hoistway doors, frames, and hinges for each floor.

---

9. You are a supervisor for the installation of an elevator in a downtown apartment complex. As part of your responsibilities, you must file for a permit to complete the job. On the permit application, you are asked to account for hoistway entrance protection. What do you record in answer to this question?

   A. Hoistway doors will be installed and will be padded according to code.

   B. A passageway will connect the hoistway to the machine room.

   C. A telephone will be connected to the hoistway.

   D. The hoistway will be based upon elevator construction drawings.

   E. The hoistway will be of standard size.

10. Six weeks after the elevator's installation, the owner of the building sends you a letter to inform you that the paint on several of the hoistway doorframes is peeling. Your response is

   F. The complaint should have been filed within thirty days.

   G. Painting of the hoistway doorframes was not part of the original work order.

   H. You will investigate within seven business days.

   J. You will contact a union representative.

   K. He must provide photographs.

From: Claire Sanchez, Loan Officer

Date: April 17

To: HECM Specialists

Subject: U.S. Department of Housing and Urban Development

Origination Services

Consistent with existing policy, the loan origination fee, which may be fully financed with Home Equity Conversion Mortgage (HECM) proceeds, includes fees paid to the Federal Housing Administration (FHA), a government program that helps people become homeowners, and approved loan correspondents. The loan origination fee also covers the origination services including:

- educating the client;
- taking information from the borrower and filling out the loan application;
- collecting related documents that are part of the application process;
- initiating/ordering appraisals;
- initiating/ordering inspections;
- providing disclosures to the borrower;
- maintaining regular contact with the borrower;
- assisting the borrower with resolving adverse property conditions;
- ordering legal documents;
- processing the loan; and
- participating in the loan closing.

Lenders may not charge the borrower any fees in addition to the origination fee to pay FHA-approved loan correspondents.

11. You are a loan officer who is a HECM specialist, and you have been asked to work with a client who has applied for a loan. The client is confused as to how to fill out the application. What should you do?

    A. Help him complete the application.

    B. Provide him with a booklet from the FHA.

    C. Discourage him from applying for a loan.

    D. Refer him to another specialist.

    E. Advise him about potential additional fees.

12. A client is very much interested in a piece of property that has recently had some minor flooding. She is concerned there may be some damage to the home. How should you assist her?

    F. Withdraw your assistance.

    G. Discourage her from continuing.

    H. Order an inspection.

    J. Refer her to another specialist.

    K. Levy additional fees.

Answers are on page 259.

Remember!

Together, policies, rules, and procedures are directives provided by employers to create a set of standard ways of conducting business. Policies made by your employer create the environment in which you work. Rules set the parameters that enable you to work and interact effectively with others. Procedures dictate specific actions that produce intended consequences. When you understand the principle behind a policy, rule, or procedure, you can adapt the principle to a different situation.

Lesson 20 ...
Determine Principles Behind Workplace Directives

Skill: Figure out the principles behind policies, rules, and procedures.

Workplace documents such as policies, rules, and procedures are provided to give employees guidance about how to act in specific situations. A policy is a high-level plan; it provides general guidelines, but it does not identify specific actions. Rules are more specific guidelines. For example, the rules of a game may establish the size of the playing field or state that the players take turns. Rules created by a governing body are known as laws. Procedures are specific guidelines that outline the steps that should be taken in certain situations.

Skill Examples

Example 1
Determine the principles behind a policy.

Excessive Tardiness and/or Absence

Tardiness: If you are tardy 12 times within 12 consecutive months, your employment may be terminated.

Absence: Any employee who accumulates 72 hours of unexcused absence within 12 months will be terminated.

In this attendance policy, the consequences of excessive tardiness and unexcused absence are identified. The principle behind this policy is employees should be present during scheduled hours.

Example 2
Determine the principles behind a rule.

Completing Your Orientation

Once a new employee completes a new-hire orientation seminar, she or he must sign a contract that states that he or she has read and understands the rules in the employee handbook.

When new employees are hired by companies, they often go through an orientation to learn about company policies and procedures. The principle behind signing the contract mentioned in the passage is to ensure that all employees verify their understanding of the policies and procedures.

Create an Expense Report

To submit an expense report, compile all receipts in order by date. Fill in the expense report form with the following information: your name, date, and an explanation of the expenses. Use the codes that appear in the box on the left hand side of the report to enter explanations. If expenses occurred during travel, list the city and purpose of the trip. All client expenses should be filled out on a separate page. There will be a delay in reimbursement if there are errors in the expense report.

Skill Practice

Use the document to the left to answer the following questions.

1. What is the principle behind this procedure?

   A. Expense reports must include all receipts.

   B. Expense reports must be filled out correctly.

   C. Expense reports are only used for employees who travel.

   D. Expense reports are only used for client expenses.

   E. Expense reports must include the date.

2. What is the principle behind the use of codes in the expense report?

   F. It helps connect the price to the receipt.

   G. It is a quick way or reviewing price.

   H. It is a quick way of providing explanations.

   J. It helps prove prices are accurate.

   K. It connects price to the trip.

Try It Out! ■ ■ ■

You are a software engineer. Tomorrow is the first Friday of the month, and no guest visits are scheduled. Based on the company dress code, which of the following outfits can you wear to work?

A. a tennis outfit

B. a pair of sweatpants and a sweatshirt that has the company logo

C. stylish frayed jeans with a polo shirt that has your college's logo

D. jeans with a short-sleeve dress shirt

E. clothing that contains political statements

Step 1 Understand the Problem ■ ■ ■

Complete the *Plan for Successful Solving.*

		Plan for Successful Solving		
What am I asked to do?	**What are the facts?**	**How do I find the answer?**	**Is there any unnecessary information?**	**What prior knowledge will help me?**
Determine which outfit you can wear to work on Friday.	The company dress policy is business casual, except for "casual Fridays."	Compare the outfit options to the guidelines in the company dress policy.	The sentence about revealing clothing is not needed to select the correct answer.	Common understanding of appropriate business casual attire.

Step 2 Find and Check Your Answer ■ ■ ■

- Confirm your understanding of the question and revise your plan as needed.

- Based on your plan, determine your solution approach: *I will check each answer to determine if it is acceptable based on the dress code. Clothing designed for sports and for exercise facilities are not acceptable. Clothing should not be frayed. Jeans are acceptable on "casual Friday." Since it is Friday, jeans and a short-sleeve dress shirt is an acceptable outfit. All of the other outfits are not acceptable.*

- Check your answer. Review all answers to determine if the answer you have selected is the best possible answer.

- **Select the correct answer:** D. jeans with a short-sleeve dress shirt
  Options A, B, and C all include at least one article of clothing that is considered inappropriate for business casual dress standards. Jeans and a short-sleeve dress shirt meet the dress code for "casual Friday."

Office Dress Code

Our standard dress code for this office is business casual. The following are clarifications as to our interpretation of business casual dress:

- Clothing that is designed for the beach, yard work, nightclubs, exercise facilities, and sports use is not considered appropriate.
- Clothing that reveals your back, your chest, your stomach, or any undergarments is not considered appropriate.
- Clothing should not be wrinkled, torn, dirty, or frayed. All seams must be finished.
- Any clothing that has words or images that may offend other employees is unacceptable and will not be tolerated.
- Clothing that has the names of sports teams, universities, and brands are generally acceptable as business casual clothing. Clothing that has the company logo is encouraged.

On Fridays, we permit "casual Friday" dress code. On these days, jeans are acceptable, as is more casual clothing that does not offend others. Business casual dress will be required on Fridays during which we will have client and/or corporate guests visiting our facility.

Problem Solving Tip

When evaluating policies, rules, and procedures, study the wording carefully. Words such as *must, will,* and *required* tell you that an instruction must be followed closely. Words such as *should, optional,* and *prefer* may indicate that you can exercise some choice in following the instructions.

Remember!

Policies are often general. Note that a dress code is a policy that varies greatly from profession to profession, industry to industry, and also has varying degrees of enforcement. Even within the same office, people's interpretations of appropriate dress may differ. Policies are set, however, to establish a basic guideline.

On Your Own ■ ■ ■

Americans with Disabilities Act Guidelines

(10) Undue hardship

(A) In general

The term "undue hardship" means an action requiring significant difficulty or expense, when considered in light of the factors set forth in subparagraph (B).

(B) Factors to be considered

In determining whether an accommodation would impose an undue hardship on a covered entity, factors to be considered include

(i) the nature and cost of the accommodation needed under this chapter;

(ii) the overall financial resources of the facility or facilities involved in the provision of the reasonable accommodation; the number of persons employed at such facility; the effect on expenses and resources, or the impact otherwise of such accommodation upon the operation of the facility;

(iii) the overall financial resources of the covered entity; the overall size of the business of a covered entity with respect to the number of its employees; the number, type, and location of its facilities; and

(iv) the type of operation or operations of the covered entity, including the composition, structure, and functions of the workforce of such entity; the geographic separateness, administrative, or fiscal relationship of the facility or facilities in question to the covered entity.

Excerpt from the Americans with Disabilities Act of 1990, as amended by the ADA Amendments Act of 2008

---

1. You are planning to start a new business, but before you do so you want to know the impact that the Americans with Disabilities Act could have on your business. In the excerpt, who or what is the "covered entity?"

   A. the local government

   B. the federal government

   C. an employer

   D. a job applicant who has a disability

   E. a customer who has a disability

2. Why is it important that the business owner read and understand the regulations of the Americans with Disabilities Act?

   F. to identify Americans who have a disability

   G. to identify businesses that discriminate against Americans who have disabilities

   H. to protect the federal government from lawsuits

   J. to eliminate discrimination against people who have a disability

   K. to identify every possible disability

From: Human Resources

Date: September 29

To: Department Managers—ALL

Subject: Retention of Records

The company's schedule for the retention and disposal of business records provides for the processing of most records created or maintained by the company. These records include invoices for office supplies, IT support, and maintenance fees incurred for cleaning and repair and/or replacement of furniture and carpeting. If a warranty exists, managers should retain records for the period of time covered in that document. The managers of the departments that created or maintained the records may destroy these records upon expiration of the retention period. This schedule authorizes, but does not require, that managers dispose of records after the expiration of the specified retention period. Local departments may require that records be retained beyond the specified periods. Nothing prevents a department from retaining records longer than the specified period.

3. You are the department manager of an engineering firm. You have recently purchased new office furniture that includes a 3-year warranty. You know that you must retain the warranty for the 3-year period that it covers. What is the principle behind your office's warranty retention policy?

   A. The policy ensures that managers will not purchase items they do not need.

   B. The policy ensures that important records are not destroyed on accident.

   C. The policy ensures that the company will be able to receive all repairs and services covered by the warranty.

   D. The policy ensures that the company will not need to purchase new equipment.

   E. The policy ensures that all departments will keep their warranties for the same length of time.

4. Why is it important to understand the record retention policy?

   F. to ensure that records are not protected for a specific period

   G. to ensure that records are protected on microfiche

   H. to ensure that records are protected on computer files

   J. to ensure that records are protected off-site

   K. to ensure that records are protected for a specific period

Memo

To: Chemical Engineers

From: Linda Mun, Department Director

RE: Procurement Requisition Procedures

The employee must request three offers. Each offer should be from a different supplier located in the United States. Select the offer that is the best choice for your project. Note that for some specialized equipment, you may not be able to get offers from three different suppliers, or the only available suppliers may not be located in the United States.

Send an e-mail to the requisition office to request procurement of the equipment. Include:

- a cover letter that indicates the equipment to be procured, the total price, and the name and location of the preferred supplier;

- a justification that explains why this supplier was selected;

- the supplier's offer, which must clearly identify the materials, the price, the date that the offer will expire, and the shipping cost.

When the complete request is received, the requisition office will start the procurement process. Please allow two weeks for the order to be placed with the supplier.

---

5. You are a chemical engineer investigating a new method of separating the components of a fluid that is a by-product of your company's production process. In order to do so, you need to order specialized equipment. What is the principle behind the rules for requesting offers from suppliers?

    A. The requestor must select the best supplier.

    B. Cost should be the main factor when selecting a supplier.

    C. Only American companies can be suppliers.

    D. Equipment can only be purchased from a list of selected suppliers.

    E. The requisition office must justify the expenditure.

6. The requisition office has returned your request and asked that you receive a revised offer from your preferred supplier. The reason they have given you is that the list of equipment and pricing on the supplier's offer seems incomplete. What is the purpose behind requesting this information?

    F. They want to be certain the supplier is located in the United States.

    G. They want to be certain of all costs before placing the order.

    H. They want to be certain the supplier can fulfill the order.

    J. They want to be certain you have received three offers.

    K. They want to be certain you have chosen the best supplier.

Memo

To: All Engineers
From: Celine Rogers, Regulations Coordinator
RE: Hazardous Waste and Pollutant Regulations

Please be aware of the following updated regulations.

A. Groundwater must be kept at the quality level stated in the regulations. No individual can violate the standards.

B. No individual can allow any pollutant to be discharged into the groundwater without the approval of the division director.

C. The Division Director will determine whether or not the Maximum Contaminant Level (MCL) is set as close to the Maximum Contaminant Level Goal (MCLG) as possible. Please note that the MCLG is determined as the level below which there is no known expected risk to health.

D. No individual can maintain or operate a facility in a manner that could result in a discharge of any pollutant into the groundwater.

E. New solid waste landfills are prohibited in areas where the groundwater is classified as suitable for drinking without treatment.

F. New facilities that are required as treatment, storage, or disposal facilities require a permit from the state. Temporary storage areas for hazardous waste are prohibited without a permit from the state.

7. As an engineer at a water treatment facility, you received the above update to the existing hazardous waste and pollutant regulations. What is the principle behind these regulations?

    A.   Landfills are not permitted.

    B.   The state issues permits regarding water storage.

    C.   Pollutants can be stored with a state permit.

    D.   Maintaining the quality of the groundwater is a high priority.

    E.   New facilities cannot be constructed.

8. Your company has hazardous material that they would like to store in a temporary site until it can be safely removed. Why must you wait for a permit from the state before doing this?

    F.   The state needs to receive approval from the Division Director.

    G.   Hazardous waste could be discharged into the groundwater if not properly stored.

    H.   It is preferred that new facilities be created for the storage or treatment of hazardous waste.

    J.   Individuals are not allowed to maintain or operate temporary facilities.

    K.   The hazardous material may change the MCLG.

Laboratory Rental Procedures

Complete the following steps three months before lab rental begins:

- Provide a lab supervisor with a written plan for storing, handling, and disposing of all hazardous materials, and containers.

- Provide a list of chemicals and other potentially hazardous materials that you will bring to the lab. Complete an information sheet for each hazardous material.

- Read this lab-safety document identifying the steps that must be completed.

- If you will be working with hazardous materials, make written operating procedures. Hazardous materials include carcinogens, reproductive toxins, and substances that have a high degree of toxicity. A more detailed list is provided on the lab's Web site. Speak to a lab supervisor if you are not sure that your materials fit into this category.

During lab rental you must strictly adhere to the following rules:

- Do not pour used laboratory chemicals down the sink. You should use necessary containers for disposal.

- Consult a lab supervisor if you need help.

- Provide a lab supervisor with a list of precautions that should be taken by any person entering your laboratory space. Leave a note as needed.

- Complete the lab-safety checklist. Contact a lab supervisor if you have any questions. Sign and submit the checklist to the lab upon completion.

- All spills, improper disposals, contact with hazardous materials, and associated accidents must be immediately reported to a lab supervisor.

---

9. Why is it important that the steps in the top portion of the procedures document be completed in advance of the lab rental?

A. to ensure that the renters are qualified and come prepared to handle any issues that might arise

B. to prepare the renters for how to complete a lab-safety checklist

C. to see if the chemicals that will be used by the renters are already in stock in the lab

D. because the lab does not have its own procedures for working with hazardous materials

E. to be certain that the renters will report all spills and other accidents to a lab supervisor

10. You have rented lab space to conduct experiments on a new furniture polish. Why is it important to have contact information for the lab supervisor?

F. in case there are concerns about lab-safety

G. in case additional supplies are needed

H. in case there is spillage of hazardous materials

J. in case you have a complaint about the condition of the lab

K. in case you cannot enter the laboratory

PROCEDURES
Submitting Article for Publication

1. Download and read the Author's Guide that is available on our Web site.

2. Follow the directions in the Author's Guide to format your article.

3. Prepare all graphics, such as charts and photos, that will be included in your article. Verify that all graphics meet the journal's requirements.

4. Edit your article, correcting errors in spelling, formatting, and content.

5. Verify that your article has been correctly prepared, based on the journal's requirements.

6. Make certain that all source material, whether directly quoted or referred to, has been clearly documented according to the method specified by this journal.

7. Write a cover letter that will accompany your article when you submit it to the journal.

8. Follow the journal's instructions to submit your manuscript to the journal.

11. As a biomedical engineer, you have written an article that you want to publish in a scientific journal. What is the purpose of the instructions provided by the journal?

    A. to teach you the publishing process

    B. to reveal your information to your peers

    C. to improve your status among your peers

    D. to make the publishing process go quickly and smoothly

    E. to verify that your research is original

12. Your article is credited to the work of a professor that you studied with in college. According to the guidelines, how, if at all, should you acknowledge that credit?

    F. dedicate the article to him

    G. document any published works of his that are part of your study

    H. there is no need to mention him at all

    J. provide narrative description of how his work influenced yours

    K. refute his ideas

Answers are on page 259.

Lesson 21
Apply Principles to New Situations

Skill: Apply general principles from the materials to similar and new situations

Remember!

A principle is created to establish a baseline, or a point of reference. Although you may understand the principle as you read it, keep in mind the importance of also understanding how to apply it to new situations.

Although company policies and procedures are often carefully detailed, you may encounter situations that are not directly stated in which you are expected to apply the company's general principles. By having a strong understanding of the general principles behind company policies and procedures, you will know how to apply these principles to any workplace situation.

Skill Examples

E-mail messages should be professional in tone and content. Writing style should be clear and concise, proofread for accuracy, and reviewed for appropriateness. Hastily written messages can sometimes seem brusque and rude to the recipient. Therefore, it is important that employees monitor the tone of their messages and responses.

Example 1
Determine the general principle of the policy or rule.

The above policy refers to being cautious before sending e-mail to others both within and outside of the company. The general principle behind the document is that employees should maintain a level of professionalism both in content and tone when communicating through e-mail or other digital formats.

Example 2
Apply principles to new situations.

Suppose you are asked to lead a conference call with outside vendors who are working with you on a project. Though the communication format for this situation is not mentioned in the above policy, the general principle of the policy—that communication should be both professional and courteous—still applies.

Skill Practice

We are in the process of making a number of strategic changes in order to meet the needs of our growing Spanish-speaking market. First, packaging designs will change. Most of the wording on our store brand packages will be displayed both in English and Spanish. All promotional materials will now be distributed in English and Spanish versions. Based on what growth trends we see from these changes, we may expand our distribution internationally to specific Latin American markets in the next few years.

Use the document to the left to answer the following questions.

1. If you are fluent in Spanish, how might you be affected by the company's new policy?

   A. You may lose your job.

   B. You will be less likely to receive promotions.

   C. You may have more job transfer or advancement opportunities.

   D. Your direct manager will probably not value your skill.

   E. Your job will probably not change.

2. Which one of the following might improve your chances of getting a sales position with this company as they move into foreign markets?

   F. You have a degree in international business.

   G. You have traveled to several countries on vacations.

   H. You like foods from the countries they plan to target.

   J. Many of your neighbors have different cultural backgrounds.

   K. You have knowledge of world currency systems.

Try It Out! ■ ■ ■

As fire captain, you are in charge of updating and enforcing your department's safety program. A resident has just submitted a complaint that in response to a recent call he made regarding a chemical spill, none of the crew that was dispatched seemed aware as to how the situation should be safely handled. Based on the guidelines to the right, how should you respond to the resident's complaint?

A. Ignore the complaint.

B. Forward the complaint to the department of labor.

C. Confirm the complaint and discipline the crew.

D. Present the complaint to the safety committee.

E. Tell the resident to develop a recommendation for how to address the issue.

> **State Guidelines: Department Safety Programs**
> 1. All fire departments shall develop and implement a written safety program. This includes establishment of a safety committee.
> 2. Each employer must develop a formal accident-prevention program tailored to the needs of the fire department and to the types of hazards involved. The department of labor and industries' consultation and compliance services division may be contacted for assistance in developing appropriate programs. The program should cover:
>   A. how and when to report injuries.
>   B. how to report unsafe conditions and practices.
>   C. the use and care of required personal protective equipment.
>   D. the proper actions to take in event of emergencies.
>   E. identification of hazardous gases, chemicals, or materials and instructions on safe use and emergency action following accidental exposure.
>   F. a description of the employer's total safety program.
> 3. Every employee has the right to submit suggestions or complaints. The safety committee must consider and respond to all suggestions.

Step 1 Understand the Problem ■ ■ ■

Complete the *Plan for Successful Solving.*

Plan for Successful Solving

What am I asked to do?	What are the facts?	How do I find the answer?	Is there any unnecessary information?	What prior knowledge will help me?
Determine the appropriate response to a complaint received from a resident.	The guidelines provide details about how fire departments should develop and implement written safety programs.	Locate any guidelines that might refer to handling resident complaints. If no guideline exists, find one that closely relates.	The information regarding who should be consulted for development is not needed.	Knowing how complaints are handled in other businesses, such as restaurants and stores.

Step 2 Find and Check Your Answer ■ ■ ■

- Confirm your understanding of the question and revise your plan as needed.

- Based on your plan, determine your solution approach: *Since the principle is to maintain the safety of department employees, and the resident's complaint relates to employee and resident safety, the steps that are outlined in item number 3 apply to this situation.*

- Check your answer. Review all answers to determine if the answer you have selected is the best possible answer.

- **Select the correct answer:** D. Present the complaint to the safety committee. The guidelines establish that employee complaints are to be submitted to the safety committee. Given this and the nature of the issue, it is likely that this committee would also review the resident's complaint.

Problem Solving Tip

Signal words such as *all, each,* and *every* may be helpful in identifying the basic details of a principle. In the *Try It Out!* example, the statements "All fire departments, " "Each employer," and "Every employee" all signal that a principle is being established.

Remember!

Sometimes the general principle in a document is stated; other times it is implied.

Memo

To: All Employees

From: Carlos Stanford, Office Manager

Re: New Office Recycling Program

Did you know that up to 77 percent of paper waste in offices like ours is recyclable? Typical businesses waste about 1.5 pounds of paper per employee each day. Recycling just one ton of paper saves about 6 cubic yards of landfill space and 17 trees. It is important that our company does its part to help the environment.

With this in mind, we are implementing a new recycling program in our offices. I encourage you to participate in our effort. The program will only take a few minutes of your time each week.

The enclosed flyer gives specific details of what materials can and cannot be recycled. As a general rule, almost all paper used in the office can be recycled. This includes letterhead, computer, notebook, and colored paper as well as magazines and newspapers. In addition to paper, cardboard, aluminum cans, and plastic and glass bottles can also be recycled.

You will receive a small container for your daily recyclables. When your container is full, please empty it in the larger containers located in each work area. Bins will also be placed near photocopiers and in the cafeteria.

Thank you for your participation. If you have any questions or concerns, please call me at extension 342.

---

1. You are a building supervisor who has thought of some suggestions to improve the recycling program. Which of these suggestions best follows the general principle of the memo?

   A. Ask employees to bring their recycling from home to the office.

   B. Ask employees to take some of their recycling home with them.

   C. Ask employees to separate high- and low- quality paper when they recycle.

   D. Ask employees to reuse paper that is only printed on one side.

   E. Ask people to donate money so that trees can be planted around the office.

2. A friend of yours owns a software design firm and would like to make improvements in his office to help the environment. Which of his suggestions would not support his goal?

   F. Offer flexible working hours so that fewer employees are in the office at one time.

   G. Encourage employees to reuse envelopes, folders, and paperclips.

   H. Install water coolers and encourage the use of reusable cups.

   J. Pay employees through electronic direct deposits as opposed to paper checks.

   K. Use energy-efficient light bulbs in the office.

MANUFACTURER'S WARRANTY

Series 3500 double-paned windows purchased and installed by us will be free from defects in material and workmanship. This warranty remains in effect for as long as the purchaser of the windows owns and resides in the home.

PVC Frame and Sashes: The welded corners will not separate. No part will chip, crack, blister, or warp.

Hardware, Balances, and other Moving Parts: All of the hardware, balances, crank mechanisms, latches, and rollers will not crack, break, or fail to work.

Screen Frame and Screening: The entire screen has warranty protection against rusting, rotting, and tearing due to manufacturer defect. A new screen frame and/or screening material will be furnished should a defect occur.

Insulated Glass Unit: The seal on the glass unit will not break and cause condensation between the glass panels. Condensation on the windows may occur due to humidity within the house and variation of inside and outdoor temperatures. This type of condensation is normal and is not covered under the warranty.

Glass Breakage: If the glass of the window breaks due to manufacturer defect, we will provide a new sealed glass unit at no charge. This warranty does not cover decorative glass units or glass in doors.

Warranty Limitations: The purchaser will pay labor costs to fix repairs and defects, except in the case of repairs or defects that occur within the first year of installation of the windows.

Exclusions: Coverage is only offered to the original purchaser of the windows who still owns and lives in the home. Removal of the windows by the owner voids this warranty. Problems as a result of natural disasters are not covered.

WILSON'S WARRANTY SUPPLEMENT

Within the first 10 years of owning your new windows, Wilson Windows will pay all labor costs associated with repair or replacement work that is covered under the manufacturer's warranty. We do not pay for labor costs already paid by the manufacturer. This warranty is valid as long as you live in and own the home.

---

3. As a service manager of Wilson Windows, you must often interpret the warranties when customers report problems. The company that makes the windows offers the Manufacturer's Warranty. Wilson's Windows—the company that installs the windows—offers the Warranty Supplement. A customer calls with the following problem: His dog ripped a hole in the window screen. He had his windows installed eight years ago. He still lives in and owns the house. According to the warranty and supplement, which of the following is true?

    A. He will not have to pay anything for the repair.

    B. He will pay only the cost of the screen.

    C. He will pay only the cost of labor.

    D. He will have to pay the cost of the screen and labor.

    E. More information is required to answer this question.

4. Another customer calls complaining that the seal in her window broke, causing condensation between the panes of glass. She has owned the windows for 12 years and still owns and lives in the house. According to the warranty and supplement, which of the following is true?

    F. She will not have to pay anything for the repair.

    G. She will pay only the cost of the glass unit.

    H. She will pay only the cost of labor.

    J. She will have to pay the cost of the glass unit and labor.

    K. More information is required to answer this question.

POCKET'S GIFT SHOPPE RETURN & REFUND POLICY

A receipt dated within 90 days is required for all returns and exchanges.

No receipt

In many cases, we can look up a receipt if a major credit card was used. The receipt look-up system only allows for purchases made in the last 90 days. If you are retuning an item that you received as a gift, you must provide the original receipt or a gift receipt. If you are returning a broken or defective item but have no receipt, you can contact the manufacturer directly.

Refunds will be given in the form of payment originally used for the purchase.

- *Cash purchases:* Refunds paid in cash.
- *Credit and debit card purchases:* Your refund will be credited to the original credit or debit card.
- *Purchase bought with gift card:* Your refund will be given in the form of a Pocket's gift card.
- *Gifts:* If your return is made with a gift receipt, your refund will be given as a Pocket's gift card.
- *Check purchases:* Your refund will be given in the form of a Pocket's gift card.

Tax: The appropriate tax amount will be included with your refund.

Discounts: If you received a discount (by sale price, coupon, etc.), the refunded amount for the item will reflect the discount.

Seasonal Merchandise: Holiday and seasonal merchandise can be returned, but the price refunded will equal that of the clearance price at the time of the return.

---

5. As a customer service representative for Pocket's Gift Shoppe, you help customers with returns. A customer bought a package of decorative candles and wants to return them. The candles are white and were originally on sale, but now the customer wants to exchange them for red candles that were, but are no longer, on sale. Which solution applies to the situation?

    A. Refuse the exchange.

    B. Exchange the candles, but charge the customer for the difference.

    C. Exchange the candles without further cost.

    D. Provide a gift card for the original amount.

    E. Provide a cash refund.

6. A customer wants to return a music box that cost $50. He paid for it with a check. Which solution applies?

    F. Do not allow the return.

    G. Contact the credit card company and ask them for a refund.

    H. Credit any other credit cards the customer has.

    J. Provide a gift card for $50.

    K. Refund cash for $50.

	Current Job	Potential Job
Title of job	Database Administrator	Database Manager
Location	Columbus, OH	Cleveland, OH
Size of company	4,850	823
Description of company	Leader in the industry of manufacturing and marketing household goods such as cleaning supplies, health and beauty, and baby products	Leader in the industry of manufacturing and marketing pet foods and supplies
Pay rate	$34 per hour overtime: 1.5 x regular rate holiday: 2 x regular rate	$39 per hour overtime: 1.5 x regular rate holiday: 2 x regular rate
Vacation	2 weeks per year (1 Paid, 1 Unpaid)	3 weeks per year (3 Paid)
Job duties	Works as part of a team to make changes to, test, and implement the database management system (DBMS) specific to the company. May help to implement security measures. Tests and corrects the DBMS. Trains database users.	Leads the process of designing, testing, and installing the company's database management system (DBMS). Also leads the database team to monitor and administer DBMS security, including adding and removing users, auditing, and checking for security problems. Trains subordinates to analyze the data stored in the database. Works with the design team when a new database is created. Supervises and evaluates database administrators.

7. You are currently working as a database administrator in Columbus, but you have been working with a career consultant to find a new job. A company in Cleveland has offered you a job. The career consultant has provided you with this information to compare and contrast the two positions. One of your primary motivators for finding a new job was to increase your pay. What information is most important to help you determine if the new job will increase your pay?

A. pay rate and title of job

B. pay rate and paid vacation

C. job duties and size of company

D. pay rate and location of job

E. paid vacation and title of job

8. What general conclusion can you reasonably make from this data?

F. The new job pays more because of its location.

G. Larger companies tend to pay more.

H. You will have to join a workers' union if you take the new job.

J. The new job pays more because the position involves more responsibilities.

K. The larger company offers better vacation benefits.

Vice President of Sales
Abcore Corp.
7893 Boston Avenue
Los Angeles, CA 90008

Dear Sir or Madam:

Please accept the following letter of recommendation for Jane Heeley. Ms. Heeley has worked for me as a sales representative for over seven years. Although I am sad to see her leave, I know that she will succeed in any new role that she chooses.

Ms. Heeley is a highly qualified sales professional. She is a self-starter with drive and energy. She has an incredible work ethic and is one of the most honest and sincere people I know. She is organized, dependable, and personable.

Ms. Heeley has been one of my top sales performers for the last five years. She has a natural talent for sales. She asks her clients the right questions, solves their problems, and closes the deal. She learns new products quickly and is very creative in her sales methods. She often amazes me with her talent to "think on her feet" when a sales solution is needed immediately. Her writing skills are as good as her speaking skills. Her ability to present a product to a client and follow up with a creatively written proposal has sealed many deals.

I can confidently recommend Ms. Heeley for any sales position.

Sincerely,

J.P. Allen

9. As the VP of Sales, you are in charge of hiring a new sales representative. You receive this letter of recommendation for one of your potential new hires. What information about Ms. Heeley does the letter provide?

A. her intention of accepting this job if it is offered to her

B. her communication skills and the details of her current job

C. her personal qualities and sales skills

D. how her coworkers feel about her skills

E. her skills as a salesperson and her goals

10. As the VP of advertising, you too are looking for a new employee. If Ms. Heeley was interviewing for a position in your department, how might the writer change the letter?

F. describe her personal characteristics in detail

G. focus more on her writing skills and creativity

H. remove references to how she communicates with clients

J. remove references to sales and creativity

K. focus more on her presentation skills and less on her writing skills

NATIONAL UNIONS FINANCIAL SERVICES

To: Members of Ironworkers Local Unions

From: Board of Trustees

Re: Pension plan

Given the current state of the economy, we would like to address concerns that you may have about your pension plan. Although the assets of the plan have been reduced since their peak last year, the Board of Trustees does not believe that we will need to reduce pensions in the near future. This includes pensions of current active participants as well as those who have retired.

Laws do not usually allow reduction of benefits that have already been earned in pension plans such as ours. However, if the assets of the plan drop to the point where they cannot meet the annual benefit payments or if funding of the plan drops significantly, changes could be made. We would like to emphasize, however, that at this point there is no need for concern. The assets of the plan are easily able to meet benefit payments in the foreseeable future.

The recent economic crisis is more severe than others we have faced. However, we are monitoring the situation closely. We pledge our commitment to protect the long-term financial stability of the plan.

11. You are a welder scheduled to retire within the coming year and you are getting your affairs in order. Based on the passage above about pension plans, what is a possible change with your 401K plan?

  A. There could be a reduction in matching contributions.

  B. The company will work to diversify funds.

  C. Laws concerning pension plans will change.

  D. There could be a rush of employee retirement.

  E. All benefits might cease.

12. What new situation could negatively impact the pension plan?

  F. The economy drastically declines.

  G. The economy drastically improves.

  H. The ironworkers see a rise in business.

  J. Retired welders elect not to receive a pension.

  K. Welders are laid off.

Answers are on page 259.

Certain formats are considered more appropriate than others for communicating specific kinds of information within the workplace.

Guidelines and Procedures: Used to explain how something should be done.

Policies and Rules: Used to establish principles and codes for workplace protocol.

Memo: Used to inform people of various things, including upcoming events, meetings, or changes in workplace procedures.

E-mail: Used for numerous types of communication, many of which are similar to memos. E-mail is unique because it is widely used for both formal and informal workplace communication.

Lesson 22
Explain the Rationale Behind Workplace Communications

Skill: Explain the rationale behind a procedure, policy, or communication

A rationale is the fundamental reason or logic that forms the basis for an idea or an action. To identify the rationale, examine the logic behind the idea or action by asking yourself why it has been established or why it makes sense.

For example, many companies require new employees to attend a new-hire orientation. The rationale behind this policy is so that new employees have an opportunity to learn about the company, its policies and procedures, and what they can expect during their employment with the company in terms of details such as work hours and benefits.

Skill Example

Identify and explain the rational behind a procedure.

> In an effort to continue to ensure the safety of all tenants in the Carson Building, all guests must be pre-registered.
>
> With at least 24 hours notice, you will need to contact your designated receptionist with your guest's arrival date and time. As guests arrive to the security desk located on the mezzanine level, their names will be verified in the system and against a valid picture ID. Upon approval of both, a name tag will be issued.

The above memo is a reminder to tenants of the standard procedures used in this office building. Similar to the main idea of a paragraph or document, the very first sentence indicates the rationale behind the communication. The memo is intended to remind tenants within the building of standard procedures for notifying security of expected guests to ensure the safety of all tenants within the building.

Skill Practice

Use the document to the left to answer the following questions.

CAMPUS FACILITIES: Arrival Time Policy

Campus facilities are tightly scheduled during the summer months. Participants may not access the campus facilities rented by the Client before the contracted start date or remain after the contracted end date without permission from the Facilities Director. Permission for such additional accommodations must be requested in writing by the Client at least two (2) weeks prior to the contracted start date. The Facilities Director will consider and respond to each request.

1. What is the rationale behind this policy?

   A. Participants are too rowdy to be allowed on campus.

   B. Participants should pay extra for additional time used.

   C. The Facilities Director wants to meet all of the participants.

   D. The facilities may be scheduled for other groups before or after this event.

   E. Early arrival would require extra preparation.

2. Who must request permission for a participant to arrive early?

   F. the client

   G. the participant

   H. the Facilities Director

   J. participants may not arrive early

   K. permission is not needed

Try It Out! ▪ ▪ ▪

As a loan officer, you have received a memo from your manager in the Mortgage Loan department. It encourages loan officers to increase the number of refinanced mortgage loans for existing clients. Based on the memo, what information should you use to encourage existing clients to refinance a mortgage loan?

A. Mortgage interest rates are rising.

B. First-time homeowners can receive incentives for financing with your company.

C. Clients can reduce their mortgage payments or terms.

D. Clients who have existing mortgages that are almost paid off will benefit from refinancing.

E. Refinancing will increase the value of a client's house.

> In order to meet our goals for this quarter, we must increase the number of refinanced loans for existing clients. The Marketing department will be sending the following letter to existing mortgage clients this week. Use the information from the letter to encourage callers to refinance their mortgage loans with us.
>
> Mortgage interest rates are falling. Because of this, refinancing during this time can provide benefits for you that will help you reduce the cost of borrowing money over the long term.
>
> • Refinancing can reduce your monthly payment for a repayment term that is similar to your existing mortgage.
> • Refinancing can reduce your repayment term while making a monthly payment that is similar to your existing mortgage.
>
> Refinancing pays off your existing mortgage loan and starts a new loan. This is more helpful during the early years of your existing mortgage, when most of the payment is applied to the loan's interest. It makes less sense to refinance an existing loan later in the loan's life cycle when payments are applied primarily to the loan principal.

Step 1 Understand the Problem ▪ ▪ ▪

Complete the *Plan for Successful Solving.*

Plan for Successful Solving

What am I asked to do?	What are the facts?	How do I find the answer?	Is there any unnecessary information?	What prior knowledge will help me?
Use information from the marketing letter to encourage existing clients to refinance a mortgage loan.	The memo includes information that explains how refinancing can reduce a client's payments or repayment term.	Read the information and determine the rationale behind it.	The fact that the company needs to meet its goals.	Basic understanding of what principal, interest, and loan terms are.

Step 2 Find and Check Your Answer ▪ ▪ ▪

- Confirm your understanding of the question and revise your plan as needed.

- Based on your plan, determine your solution approach: *I will read the letter to customers and note the benefits that come from refinancing. I see that the two main benefits listed are reduced payments and shorter terms. I will choose the answer that is closest to either or both of these benefits.*

- Check your answer. Review all answers to determine if the answer you have selected is the best possible answer.

- **Select the correct answer:** **C.** Clients can reduce their mortgage payments or terms.
  Refinancing is a way to reduce mortgage payments and this is the best answer for why a person should refinance a loan.

Problem Solving Tip

To determine a rationale, look for words or phrases that indicate a cause or reason for action, such as *in order to, because, therefore, thus,* and *as a result.* In the *Try It Out!* example, the second sentence of the letter to customers begins, "Because of this" to signal the cause-and-effect relationship that since mortgage rates are falling (cause), you can refinance and reduce your mortgage payment (effect). This helps give the customer a rationale for why they should refinance.

Remember!

Asking *why* can help you identify the rationale behind an action, an idea, or workplace communication.

Daily Vehicle Inspection Procedure

1. Police officers will inspect their assigned police vehicle before and after each tour of duty. They should carefully check each of the following items and complete Form A1:

   a. Verify that the vehicle is clean inside and outside. Remove any unauthorized bumper stickers or other markings.

   b. Verify that the tires are properly inflated and undamaged.

   c. Report any dents or damage affecting the vehicle's body.

   d. Verify that the lights are functional and the lenses are clean.

   e. Check the windows for damage. Verify that visibility is not impeded.

   f. Check and maintain the following fluid levels: oil, transmission, steering, windshield washer, and coolant.

   g. Verify that the brakes and the emergency brake function correctly.

   h. Verify that the steering is not too tight or too loose.

   i. Verify that the windshield wipers work correctly.

   j. Verify that the dashboard instruments and lights work.

   k. Verify that the seats are operational and adjust easily.

   l. Verify that the siren/emergency lights, spotlights, and auxiliary lights work properly.

   m. Verify that the radio, mobile video recorder, and mobile data computer are working correctly. Record the serial numbers on the form.

   n. Inspect the license plate recognition equipment, including the cameras, drive, and cables.

   o. Verify that the radar equipment is present and functional.

---

1. You are a police officer who must complete the inspection procedure. What is the rationale behind the required procedure?

   A. to meet the demand of taxpayers, who require the inspections

   B. to ensure that the vehicle is the one assigned to you

   C. to ensure that the fluid levels in the vehicle are maintained

   D. to increase your safety during your shift

   E. to increase the cost of vehicle maintenance

2. Why must the inspection procedure be performed before each tour of duty?

   F. It ensures that the fluids are replaced daily.

   G. It ensures that the vehicle has not been damaged since it was last used.

   H. The inspection at the end of the previous shift was not performed.

   J. The inspection form must be completed.

   K. The equipment is not well maintained and it often breaks down.

Fire Drill Procedure

- The employee who serves as the Fire Safety Director must schedule a fire drill when most employees are in the building.

- The Fire Safety Director must inform the local police and fire department, the company's security officers and maintenance personnel, and the building supervisor of the exact time that the fire drill will begin.

- The Fire Safety Director will activate the fire alarm.

- All occupants will evacuate the building when the fire alarm sounds. Based on state law, an occupant can be prosecuted for failing to leave the building or preventing another person from leaving the building.

- During the evacuation, the Fire Safety Director must verify that elevators are not used.

- The Fire Safety Director must verify that all building occupants assemble at the designated outside location.

- The Fire Safety Director must verify that any individuals requiring assistance to leave the building reach the designated assembly location.

- When the Fire Safety Director has verified that all occupants have left the building, the alarm will be reset and the occupants can return to the building.

---

3. As an electrical engineer in this building, you have been asked by the Fire Safety Director to assist another engineer who has a severe hearing impairment. Which item within the procedure addresses this situation?

    A. The employee who serves as the Fire Safety Director must schedule a fire drill when most employees are in the building.

    B. The Fire Safety Director will activate the alarm.

    C. During the evacuation, the Fire Safety Director must verify that elevators are not used.

    D. The Fire Safety Director must verify that all building occupants assemble at the designated outside location.

    E. The Fire Safety Director must verify that any individuals requiring assistance to leave the building reach the designated assembly location.

4. According to the procedures, why must the Fire Safety Director verify that all occupants have left the building after a fire drill?

    F. to notify the city fire department

    G. to notify the building manager

    H. to notify the department supervisor

    J. to reset the alarm and allow the occupants to return

    K. to determine whether or not an emergency really does exist

United States Space Program Policies

U.S. policies related to space programs are guided by several principles:

- The United States supports the concept of the exploration and use of outer space by all nations for peaceful purposes. This allows for U.S. defense and intelligence-related activities in pursuit of national interests.

- The United States rejects any claims to sovereignty or ownership made by any nation over outer space or any portion of outer space.

- The United States will cooperate with other nations to advance the peaceful use of outer space and enhance space exploration, an effort that can promote freedom for all nations.

- The United States believes that space systems belonging to any nation have the right to operate in space without interference. The United States views any purposeful interference with its space systems as an infringement on its rights.

- The United States encourages the entrepreneurial U.S. commercial space sector by using U.S. commercial space capabilities to the maximum practical extent, consistent with national security.

5. As an aerospace engineer, you work for a private company that is researching new technology for a communication satellite. Based on this policy information, how is your company affected by this policy?

   A. Your company's activities must be halted.

   B. Your company's research will be confiscated by the government.

   C. Your company will be forced to work with other nations to develop the new technology.

   D. Your company will remain independent, but you must sell your technology to the U.S. space program.

   E. Your company is not affected.

6. What is the rationale behind the U.S. policies related to space programs?

   F. The United States plans to control outer space.

   G. Outer space is not important.

   H. The United States does not want other countries to explore outer space.

   J. The United States plans to colonize outer space, thereby claiming it as U.S. territory.

   K. The United States supports the peaceful use of outer space by all nations.

General Returns Policy

You may return most new, unopened items purchased from our Web site within 30 days of delivery for a full refund. We will pay the return shipping costs if the return was caused by our error. For a full refund, please return items in their original packaging. Visit the Returns section on our Web site to print a return mailing label that must be clearly visible on the outside of the box used to return the item. Any package without the return mailing label will be refused by our Receiving Department.

- You will receive an 80% refund of the item's price for any opened computer equipment returned within 30 days of delivery.

- You will receive a 75% refund of the item's price for any unopened media item in its original condition that is returned more than 30 days after delivery.

- You will receive a 70% refund of the item's price for any book that has obvious signs of use.

- You will not receive a refund for any electronic medium, such as a CD, a DVD, software, or a video game that has been removed from its packaging.

- You will receive a maximum of a 50% refund of the item's price for any item that is not in its original condition for reasons that are not caused by an error on our part.

---

7. You are a customer service representative. A customer calls because she returned an opened video game but did not get a refund. She explains that the video game wasn't damaged, but that her son already owns a copy of the game. Which of the following rationales best explains the company policy?

  A. The game could have been damaged or copied.

  B. The game could have been purchased by another company.

  C. The game should have been returned within 24 hours.

  D. The game is no longer made by your company.

  E. The game is currently on sale.

8. What is the rationale for requiring the return mailing label printed from the supplier's Web site?

  F. It increases the number of legitimate returns.

  G. It increases the supplier's cost.

  H. It makes the return process work more smoothly.

  J. It increases the cost of restocking the item.

  K. It encourages the customer to look for a different supplier.

Chain Saw Safety Precautions

- Check controls, chain tension, bolts, and handles before starting a chain saw.

- Start the saw on the ground or on a firm support.

- Start the saw at least 10 feet away from the fueling area or any potential source of ignition. Use a funnel or a flexible hose to pour fuel into the saw.

- Do not pour fuel into a hot saw.

- Before cutting, remove dirt, debris, small tree branches, and rocks from the saw's path. Verify that a tree does not have nails or other metal.

- Turn off the saw or engage its chain brake when you are carrying it on uneven terrain.

- Keep your hands on the saw's handles and securely plant your feet while operating the saw.

- When operating the saw, do not wear loose clothing. Wear protective equipment, including hand, foot, leg, head, eye, face, and hearing protection.

- Watch for branches that are under tension because they may cause an injury by springing out when cut.

9. As an environmental engineer hired by a logging company to create a plan to maintain an area of old woods, you are required to read the chain saw safety precautions. Based on the precautions, why should you engage the chain brake?

   A. to refuel the chain saw

   B. to cut branches under tension

   C. to slow down the chain saw

   D. to keep the chain saw sharp

   E. to carry the chain saw over uneven terrain

10. What is the rationale behind requiring all employees to read the chain saw safety precautions?

   F. It should not be a requirement. All employees do not use a chain saw.

   G. All employees use chain saws.

   H. Improper use of a chainsaw caused several lawsuits filed against the company.

   J. It is a safety precaution.

   K. A new chainsaw model was recently purchased so all employees must become familiar with the new safety precautions.

Regulations for Outdoor Seating for Restaurants

A. An outdoor seating area must be structurally attached to the restaurant.

B. An outdoor seating area must be enclosed by masonry walls or decorative fencing that is at least four feet in height. The seating area should be accessed only from the interior of the restaurant.

C. All lighting shall be directed down and away from adjacent properties.

D. The restaurant must provide parking spaces for the outdoor seating area in addition to the parking that is required for the restaurant. The number of spaces is calculated as required for the principal building/use.

E. Public entertainment equipment, such as loudspeakers and public address systems, may be permitted.

F. Adequate facilities must be provided for the disposal of refuse within and around the outdoor seating area.

G. The Fire Marshal must review the proposed outdoor seating area(s) and certify that the area conforms to applicable fire-safety codes.

H. The Police Department must review the proposed outdoor seating area and certify that the area conforms to applicable safety concerns.

I. The Planning Commission may require that the seating area meet additional conditions concerning appearance and noise control to ensure that the outdoor seating area is designed to have minimal impact on adjacent businesses.

11. You are a restaurant owner who is building an outdoor seating area. What is the rationale behind the regulations governing the construction of an outdoor seating area?

    A. The outdoor seating area should be safe, attractive, and compatible with nearby businesses.

    B. The regulations increase the restaurant's profitability.

    C. The regulations prevent traffic congestion in the area.

    D. The regulations prevent the restaurant from competing with a similar nearby restaurant.

    E. The regulations prevent criminal behavior in the area.

12. You work for the police department and you have received a proposal from a restaurant owner to provide an outdoor dining area with no added cost to the city because he is not expanding the parking lot. You reject the proposal because

    F. Fire safety codes do not permit outside dining areas.

    G. Outside lighting and loudspeakers are not allowed.

    H. There is no mention of refuse disposal provisions.

    J. The owner is not providing parking spaces for the additional patrons.

    K. Public safety is not ensured.

Answers are on page 259.

Level 6 Performance Assessment

The following problems will test your ability to answer questions at a Level 6 rating of difficulty. These problems are similar to those that appear on a Career Readiness Certificate test. For each question, you can refer to the answer key for answer justifications. The answer justifications provide an explanation of why each answer option is either correct or incorrect and indicate the skill lesson that should be referred to if further review of a particular skill is needed.

From: Jarrod and Marietta Boscow   Date: February 22
To: Loan Servicing Vice President, Peabody Bank
Subject: Application for loan modification

To Whom It May Concern:

This message is to support our application for a modification plan that will help us to resume affordable mortgage payments.

Our youngest son has a learning disability and attends an exceptional special-education program at his public school. If we lose our home, we will likely be forced to move out of our current school district. Few rental properties are available in the area, so renting or leasing is not a probable option. We fell behind on our mortgage payments due to loss of income. Jarrod was laid off by his prior employer last September. Marietta was able to increase her hours as a school aid, but we were unable to make full mortgage payments for December through April.

On April 15, Jarrod found part-time employment, and the job is expected to change to a full-time position on July 1. Jarrod's new employer has been in business for 35 years. His income will be slightly less than his previous wage, but with the extra pay earned by Marietta, our total income will amount to 90 percent of its previous amount. Our financial details are enclosed. If you can arrange a loan modification that involves payments of $800 or less per month, we are certain that we can work it into our budget. Thank you in advance for your help.

---

1. As the assistant vice president of loan servicing at a lender, you receive a letter from a couple who is in jeopardy of losing their house because of missed or partial payments. Read the e-mail and identify the detail that is implied about the consequence of moving.

   A. They will not be able to pay rent or lease an apartment elsewhere.

   B. Marietta will lose her job if she moves from the school district.

   C. The development of their son will be disrupted because he will have to change schools.

   D. They will not be able to afford the cost of professional movers.

   E. Jarrod will not be able to find work in a new city.

2. What is implied about their future?

   F. If necessary, Marietta will get a second job in order to keep their house.

   G. Jarrod's new employer and job are stable.

   H. If they are given a short reprieve on their past-due payments, they will be able to afford their current house payments beginning in July.

   J. As soon as they can afford to do so, they will sell their house and rent a property in their current district.

   K. They will move when they find another school that can meet the needs of their son.

Memo

From: Elizabeth Martinez, Executive Director

To: Library Staff-ALL

RE: Exciting new library programs

The Fairview Public Library is always trying to maintain visibility in the township and promote a sense of belonging to our patrons. In order to further our bond with our neighbors, we need your help. We'd like our customers to feel a personal connection with each of you. In that light, we are kicking off our *What's on Your Bookshelf?* program. If you choose to participate, we will post your photograph and a short bio on the wall beside the checkout desk. After your bio, we'd like to hear about a couple of your favorite books and/or what you're reading right now. A sample bio could look like this:

Barb Zeke

Barb Zeke has been a librarian at Fairview for four years. In her spare time she likes to read, bike, paint, and spend time with her family. You'll often find Barb at the park with her dog, Ziggy.

What's on Barb's bookshelf? Barb's all-time favorites include *The Secret Life of Bees* by Sue Monk Kidd and *Without Reservations* by Alice Steinbach.

In addition to this program, we will continue to expand our *Friends of the Library* volunteer group. As you may recall, the goal of this group is to help provide library services to people who cannot leave their homes. Watch for announcements of exciting new programs from *Friends* later this spring.

---

3. You are a librarian at Fairview. Which of the following goals of the library does the *What's On Your Bookshelf?* program support?

A. Satisfy its members' recreational and practical interests by use of traditional and emerging technologies.

B. Anticipate and meet changing needs.

C. Educate the public regarding library standards.

D. Encourage a love of reading and learning in children.

E. Promote a sense of community for library patrons.

4. The *Friends of the Library* volunteer group works to help homebound people borrow books of their choice from the library. Which of the following programs would best achieve this goal?

F. Allow homebound people to view descriptions of books online.

G. Set up book displays at local grocery stores or nursing homes.

H. Recruit volunteers who will deliver and return books to homebound people who have placed requests by phone or online.

J. Ask their relatives to pick out books for them.

K. Let homebound people order books by phone or online, and then ask the library to mail the books to them.

Health and Safety Waiver

Heat-Related Illness

When your body cannot cool itself adequately by sweating, heat-induced illnesses, including heat exhaustion and heat stroke, can occur. Heat-related illness can cause death.

Environmental causes: High temperature, high humidity, direct sun or a direct heat source, and limited air movement are common environmental causes.

Personal Factors: Physical exertion, poor physical condition, medication, or low heat tolerance are personal factors.

Symptoms of Heat Exhaustion

- Headache, dizziness, weakness, lightheadedness, or fainting
- Moist skin, nausea, or vomiting
- Mood change, particularly irritability or confusion

Symptoms of Heat Stroke

- Dry hot skin
- Mental confusion or losing consciousness
- Seizures or convulsions

If a Heat-Related Illness Occurs

- Call 911 immediately.
- Move the person to a cooler shaded area.
- Loosen or remove heavy clothing.
- Provide cool drinking water.
- Fan the person and mist him or her with water.

Students must sign and certify that they understand these procedures and will abide by them.

---

5. As an archaeology professor, you are accustomed to long hours outside while working at a site. However, you must educate your students at the beginning of each excavation on how to avoid heat-related illness. What is the basic condition of the human body that causes heat-related illness?

A. when you have a headache, dizziness, or weakness

B. when the body cannot cool itself adequately

C. when you cannot drink enough coffee to stay hydrated

D. when the body has seizures or convulsions

E. when you have dry, hot skin

6. Students are required to certify that they understand and will follow these procedures. Why is this a requirement?

F. to ensure the safety of the professor

G. to provide for their own safety in case of an emergency

H. to allow travel to potentially dangerous sites

J. to prepare students considering medical school

K. solely for insurance purposes

To: Owner Big Sky Steakhouse

From: Patricia Amos, Sales Manager, Restaurant Systems, Inc.

Subject: New technology

Date: January 15

Dear Sir or Madam:

As the owner of a restaurant, you know that technology plays an important role in enhancing the efficiency and productivity of your staff. Your restaurant chain already uses one of our systems to track your inventory. I believe that you will also appreciate the benefits of our newest point-of-sale order system. Using this system, your servers carry hand-held, wireless terminals. Servers use the convenient touch screens on these devices to enter patrons' orders as they take them at the table. As customers place their orders, the terminal also reminds the server to ask important questions, such as the how the customer would like his or her meat cooked. It also prompts the server to suggestive sell. For instance, it could prompt them to ask the patron if they would like to add a soup or salad to their meal. Once an order is complete, it is automatically and immediately sent to the kitchen for preparation.

The benefits of this system are numerous. Speed of service for your customers is dramatically increased. It also improves service because your servers do not need to leave the floor to place orders. This allows each server to handle more tables. The increased speed in ordering and serving allows more table turnover and lower wait times for your patrons. In short, the system benefits you, your servers, and most importantly, your customers. Please contact us for more information about how this fabulous new system can save you time and money.

---

7. You are the owner of a restaurant, and you are looking for ways to save time and money. You receive this letter from a company selling a wireless ordering system. The ordering system encourages suggestive selling by the servers. In which of the following jobs would an employee most likely use **suggestive selling**?

    A.   a manager at a hotel

    B.   a salesperson at a store that sells men's business clothing

    C.   a pharmacist at a drug store

    D.   a payroll specialist at an insurance company

    E.   a teacher at a private school

8. Which of the following situations would benefit from using a **point-of-sale** order system similar to the one described in this letter?

    F.   A public relations specialist could send press releases to several media sources at one time.

    G.   A loan officer could approve loans for clients.

    H.   A legal assistant could schedule client appointments.

    J.   An engineer could estimate labor needed for a project.

    K.   A physician could quickly send a prescription directly to a pharmacy.

Employee Handbook

E-mail Policy

Employees can use e-mail for personal reasons in limited circumstances. Employees can use e-mail during their normal work hours to send messages for personal reasons as long as it does not interfere with the employee's duties. Messages cannot be obscene, defamatory, or inappropriate. If obscene, defamatory, or inappropriate messages are sent, the action will be treated as misconduct. In serious cases, the action is regarded to be gross misconduct and it could lead to dismissal.

Before opening any attachment to a personal e-mail they receive, employees must be confident that the content is not obscene or defamatory. If an employee receives an e-mail that is obscene or defamatory from any source, the message must immediately be sent to the investigator in the Information Technology department.

If the company has a reasonable suspicion that an employee is misusing e-mail in scale of use or content, it reserves the right to monitor the destination, source, and content of e-mail messages to and from a particular address.

The university reserves the right to access an employee's e-mail account if an employee is unexpectedly absent for three or more days. If possible, the employee will be contacted before this is done.

---

9. Based on the e-mail policy, what can be assumed about the company's Internet access policy?

    A.   All Internet access is monitored.

    B.   Accessing the Internet for personal reasons is not permitted.

    C.   Internet access is limited to business use only.

    D.   Accessing the Internet for personal use is allowed, but should not interfere with the employee's duties.

    E.   Accessing the Internet is only permitted outside of working hours.

10. Why does the university reserve the right to monitor its employee's e-mail?

    F.   to expand its e-mailing list

    G.   to protect the employee from potentially harmful contacts

    H.   to conduct research about spam mail

    J.   to maintain acceptable standards of professional conduct

    K.   to conduct market research

> From: Human Resources
>
> To: Department Administrators
>
> Subject: COMPLETING THE BUDGET REPORT
>
> Date: April 26
>
> ---
>
> The Annual Budget Report form has been replaced. You will now enter all data through the terminal, or computer entry system. The terminal entry of the data into the computer-based Annual Budget Report form should speed preparation of the final report.
>
> At this point, you should have received a user name and password for logging into the new system. When you first log in, the opening window will prompt you to set a new password. Links are also provided that will direct you to tutorials on how to enter data into the new system.
>
> As you familiarize yourself with the new system, please direct your questions on technical issues to the Informational Technology (IT) department and direct questions on budget issues to the finance office.

11. As the administrator of your department at the university, you are responsible for preparing the annual budget report. What is the meaning of **terminal** in the context of the above e-mail?

A. final

B. adding machine

C. computer station

D. fax machine

E. register

12. What does the word **window** mean as it is used in the second paragraph of the e-mail?

F. an opening in the side of a building filled with glass

G. a period of available time

H. a frame on a computer screen that displays or prompts for information

J. an opportunity to experience something new

K. a place where questions can be directed

> ### RULE 151: BRIEFS
>
> **Service:** Each brief will be served by the Clerk promptly upon the opposite party after it is filed, except in partnership actions, except where it bears a notation that it has already been served by the party submitting it, and except that, in the event of simultaneous briefs, such brief will not be served until the corresponding brief of the other party has been filed, unless the Court directs otherwise. Delinquent briefs will not be accepted unless accompanied by a motion setting forth reasons deemed sufficient by the Court to account for the delay. In the case of simultaneous briefs, the Court may return without filing a delinquent brief from a party after such party's adversary's brief has been served upon such party. In partnership actions, briefs shall be served by the parties. For the rules regarding service of papers in partnership actions, see Rule 246 (c).

13. You are a Clerk at a District court. An attorney has filed a delinquent brief and you are not certain whether or not to accept it. What should influence your decision?

    A. whether or not the case merits a brief

    B. whether or not the Court has directed you to accept it

    C. whether or not the filing attorney has also filed a written petition

    D. whether or not the brief is pertinent to the case

    E. whether or not the senior attorney filed the brief

14. You receive a brief that bears a notation indicating that it has already been served to the opposing party. What should your response be?

    F. serve the brief anyway

    G. seek a judgment from the court

    H. consider the brief already served

    J. contact the opposing party to verify

    K. seek a contempt citation against the attorney

Processing a Payroll Dispute

Once an administrative assistant in your department has logged in a payroll dispute, you must classify the claim as *RECEIVED*. You will then have 45 days to notify the employee of the final decision. You must verify all details of the employee's claim with his or her supervisor and by checking against the database of employee log-on/log-off times and dates.

Post-6-Month Dispute

Use the guidelines outlined in the company policy manual to approve the dispute, reject the dispute, or request further documentation for verification. In the event that the employee files a claim for the dispute 6 months after the incident takes place, you will have 60 days to notify the employee of the final decision.

---

15. As the director of the human resources department at an engineering firm, you are responsible for making decisions about employee payroll disputes. What is the meaning of the term **log-on/log-off**?

   A. agree/disagree with a computer network

   B. accept/reject a decision about a computer network

   C. initiate/terminate interaction with a computer network

   D. start/end an agreement with a computer network

   E. start/finalize a dispute with a computer network

16. As the human resources director, how would you make a final decision about a payroll dispute for an employee who files a **post-6-month dispute**?

   F. follow regular procedures; you will have 45 days instead of 60 days to notify the employee

   G. classify as *RECEIVED/POST-6*; approve the dispute as outlined in the company policy manual

   H. follow regular procedures; you will have 6 months instead of 45 days to notify the employee

   J. follow regular procedures; you will have 60 days instead of 45 days to notify the employee

   K. request documentation; ask for verification as outlined in the company policy manual

From: Miriam Shriver, Construction Site Supervisor   Date: May 10
To: All Workers
Subject: Concrete Curing

As you know, there have been ongoing discussions over the past several months about the importance of having all workers follow consistent procedures in regard to curing concrete. As you continue your work on this important project, please use the list of reminders below:

- In order to increase the durability of concrete you must cure it.

- Remember that the surface of the concrete must be kept wet during this period.

- The chemical reaction between the water and the cement is what cures the concrete.

- Because temperature is important, use soaking hoses to keep the concrete wet.

- Remember to use sealing compounds, as uncured concrete will not weather well.

17. You are a construction worker, and you must be familiar with the materials being used on the site. What is the meaning of the word **cure** in these instructions?

A.   diagnose the problem

B.   finish by a chemical process

C.   wash thoroughly

D.   smooth with a trowel

E.   heal or make better

18. In relation to your work as a construction worker, what does the word **weather** mean as used in the above memo?

F.   settle

G.   expand

H.   deteriorate

J.   endure or stay intact

K.   shine

Answers are on page 259.

Level 7 Introduction ...

The lesson and practice pages that follow will give you the opportunity to develop and practice the comprehension skills needed to answer work-related questions at a Level 7 rating of difficulty. The *On Your Own* practice problems provide a review of key reading skills along with instruction and practice applying these skills through effective problem-solving strategies. The *Performance Assessment* provides problems similar to those you will encounter on a Career Readiness Certificate test. By completing the Level 7 *On Your Own* and *Performance Assessment* questions, you will gain the ability to confidently approach workplace scenarios that require understanding and application of the reading skills featured in the following lessons:

Lesson 23: Determine Meaning of Uncommon Words

Lesson 24: Determine Meaning of Technical Terms and Jargon

Lesson 25: Apply Principles and Policies to New Situations

These skills are intended to help you successfully read and understand workplace documents, such as procedures manuals, policy statements, and bulletins. Reading these types of documents often requires the ability to:

- understand uncommon words as well as technical terms and jargon used in the text,
- understand the general principles underlying policies and apply them to different situations.

Through answering document-related questions at this level, you will continue to develop problem-solving approaches and strategies that will help you determine the correct answer in real-world and test-taking situations.

Lesson 23 ▪ ▪ ▪
Determine Meaning of Uncommon Words

Skill: Figure out the definitions of difficult, uncommon words based on how they are used

Sometimes workplace documents include difficult or uncommon words. Advanced words such as *reimburse* or *expedite* are sometimes used in more formal workplace communications to make them sound more professional. They may also be used because, though uncommon in everyday conversation, they are used regularly in a workplace setting. It is often possible to determine the meaning of such words based on how they are used in the document.

Remember!

When you encounter an uncommon word while reading, it helps to see if the word looks or is spelled similar to other, more familiar words. In question 1 of *Skill Practice*, the word *surveillance* is similar to the word *survey*. If you have ever taken a survey, which is used by companies or organizations to better understand what their customers or members want, it might help you determine the meaning of *surveillance*.

Skill Examples

It is important that everyone working in the hospital's accounts department understands how to read forms from insurance companies. Checking each company's codes against the procedures and services performed at the hospital ensures that we are fully reimbursed for all treatment we have provided to the patient. Submitting forms correctly helps expedite, or speed up, the time it takes for us to receive payment. Submitting incorrect forms may result in nonpayment or underpayment.

Example 1:
Use context clues to determine the meaning of a difficult word.

The passage is about the procedure the accounts department must follow to make sure that the hospital receives payment. The word *reimbursed* is used in the second sentence. The sentences that follow help you determine that *reimbursed* refers to payments.

Example 2:
Use directly stated definitions to determine the meaning of an uncommon word.

The word *expedite*, used in the third sentence, is followed by the definition "speed up." The last part of the sentence helps you determine that in this context, *expedite* means to shorten the time it takes to receive payment.

Fighting Wildfires

The primary responsibility of firefighters who fight wildfires is to prevent loss of life. Aerial surveillance can determine the extent and movement of the fire. The surveillance crew will inform you about the direction in which the fire is moving and if there are homes in that area. If a wildfire encroaches on a residential area, residents may have to be evacuated for their own safety. In these cases, preventing loss of life is paramount even if it entails the sacrifice of property.

Skill Practice

Use the document to the left to answer the following questions.

1. As a firefighter working to contain a wildfire, you are given information from the surveillance crew. What is the meaning of the word **surveillance**?

   A. hosing

   B. observation

   C. extinguishing

   D. rescue

   E. weather monitoring

2. What does it mean for a fire to **encroach** on an area?

   F. It burns the area.

   G. It has charred houses.

   H. Fire has harmed residents.

   J. It is closely approaching an area.

   K. It cannot be stopped from spreading to the area.

Try It Out! ▪ ▪ ▪

You are a pilot trainee at this airline. What are you responding to when you encounter **wind shear** in the flight simulator?

   A. a storm

   B. a type of tornado

   C. a high-altitude air pocket

   D. a dangerous crosswind

   E. a sudden loss of engine power

> All airline pilot trainees must successfully complete our training program. Training takes place in a simulator where a wide range of flying conditions faces the pilot trainee, who must correctly and safely respond to them. The conditions presented in the simulator are controlled by a computer, which also records the pilot trainee's responses. The pilot trainee will be exposed to conditions encountered during all types of adverse weather and to potential problems during takeoff and landing.
>
> Learning to recognize and respond to wind shear is a primary focus of our training program. These sudden shifts in wind speed and direction must be dealt with quickly and aggressively in order to guide the plane safely through them.

 Step 1 ## Understand the Problem ▪ ▪ ▪

Complete the *Plan for Successful Solving.*

Plan for Successful Solving

What am I asked to do?	What are the facts?	How do I find the answer?	Is there any unnecessary information?	What prior knowledge will help me?
Determine the meaning of the term *wind shear.*	The term *wind shear* refers to a condition you must respond to as a pilot.	Locate where *wind shear* is introduced. Find context clues from the sentence(s) in which it is used.	The entire first paragraph makes no mention of *wind shear.*	Because the word *wind* is in the term *wind shear,* it may have something to do with severe wind or weather.

 Step 2 ## Find and Check Your Answer ▪ ▪ ▪

- Confirm your understanding of the question and revise your plan as needed.

- Based on your plan, determine your solution approach: *The paragraph describes what a pilot trainee is instructed to do. It states that training to deal with wind shear is very important. The term* wind shear *is introduced in the second paragraph. The context clues indicate that wind shear refers to "sudden shifts in wind speed and direction." Safety is mentioned. Among all the answer choices, D best describes this condition.*

- Check your answer. Review all answers to determine if the answer you have selected is the best possible answer.

- **Select the correct answer:**   D. a dangerous crosswind
  The passage states that wind shears are "sudden shifts in wind speed and direction that must be dealt with quickly and aggressively in order to guide the plane safely through them." Therefore, *wind shear* means "a dangerous crosswind."

Problem Solving Tip

Sometimes there are clues within a word or phrase that can help you determine its meaning. In the *Try It Out!* example, the fact that the word *wind* is part of *wind shear* helps you understand that *wind shear* must have something to do with wind. Using this knowledge, you can eliminate answer options C and E. This helps you reduce the number of answer options from which to choose.

Remember!

Find the sentence that contains the uncommon word. Read it carefully to see if there are hints about the meaning of the word or phrase. Look for other words or phrases in the passage that might give you clues about the meaning.

On Your Own ▪ ■ ▪

EMPLOYEE HANDBOOK

New Jewelers' Technology

All jewelers and gemologists in our newly equipped jewelry department must familiarize themselves with our new laser instruments. Gemologists should use the laser for stone cutting. After scrutinizing the gemstone under high magnification, the gemologist should plan a cut that emphasizes the stone's best facets and minimizes its flaws. The cut should reflect this enhancement and conceal, to the greatest degree possible, the stone's blemishes. Once the technique is mastered, you will find that laser stonecutting is far more precise and far less time consuming than cutting with hand instruments.

Jewelers can also use the laser for welding. The laser beam is so hot and precise that jewelers often need little or no solder to weld two pieces of metal together when fabricating an item of jewelry. Laser welding can be accomplished in milliseconds, which greatly improves jewelry-making efficiency.

---

1. You work as a jeweler in a company that makes fine jewelry. Gemology is part of your training. What does a **gemologist** do?

    A. removes flaws from all gems

    B. evaluates and cuts gemstones

    C. sets gemstones in gold settings

    D. polishes the best facets of gemstones

    E. separates gemstones from their parent rock

2. What is the purpose of **solder**?

    F. to bond metal

    G. to cut gemstones

    H. to control lasers

    J. to fabricate gems

    K. to magnify flaws

New Building Site Planning Guidelines

When planning new construction of an energy-efficient building, the site must be analyzed to ensure that the structure is situated optimally for greatest energy savings. Building orientation should be north-south, with south-facing windows placed to absorb as much solar thermal energy as possible during cool months.

The south-facing windows must be shaded during the hot summer months to reduce direct solar gain and glare. West-facing windows should also be protected from excess solar gain during the summer. The best solution for reducing summer solar gain is landscaping with deciduous shade trees. The trees should be placed an appropriate distance from the structure to ensure proper shading. Deciduous trees provide shade in summer when they leaf out, while allowing solar heating during the winter when leaves are dropped.

In planning building construction, thermal loss from drafts and degradation of building materials must be accounted for. Durable building envelope materials and well-planned landscaping features can prevent thermal loss and protect structures from the wear and tear of snow, sand, dust, and other materials that may compromise their insulating qualities.

3. As a planner with a company that builds energy-efficient homes, you need to consider a building's orientation. What do you consider when planning a building's **orientation**?

    A.   its sun-angle

    B.   its shading

    C.   its landscaping

    D.   its positioning

    E.   its latitude and longitude

4. What does the word **thermal** refer to?

    F.   efficiency

    G.   the sun

    H.   heat

    J.   glare

    K.   seasons

From: Dillon Brown

Date: May 2

To: Anthony Charles

Subject: Promotion

Dear Anthony,

Your expertise using the complex instruments in our state-of-the-art computer laboratory has earned you a position in our Research and Development (R&D) department. Here, you will work directly with the brightest computer programmers to produce new and useful software. Under the tutelage of these programmers, you are sure to learn a great deal! You will be working on a variety of innovative programs using the newest technology. If I can be of any assistance in your new position, please do not hesitate to ask. Good luck and congratulations on your new position!

Regards,

Dillon

5. You are a software technician at this company, and you have just been promoted to work in the R&D department. What does **tutelage** mean?

A. instruments

B. guidance

C. assistance

D. programmers

E. research

6. What are **innovative** programs?

F. software

G. developmental

H. forward-looking

J. fundamental

K. old

From: Sarah Wilson, Director XYZ Biologics, Inc.

To: New Technicians

Subject: Training

Date: November 13

All recently hired clinical laboratory technicians will train in several areas of clinical lab work. Everyone will spend two weeks mastering the techniques and tests used in each of the following laboratories.

- Clinical chemistry. In this lab, you will learn how to prepare specimens and conduct analytical tests. We are a leader in the field of hormonal chemical analysis, and you will receive extensive training in the advanced analysis of the body's hormones.
- Microbiology. As a technologist in the microbiology lab, you will get experience analyzing tissues that may harbor microorganisms. You will learn how to prepare slides for microscopic examination and to identify pathogens within tissue that cause disease.
- Immunology. As a technician in this department, you will learn to examine elements of the immune system. You will also test the immune system's response to specific foreign bodies introduced into the tissue or cells.
- Cytotechnology. You will prepare slides of all types of body cells. You will examine these cells microscopically to determine if they have any anomalies that may signal the onset of serious disease.
- Molecular biology. In this lab you will learn to perform complex protein and nucleic acid testing on cell and tissue samples.

7. As a new chemical technician at XYZ Biologics, Inc., you receive the above e-mail. What does the word **harbor** mean?

    A.   create

    B.   infect

    C.   contain

    D.   reproduce

    E.   destroy

8. If while working in the Cytotechnology lab you are asked to look for **anomalies**, you should look for

    F.   cells.

    G.   abnormalities.

    H.   tissues.

    J.   pathogens.

    K.   microorganisms.

Geothermal Drilling Records

Prior to the installation of a geothermal system, the drilling technician must keep a log of materials and conditions encountered at each subsurface layer during the drilling process. The log must contain the following information:

1. The reference point for all depth measurements

2. The depth at which each layer changes

3. The depth at which the first water is encountered

4. The depth at which each layer was encountered

5. The thickness of each of these layers

6. The identification of any of the following materials within each stratum

    a. clay

    b. sand or silt

    c. gravel (indicate if loose or tight, angular or smooth; indicate color)

    d. cemented formation (indicate if natural cementing; i.e., with silica or calcite)

7. The depth at which each sample is taken

8. The depth at which the hole diameters change (i.e., bit sizes)

---

9. You are a driller installing the pipes in a geothermal energy system. Based on what you must write in your log, what does **subsurface** mean?

    A. rocky

    B. striped

    C. underground

    D. a type of drill

    E. a type of well

10. What is an **angular** piece of gravel?

    F. gravel made of clay

    G. gravel mixed with water

    H. very hard gravel

    J. sharp-edged gravel

    K. gravel cemented to silt

Family Services Report (Confidential)

With the help of our agency, the Jones family is beginning to resolve its problems. Though the parents are still unemployed, the agency has found temporary shelter for the family, so they no longer face the threat of homelessness. This provisional solution will ease some of the stress on the family, but there remain serious issues that need to be dealt with. The elderly paternal grandmother resides with the parents and the three children. Brief conversations with her, and observations of her behavior, show that she is often confused and indicate the possible onset of dementia. She has other health problems as well. The agency will arrange a consultation for her with a gerontologist to evaluate her overall condition and make recommendations for treatment.

The family has three sons, aged 10, 8, and 6. All are in school. My evaluations of the children have been confirmed during interviews with their teachers. The oldest and youngest boys are doing fairly well in school, and the oldest sometimes even reads to his youngest brother. The eight year old, however, shows signs of cognitive problems. These are most likely due to dyslexia, which was diagnosed by his school last year. I strongly recommend that the agency provide a tutor for this child. His inability to keep up at school is beginning to affect his behavior, and he is acting out. If he can overcome this disability with our help, I feel that his school performance and behavior will improve. We are working with other agencies to help the parents find employment. Once they are working, the family should regain stability.

11. As a family social worker, what are the **provisional** solutions you sometimes must find for a family?

   A. positive

   B. financial

   C. therapeutic

   D. temporary

   E. re-established

12. What does a **cognitive** problem refer to?

   F. memory

   G. temper

   H. physical handicap

   J. mental illness

   K. learning ability

Answers are on page 262.

Lesson 24 ■ ■ ■
Determine Meaning of Technical Terms and Jargon

Skill: Figure out the meaning of jargon or technical terms based on how they are used

Workplace documents may be difficult to understand because they often include technical terms and jargon. A technical term is a word or phrase that refers to a certain aspect of a job. For example, in a quarterly sales memo, the president of a technology supplies company reports increased profits due to having outsourced work to India. Even if you are not familiar with the term *outsource*, you can use the context of the geographical location mentioned, as well as the fact that the word *out* is a part of the word *outsource*, to determine that *outsource* might mean to hire an organization in another country to perform part of the work your company does. Jargon, such as *server* in the computer field, is language that is specific to a particular industry or field.

Remember!

When you encounter a technical term or jargon within documents, understanding the main idea of the document can help you determine the meaning of the word. Sentences, phrases, or words within the passage often provide the reader with context clues about the word's meaning. When available, graphics or illustrations can also be helpful.

Skill Example

Determine the meaning of a technical term based on the description of its use.

Frequently, paramedics will respond when a person is experiencing a heart attack. Often, the heartbeat is erratic, beating in a rapid and uncontrolled manner. When the paramedic encounters a patient in this condition, defibrillation should be applied immediately. The defibrillator is used until the patient's heartbeat approaches a normal rhythm. The patient should be transported immediately to the nearest hospital for treatment.

The passage is about the procedure a paramedic should use on patients with a rapid and irregular heartbeat. After the term *defibrillation* is introduced, the sentence that follows clarifies its intended effect. You can conclude that *defibrillation* is a procedure that restores a normal heartbeat to someone having a heart attack.

ABOUT US

All new employees will learn about various aspects of aerospace engineering. They will also have the opportunity to advance into employment at one of a number of specialized departments at our company. Technicians may decide to apply for a position in thermodynamics, where they can begin a career developing satellite materials that can withstand the heat of reentry. Perhaps a qualified trainee may choose to work in the jet propulsion lab, where new fuels and new engines are developed to propel rockets forward. These are just two of the many exciting opportunities available to trainees who have successfully completed our training program for aerospace technicians.

Skill Practice

Use the passage to the left to answer the following questions.

1. As a potential employee for an aerospace company, you are researching the company on their Web site. What does **thermodynamics** refer to?

   A. orbit

   B. splashdown

   C. air flow

   D. aerodynamics

   E. heat mechanics

2. What is **propulsion**?

   F. force of forward motion

   G. airflow in a jet engine

   H. a positive feedback or result

   J. the act of throwing something

   K. a very efficient engine fuel

Try It Out! ■ ■ ■

You are a financial planner. When reviewing a client's **portfolio**, what are you looking at?

A. a type of stock

B. a type of risk assessment

C. an investment in a money market

D. a high-yield, risky investment

E. a group of different investments

Step 1 Understand the Problem ■ ■ ■

Complete the *Plan for Successful Solving.*

Plan for Successful Solving

What am I asked to do?	What are the facts?	How do I find the answer?	Is there any unnecessary information?	What prior knowledge will help me?
Find the meaning of the word *portfolio*.	The word *portfolio* refers to money and investments.	Find where the word *portfolio* is used in the document and look for clues to its meaning.	Many of the sentences do not contain the word *portfolio*, but they do provide context clues.	I have heard the term *portfolio* used in reference to investments.

Step 2 Find and Check Your Answer ■ ■ ■

- Confirm your understanding of the question and revise your plan as needed.

- Based on your plan, determine your solution approach: *The paragraph describes what a financial planner does. It explains that financial planners help people build a portfolio, which includes stocks, bonds, and cash. So a portfolio contains a variety of things you can invest in or do with your money. Among all the answer choices, option E is the best description of a portfolio.*

- Check your answer. Review all answers to determine if the answer you have selected is the best possible answer.

- **Select the correct answer:** E. a group of different investments
  The passage states that a financial planner ensures that the client's portfolio includes "the right balance of stocks, bonds, and cash." It also states that portfolios may contain investments with different levels of risk. From this you can conclude that a *portfolio* means "a group of different investments."

A certified financial planner is trained to help individuals and families manage their money. This may involve helping set up a budget. More often, it involves giving advice on increasing the client's assets for current use or for retirement. The financial planner helps balance the client's portfolio to ensure that it contains the right balance of stocks, bonds, and cash, such as money market accounts. The financial planner may also recommend stocks that will likely yield the highest return on investment. He or she will also assess the amount of investment risk the client can tolerate and recommend investments accordingly. For example, a financial planner will advise risk-averse clients to have more bonds and cash in their portfolios, even though these investments yield lower returns.

Problem Solving Tip

Find the sentence that contains the word. Read it carefully to see if it has hints about the word's meaning. Look for other words or phrases in the passage that give you additional clues about the word's meaning.

Remember!

Many technical terms and jargon have similar meanings across different jobs or industries. In the *Try It Out!* example, the term *portfolio* refers to a group of different investments. However, for people who work in jobs such as graphic arts or photography, the term *portfolio* refers to a variety of works that demonstrate the person's artistic talent. While these two definitions are similar, each has a technical meaning specific to a particular industry.

On Your Own ▦ ▪ ▦

MEMORIAL HEIGHTS HOSPITAL
Responsibilities of a Cardiovascular Technician

Cardiovascular technicians at our hospital assist cardiac specialists and heart surgeons by performing diagnostic tests and, in some cases, assisting the cardiologist during certain procedures, especially catheterization. After placing the patient in the correct position, the technician prepares the patient for cardiac catheterization. The technician assists as the physician inserts a small-diameter catheter into an artery and carefully threads it through arteries toward the heart. Then the technician introduces contrast fluid that enables visualization of blood flow to the heart. The technician uses a monitor to observe blood flow and determine if there is a blockage in the blood vessels that supply the heart with blood. The images on the monitor are saved automatically and must be analyzed by the cardiologist.

A cardiologist may also request the assistance of a technician in opening blocked blood vessels. During these procedures, the technician may assist the cardiologist with the insertion of a balloon that, once inflated, opens the clogged blood vessel. A similar procedure involves the insertion of a stent that expands the blocked blood vessel. As the technician gains experience, he or she may prepare and monitor patients in open-heart surgery for the placement of a cardiac pacemaker or with other procedures that correct arterial blockages or cardiac arrhythmias.

1. As a new cardiovascular technician at this hospital, you are reading about the ways in which you will assist cardiac specialists and heart surgeons in your new role. If you are assisting with a cardiac **catheterization**, which of the following items will be inserted into the patient's artery?

    A. a ring

    B. a tube

    C. a syringe

    D. a scalpel

    E. a balloon

2. Based on its use in the passage above, what does a cardiac **stent** do?

    F. inflates a balloon

    G. shows a blood flow

    H. opens a clogged artery

    J. maintains the heartbeat

    K. normalizes arrhythmias

From: Elizabeth Mullin, Technical Supervisor   **Date:** October 15

To: *Paralegals—All*

Subject: Software Upgrade

Next week we will be installing new software that will make it far easier for you to find and assemble legal documents needed for each type of litigation handled by our lawyers. The new software is very efficient and affords you more time to concentrate on the preparation of court cases. The attorneys at our firm value the help of paralegals in obtaining and witnessing the affidavits provided by clients, witnesses, and relevant experts, whose official input is so essential to preparing and winning a case. This software will make it easier than ever to file required papers, such as defendant pleadings and legal motions made by our attorneys on behalf of our clients, with the courts.

The organizational efficiency of the new software will surely make it easier for you to do your job and make you an even more invaluable aide to the attorneys with whom you work.

---

3. You are a paralegal at this law firm. You receive the above e-mail that outlines how this new software will be helpful when organizing litigation. What is **litigation**?

    A.   research

    B.   a witness

    C.   a precedent

    D.   a lawsuit

    E.   testimony

4. What does a paralegal obtain in an **affidavit**?

    F.   a sworn statement

    G.   concrete evidence

    H.   an official pleading

    J.   a legal motion

    K.   an oath of confession

Procedures for Installing Combo Heating and Cooling Systems

When installing a combination heating and cooling system, the following procedures should be followed by all technicians.

1. Verify that the installation procedure is in compliance with both municipal and manufacturer's start-up guidelines.

2. Check the refrigerant charge by using the superheat test or other method as specified by the manufacturer.

3. Make sure that the burner is set to fire at the nameplate input rating.

4. Ensure that the heat reduction across the evaporator is within the manufacturer's recommended range.

5. Test and verify the air flow in the system to within 10% of the initial design air flow.

6. Check the static pressure inside the duct system. This unmoving air must be at a pressure that is within the acceptable range as given by the manufacturer.

5. As an HVAC technician installing a new heating and cooling system, you inspect the evaporator. What occurs at the site of the **evaporator**?

   A.   Air flow increases.

   B.   Refrigerant charges.

   C.   Temperature drops.

   D.   The nameplate fires.

   E.   Heat flows into ducts.

6. What is **static** pressure within the ducts?

   F.   heated

   G.   stationary

   H.   refrigerated

   J.   blowing

   K.   fire

EMPLOYEE HANDBOOK
Veterinary Technician

As a veterinary technician at Furry Friends Clinic, you will assist our veterinarians in nearly all aspects of companion animal diagnosis and treatment. You will help in weighing each animal, getting a medical history, and holding the animal in the proper position during the veterinary examination. You will be trained to obtain radiographs if the veterinarian requests the imaging of bones and internal organs.

You will also assist during teeth cleaning, which requires anesthesia. After the veterinarian has administered general anesthesia, you will be required to assist with dental prophylaxis, a common preventive procedure that helps prevent the kidney disease that is often caused by gum and tooth decay. The veterinarian may require you to explain to clients the importance of teeth cleaning to avoid the onset of serious, debilitating, or even fatal renal failure.

7. You are a new technician at this veterinary clinic. What is a common **radiograph** you will be trained to obtain?

    A.   an X-ray

    B.   a pulse

    C.   a blood sample

    D.   an angioplasty

    E.   an electrocardiogram

8. What does **prophylaxis** refer to?

    F.   tooth pulling

    G.   general anesthesia

    H.   kidney failure

    J.   disease prevention

    K.   fatal illnesses

New City Bank

Dear Mr. Phillips:

We at bank headquarters are delighted that you have been promoted to the post of regional financial manager. We are sure you will do an excellent job, as you have extensive experience in preparing bank financial statements, in analysis of current and projected earnings and expenses, and as a liaison with government regulators. In this latter regard, we know you will competently oversee the new guidelines regarding leverage, ensuring that the banks in your region increase the amount of cash on hand to cover loans.

During the upcoming quarter, we expect you to monitor the flow of cash receipts and disbursements until all our branches are in compliance with the new leveraging rules. We are confident that you will accomplish this important task efficiently. Once again, we offer our sincere congratulations.

Regards,

Tucker Anderson

---

9. As the new regional financial manager of a bank, you are responsible for overseeing bank implementation of the new leveraging regulations. What do the new **leveraging** rules regulate?

    A.   the number of loans made

    B.   the dollar amount of loans made

    C.   the amount of money on deposit

    D.   the amount of cash relative to debt

    E.   the statement of projected earnings

10. What is a **disbursement**?

    F.   a type of merger

    G.   a form of capital

    H.   a type of stock

    J.   money received

    K.   money paid out

From: Tanya Gbur, Production Specialist

Sent: June 1

To: School Editorial Group

Subject: Streamline Monthly Service Maintenance

Dear School Editorial Group,

We have to perform our Streamline monthly server maintenance on June 3.

This will only affect the Math and History projects in Streamline.

Everyone must be logged out of Streamline by 5:30 P.M. Eastern/4:30 P.M. Central on June 3. It is OK to have articles checked out to work on during this time, as I do not foresee that these files you have opened from the server and are editing will be interrupted. If you are concerned about losing articles and the changes you have made to them, it is advised that you check in all articles you are currently working on by no later than 5:00 P.M. Eastern/4:00 P.M. Central on June 3. I will send out a notification when the server is back up. The server should only be down for about 2 hours.

Please notify everyone on your team of this down time, and make sure everyone logs out of Streamline on June 3 by 5:30 P.M. Eastern/4:30 P.M. Central.

Thanks,

Tanya

11. You are an editor at this publishing company. Based on the information in the passage, what is an **article**?

A. a server

B. maintenance

C. a notification

D. a log out

E. a file

12. What occurs when an article is **checked out**?

F. a file is opened from the server

G. teams have down time

H. the server is back up

J. the files are shut down

K. maintenance is performed

Answers are on page 262.

Lesson 25 ▪ ▪ ▪
Apply Principles and Policies to New Situations

Skill: Figure out the general principles behind policies and apply them to situations that are quite different from any described in the materials

Remember!

Principles are established to set guidelines for employee performance and how a business should function. A particular principle may be a general description of business practices, or it may refer to one specific aspect of the business. It is important to understand what the principles mean, but it is equally important that you be able to apply the same principles to new and different situations.

When reading documents that describe company policies and procedures, you need to be able to understand the principles upon which they are based. General principles can often be applied to a wide variety of workplace situations. For example, a company has established a specific procedure for carrying out recycling duties and has posted a schedule that informs employees when it is their turn to take out the recycling bin. The company later initiates a community clean up program, and employees are required to participate on a bi-weekly basis. The company decides to use the principles of the recycling program procedure—sharing workplace responsibilities—to establish a schedule.

Skill Examples

Return Policy: We offer full refunds within 30 days of purchase for most goods that meet certain criteria: they retain their tags, they are returned with the sales receipt, and they have not been used.

Example 1
Identify how the principle can be applied to a different situation.

During a special weekend sale, a new situation arises. All items that are marked 60% off the original price have tags that read "SALE ITEMS FINAL—NO RETURNS." In this case, the store's return policy would apply only to those items without the tag.

Example 2
Apply the general principle to a different situation.

One principle behind the return policy is to prevent customers from using items once and then returning them. However, if a customer returns an item that has been used but does not work, the return policy would likely still be applied because the customer is not to blame for the faulty item.

District-Wide Healthy Foods Policy

All district schools will be implementing a new, healthier menu in their cafeterias. School cafeterias will no longer serve cheeseburgers, fries, and other fried or fatty foods. Sugary foods and beverages will also be taken off cafeteria menus. The new main lunch menu will always offer a choice of at least two fresh salads, a variety of steamed fresh green vegetables, baked potato, and other low-fat vegetable dishes. There will be various fruits for dessert, including freshly made pie, when possible.

Skill Practice

Use the document to the left to answer the following questions.

1. As a nutritionist in this district, what type of vegetable would you include in the new lunch menu?

   A. baked beans

   B. fried onion rings

   C. potato puffs

   D. steamed broccoli

   E. creamed spinach

2. What dessert should you avoid serving at home if you want your child to eat healthful foods like those at school?

   F. peaches and nonfat yogurt

   G. pineapple slices

   H. no sugar added blueberry pie

   J. ice cream sundae

   K. watermelon

Try It Out! ▪ ▪ ▪

You are visiting an office in the Executive Park to interview for a job opening at a consulting firm. As you enter the parking lot, you see the warning signs for nonemployees who park in the lot. What should you do to avoid having your car ticketed or towed?

   A. park at the mall

   B. put some identification on the dashboard

   C. a put a memo on your dashboard explaining your visit

   D. back into the parking space

   E. ask the firm for a temporary parking tag

To: All Executive Park Lessees
Subject: Parking

Management will implement a new parking policy beginning next week. Steps have been taken to deter mall-goers from parking in the Executive Park lot. By next week, signs will be erected indicating that our parking lot is for Executive Park employees only. The signs will warn shoppers that their cars will be ticketed and towed if they park here.

Management will distribute parking tags to all businesses in Executive Park. By the end of next week, every employee must display the ID tag in the lower right corner of his or her car's rear window. To make the tags easy to see, all cars must be parked head in, not head out, in that business's designated parking spaces. Anyone who finds an illegally parked car in our lot is to notify maintenance immediately. They will contact the police, if necessary.

 Step 1 ## Understand the Problem ▪ ▪ ▪

Complete the *Plan for Successful Solving.*

Plan for Successful Solving

What am I asked to do?	What are the facts?	How do I find the answer?	Is there any unnecessary information?	What prior knowledge will help me?
Understand how the new parking policy applies to visitors.	Employees will have to display tags on their cars. Illegally parked cars will be ticketed and towed.	Identify the general principle to determine the best way to comply with in the new situation.	Yes. Details regarding how to report illegally parked vehicles do not help answer the question.	Familiarity with common parking rules and regulations at private lots.

 Step 2 ## Find and Check Your Answer ▪ ▪ ▪

- Confirm your understanding of the question and revise your plan as needed.

- Based on your plan, determine your solution approach: *The principle behind the new policy is to keep mall shoppers from parking in the Executive Park parking lot. The memo states that employees who park in the lot must show an identification tag. So I must determine which answer choice makes the most sense in applying the ID tag rule to visitors of the Executive Park. Among all the answer options, E seems like the best choice because it meets the requirement that all parked cars have ID tags. I'll select option E as the answer.*

- Check your answer. Review all answers to determine if the answer you have selected is the best possible answer.

- **Select the correct answer:**   **E.** ask the firm for a temporary parking tag
  The passage states that cars lacking a legitimate ID tag will be ticketed and towed. Therefore, as a visitor of the Executive Park, you should be able to obtain a parking tag so you can legally park in the lot.

Problem Solving Tip

The passage states a principle that refers to limited situations—that of employees and mall shoppers who park in the Executive Park lot. Look for details contained within the principle that best apply to the new and different situation. In this case, all employee cars must show an official ID tag. This key piece of information can be applied to the new situation and help you determine the correct answer.

Remember!

Read the passage carefully to understand the principle or policy and where, when, why, how, and to whom it should be applied in different situations.

Proper Use of Traffic Radar Equipment

All highway patrol officers must be trained in using extremely low-frequency (ELF) radiation and pass a test to be certified in the use of traffic radar equipment. Ongoing research indicates that ELF radiation may have adverse health effects, so the following protocols must be strictly adhered to when operating equipment that uses it.

1. Always point an unfixed device away from your body or your partner's body while it is turned on. Keep an unfixed device in a mount to keep it steady and prevent accidental activation.

2. Mount fixed radar antennas so that the beam is not pointed at anyone in the patrol car.

3. For hand-held units, turn the device off when it is not in use. Units that have a stand-by mode should be set on stand-by whenever they are not in use. Never rest the unit against your body when it is turned on.

4. When the device is turned on, avoid pointing it at any metal surfaces inside the patrol car. ELF radiation striking metal can reflect microwave radiation back toward the device and persons inside the car. Far less microwave reflection occurs when ELF radiation strikes nonmetal surfaces, such as auto window glass.

5. Radar antennas, both mounted and hand-held, must be properly secured to protect officers during emergency vehicle maneuvers.

6. New regulations are coming into effect to eliminate radar devices with trigger locks that keep them in the on position. Regulations will soon also require that all radar device mountings be located on the exterior of the patrol car.

1. You are a highway patrol officer, certified in using radar equipment. You helped your supervising officer write the above principles for using radar in a patrol car. What was your main concern in setting out these principles for the use of ELF radar?

A. explaining how the radar equipment should be used

B. describing what extremely low energy radiation is

C. regulating the conditions in which traffic radar should be used

D. describing how to adapt radar equipment to older police vehicles

E. explaining how to safely use and store traffic radar equipment

2. You work at a firm that has been contracted by the police department to design the external radar mounting devices for police cars. What is the most important specification for you to incorporate into your design?

F. Enable the trigger to be turned on while the radar device is still in the mounting.

G. Make sure the external mount does not attach to a metal surface.

H. Design the mounting with an opening facing the front of the car.

J. Create a mounting device that is not made of any metallic material.

K. Create a mounting device that does not contain an antenna.

Safety Guidelines:

OSHA Injury Recording Guidelines

Some on-the-job injuries must be recorded and the record sent to the appropriate section of the Occupational Safety and Health Administration (OSHA). The following flowchart will help supervisors, human resources managers, plant managers, and others determine if a particular injury is recordable.

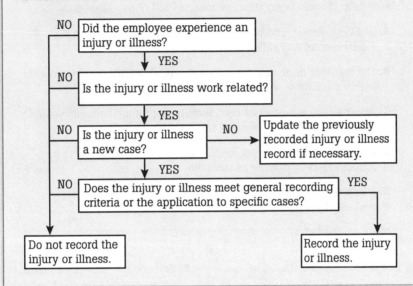

3. As a human resources manager at a factory, you are responsible for determining if your company must file a record of employee injuries. Based on the above flowchart, what criteria determine whether or not you must file a record of the injury?

    A. which part of the employee's body was injured

    B. if the employee was working safely

    C. if the injury is new and occurred on the job

    D. if the employee can do less strenuous work

    E. if another employee was at fault

4. Which of the following situations would not be recorded as a work-related injury?

    F. a sprained ankle sustained the previous week while loading cartons onto a truck

    G. a skin infection that spread from an untreated cut received when fixing a copying machine a month ago

    H. nausea and headaches that continued at home after first experiencing them when new carpeting was installed in the office reception area

    J. lower back injury incurred in a car accident while driving home

    K. concussion and blackouts resulting from a shelf that collapsed in an office storage area

State Mining Procedures

The following policies apply to all mining operations in our state.

I. All welding, arc cutting, and soldering operations in a mine, especially a coal mine, are inherently dangerous. The danger comes primarily from potentially explosive methane gas and, in coal mines, coal dust.

II. Open flames, molten metal, and sparks may ignite these explosive materials. The following safety procedures MUST be adhered to.

 A. Welding, cutting, and/or soldering must be done under the supervision of a qualified manager.

 B. The manager must conduct a diligent search for fire during and after any or all of these activities.

 C. The qualified person must continuously test for methane immediately before and during any or all of the activities.

 D. Welding, cutting, and/or soldering shall NOT be conducted in air containing 1.0% or more of methane.

 E. A sufficient number of fire extinguishers shall be immediately available for use during any or all of these activities.

5. You are a manager in a mine. What are the guidelines you must enforce at the mine intended to help you identify?

 A. fire potential

 B. lung damage from dust

 C. malfunctioning equipment

 D. the ratio of methane to oxygen in the air

 E. what type of solder is best to use in the mine

6. Propane has similar properties to methane (both are hydrocarbons). You heat your home with propane, and at the site where the propane pipe enters your home there is a detector that sounds an alarm if it detects propane leaking from the pipe into your house. Why does the propane supplier most likely insist that you call their emergency repair line when the alarm goes off?

 F. because propane is poisonous

 G. because propane is odorless and colorless

 H. because propane can contaminate drinking water

 J. because propane becomes liquid at room temperature

 K. because propane is highly flammable and explosive

Community Hospital

Nurses' Guidelines for Avian Influenza

All hospital workers should follow these guidelines with Avian Influenza (AI) patients

I. Standard Precautions:

    A. Hand washing before and after all patient contact, and after contact with all potentially contaminated items.

II. Contact Precautions:

    A. Use gloves and gown for all patient contact.

    B. Use only disposable equipment or equipment that can be sterilized.

III. Droplet Precautions:

    A. Wear goggles or face shields within 3 feet of the patient.

    B. NOTE: face shields not intended for use with infectious patients afford no protection against airborne pathogens.

IV. Airborne Precautions:

    A. Place the patient in an airborne infection isolation room that has negative air pressure in relation to the hospital corridor. If one is not available, have an engineer install a high-efficiency particulate filter.

    B. Exhaust room air directly to the outside or recirculate after high-efficiency particulate filtering.

    C. Keep patient door closed.

    D. Wear a fit-tested, N-95 disposable respirator mask.

V. Transmission Precautions:

    A. Put AI patients in the same room. If this is impossible, put an AI patient in a single room. Do not put together patients with seasonal influenza and those with AI.

    B. Minimize transport of AI patients. Limit the number of attending healthcare workers.

---

7. As a nurse in the infectious diseases unit at Community Hospital, you must read and understand the above guidelines. A patient who has AI is admitted to the hospital's infectious diseases unit. You put this patient in an airborne infection isolation room. Why do the guidelines recommend this policy?

    A. because it is a single room

    B. because it keeps room air from escaping and spreading the infection

    C. because the sick-room air is contained in a small space

    D. because only isolation rooms are disinfected after a patient is released

    E. because it will limit the number of health care workers attending the patient

8. One of your three children has come down with an upper respiratory infection. After a visit to the doctor, you return home with your sick child. What might you do to prevent your other children from becoming infected?

    F. Keep the ill child alone in the guest room.

    G. Do not let your other children wash their hands.

    H. Turn off the air filter in the ill child's bedroom.

    J. Do not permit any of the children to wear face masks.

    K. Take your other children to the doctor.

ClearVu Windows: Required Procedures

WINDOW FRAME MANUFACTURING HAZARD MITIGATION

Hazard	Mitigation
Saws	Attach fixed tunnel guards to enclose the saw blade. If that is impractical, add an adjustable guard to enclose the saw blade.
Drilling machines	Fit drilling machines with operator-run controls. The controls should require using two hands on separate devices that are operated with push buttons or triggers. The equipment should be designed so that removing one hand from the controls stops the drill.
Welding machines	Protection from heat is needed. Provide fixed guards or automatic guards that move into position before welding begins and heat is generated.
Knives and cutting machines	Attach fixed guards to the front of the machine to prevent any part of the body from coming into contact with the knives and cutters. If spinning cutters are used, a control should be installed that stops the spinning cutter when the door to the blade housing is opened.
Milling machines	Milling machines contain cutters that are accessed through a feed opening. To prevent injury, the size of the feed opening should be limited to less than the diameter of a finger.

9. You are a worker in this window manufacturing plant. What do the guidelines instruct workers to do during the manufacturing process?

   A. Use adjustable safety guards.

   B. Wear protective clothing and gear.

   C. Operate all machinery using two hands.

   D. Make sure their machinery has proper safety devices.

   E. Turn off machinery if it generates too much heat.

10. You use a cutting machine (without a spinning cutter) for your job, but your supervisor advised you that you must mitigate the hazard level of the equipment. How would you minimize your cutting machine's hazard level?

   F. Keep it protected from the welding machines.

   G. Install a control that starts the spinning cutter when the door housing is open.

   H. Attach fixed guards to the front of the machine to prevent contact with the cutters.

   J. Fit drilling machines with operator-run controls.

   K. Limit the size of the feed opening to less than the diameter of a finger.

Emergency Air-Traffic Control Procedures

All air-traffic control (ATC) centers have an automatic response tool that is to be activated when a potential or actual emergency plan is required. Emergency plan triggers include:

I. loss of air-ground communications

II. loss of ground-ground communications [telephony];

III. loss of critical automation systems;

IV. loss of power, including backup;

V. significant reduction in staffing; and

VI. loss of surveillance, e.g., radar.

If one or more of the above occurs, the following procedures apply:

VII. Declare that an emergency plan has been implemented. Contact the ATC Command Center. Their Operations Manager will issue an alert and take measures to ensure continued safe operation.

    A. The Operations Manager may have another facility take over air traffic controls.

    B. The Operations Manager will organize and have implemented corrective measures.

VIII. If the recovery from an ATC alert will take a long time, the emergency plan must revert to a Contingency Plan until restoration is achieved.

IX. The Operations Manager must notify the Federal Aviation Administration (FAA) of the event. Technical Operations Officers at the FAA will contact the ATC facility.

X. All facility airspace must be divested during the event. ATC operations in the affected airspace must be stabilized and under control. Stabilization must be reported to the Command Center.

XI. Once the event has been resolved, the Command Center must be notified before the facility returns to normal operations. The Operations Manager must authorize resumption of normal operations before the facility can resume control of its airspace.

---

11. As an air traffic controller, you must be familiar with emergency procedures. What principle underlies the emergency procedure guidelines described above?

    A. Too much airplane congestion at most airports is dangerous.

    B. The delays caused by security screening are inconvenient.

    C. Constant oversight by a national command center is not always necessary.

    D. The stress experienced by ATC workers creates high turnover rates.

    E. The safety of airline passengers is the first priority.

12. In your work as an air traffic controller, you must notify a pilot of sudden severe weather. What directive will you give the pilot?

    F. Have the pilot circle the home airport until the weather clears.

    G. Tell the pilot to follow another plane to lead him or her away from the local area.

    H. Have the pilot land at the airport using only her or his radar for guidance.

    J. Inform the pilot of the nearest airport for safe landing.

    K. Ask the pilot if the plane can withstand the severe weather.

Answers are on page 262.

Level 7 Performance Assessment

The following problems will test your ability to answer questions at a Level 7 rating of difficulty. These problems are similar to those that appear on a Career Readiness Certificate test. For each question, you can refer to the answer key for answer justifications. The answer justifications provide an explanation of why each answer option is either correct or incorrect and indicate the skill lesson that should be referred to if further review of a particular skill is needed.

Multitrack Recording Software Instructions

An electronic media producer is responsible for the recording of separate tracks of sound and then assembling them into a harmonious or desired recording. Computer-based multitracking allows the technician to lay down an unlimited number of tracks. Each vocalist, musical instrument, and/or sound effect can be recorded separately and saved. Those tracks that are subpar can be erased, and new tracks of higher quality can be rerecorded or added. Thus, a recording artist can obtain a vast number of takes for each track.

Once all tracks have been recorded, the technician and the producer mix the tracks to achieve a recording with the best aural quality and the best mix of sounds. To accomplish this, the technician must be adept at synchronizing all the tracks to be included in the final recording. Multitracking also permits artists to listen to selected tracks while they are recording their own track. For example, a singer can listen to instrumental tracks through headphones while recording the vocals.

---

1. You are an electronic media producer using new multitrack recording software in a recording studio. What is a **subpar** track?

    A.   a track that doesn't measure up to standards

    B.   a track with too many recordings

    C.   a track with musical instruments

    D.   a track that measures up to standards

    E.   a track with too few recordings

2. What are you doing when you are **synchronizing** the tracks?

    F.   erasing bad tracks

    G.   evaluating all tracks

    H.   blending tracks together

    J.   recording an instrumental track

    K.   recording separate tracks

Lighting Industries Inc.

October 13

Welcome to all the Lighting Staff,

As the cinematographer, I want to welcome you all to the filming of this feature. We are extremely excited both about the ambitious project that lies before us and the talented cast and crew that we have assembled to help make it all come together smoothly.

I wanted to give you a brief introduction as to how we will work together, as well as the decisions that have been made up to this point. Ellen Roberts is the gaffer and will be the main liaison between me and the rest of the lighting crew. As the gaffer, Ellen will execute on the set the decisions that have been made between me and the director. She will instruct Jorge Rojas about what type of lighting is wanted. As the lighting foreman, Jorge will coordinate the other lighting and electrical staff to prepare the lights so the set is lit for the scene we are about to shoot. The best boy should maintain excellent communication with the grip department to make sure that all the electrical equipment, including cables and fixtures, is in good working order and is placed where it should be for each scene.

We are incredibly anxious to get started on filming. I look forward to working with each and every one of you.

Cheers,

Michael

---

3. As a member of the lighting crew on this movie, you receive the above letter. What does the **gaffer** do?

A. shoots the picture

B. provides film for the cameras

C. makes sure that all electrical equipment works

D. gets directions from the cinematographer

E. consults with the film director

4. You work in the **grip** department. What is a part of your job?

F. moving electrical wires

G. directing the lighting foreman

H. positioning the movie camera

J. consulting with the film director

K. serving as liaison with the cinematographer

East Elbow Hotel

Dear Hotel Staff,

As the new manager of the East Elbow Hotel, it is my job to reorganize the running of the hotel to improve its efficiency, profitability, and service. My personal belief is that a hotel exists to provide excellent service to its customers.

In order to increase customer satisfaction, I will be reviewing our allocation of funds, as well as personnel, and shifting where we focus our resources to those areas where they are needed most and where improvements will be most visible to and appreciated by our customers. I can tell you that I've already decided to increase staff in the housekeeping, dining, and room service divisions. Another area of hotel service I want to expand is conference hosting. I am engaged in ongoing discussions with corporate headquarters regarding a reconfiguration of the space on our first two floors. I hope to configure the available space to make our hotel more attractive for small- and medium-sized conferences. Altering these spaces will also make our hotel a more desirable location for special occasions both large and small, such as corporate functions and wedding receptions.

As always, we highly value and welcome the input of all our team members regarding how we can make improvements both for our customers and for our East Elbow team. As staffing, funding, and space decisions are made, I will do my best to keep all of you informed as to what is being done and how it will impact your day-to-day business.

Sincerely,

Sofia Lowe

---

5. You are the operations consultant of the East Elbow Hotel and you have many ideas about changing how it operates. What does **allocation** mean?

A. location

B. distribution

C. allowable

D. satisfaction

E. improvement

6. To **configure** the available space means

F. to open it

G. to increase it

H. to join it

J. to arrange it

K. to complete it

From: Miriam Thompson

To: Mark Hildebrand

Subject: RE: Advising Clients to Short a Stock

Date: April 28

Mark,

    First let me congratulate you on the great job you're doing bringing in new clients. Your telephone solicitation skills are first rate, and you have performed well for the new clients you have brought to our brokerage firm. Your equity trading skills are also very good. You have advised our clients to buy worthwhile stocks that have appreciated in value and made them money—and that is obviously the number one way we can keep our clients happy and loyal.

    To answer your question from a previous e-mail, under no circumstances is a broker to advise a client to short a stock without prior permission from a supervisor. The assumption involved with borrowing stock to sell at a high price in anticipation that this same stock will be available to buy back at a lower price (helping the investor to turn a profit) involves a high level of risk. Approval for shorting stock is therefore subject to an additional approval and application process, in which the supervisor will determine if the investor meets our firm's requirements.

    Hope this answers your question. Keep up the good work.

Best regards,

Miriam

---

7. What does it mean when stocks have **appreciated** in value?

    A.   They have been sold.

    B.   They have decreased in value.

    C.   They have increased in value.

    D.   They bring in new clients.

    E.   They have lost money.

8. What does it mean to **short** a stock?

    F.   to buy and sell shares of the same stock

    G.   to borrow, buy, and sell shares of different stocks

    H.   to borrow, sell, and buy back shares of the same stock

    J.   to borrow, sell, and buy back shares of different stocks

    K.   to buy shares when the prices are low

Professional Staffing Inc.

To: All Employees
From: Dania Snow, Office Manager
RE: Emergency Evacuation Plan

The Occupational Safety and Health Administration (OSHA) requires all businesses to implement an emergency evacuation plan. As office manager, I have established the following plan.

1. Alarms in every office and corridor are automatically activated if a fire is detected by the smoke detector system. In case of other emergencies, any personnel may activate the alarm by pulling down on the alarm lever. An activated alarm triggers a siren and a flashing red light, and also automatically contacts security and the fire department. (Note: activation of the alarm when there is no emergency is cause for dismissal.)

2. There are floor plans posted in all offices and corridors near elevators and stairwells. Each floor plan shows its location and the route personnel should take to reach the nearest emergency exit. The routes have been set out to avoid overcrowding in exits. During an emergency, all personnel in a given area should proceed calmly by walking quickly, not running, to the designated emergency exit.

3. All alarms are checked frequently to make sure they are working. If for some reason an alarm is not working, anyone who notices a fire or other emergency should activate the alarm by pulling the manual alarm lever down. If the alarm lever is broken, dial 555 on the phone to be instantly connected to security, who will activate the alarm.

4 Each office or department has several people who form a chain of command during an emergency. The person highest on this chain oversees the evacuation. Each office and department also has personnel who are responsible for the safe evacuation of physically handicapped employees.

5. Periodic emergency evacuation drills will be held and evaluated.

9. You are a supervisor at Professional Staffing Inc., and have been asked to manage a satellite office that your company is opening in a busy shopping mall. The new office will be located on the ground level and there will be no security office. Your district manager asks you to establish an emergency evacuation plan for your office based on the principles of the home office's plan. Which of the following procedures will only apply to your new office's plan?

   A. Note the appropriate supervisor to contact in case of an emergency.

   B. Post a floor plan that shows the nearest exit to take in case of an emergency.

   C. Identify the proper stairwell to take to evacuate the building.

   D. Instruct all personnel to dial 555 in case of an emergency.

   E. Designate a subordinate to oversee all evacuations.

10. During a company event at a local restaurant, the weather becomes inclement and threatening, and all employees must leave the restaurant safely and quickly. Which of the following actions, based on the company's emergency evacuation plan, would be appropriate?

   F. Pull the manual alarm lever down; dial 555 if broken.

   G. Assist physically handicapped co-workers to safety.

   H. Wait for your department supervisor to oversee the evacuation.

   J. Follow the floor plan to determine your exit route.

   K. Walking calmly to avoid overcrowding in the stairwells.

Crane Operation Procedures

Before a crane is used at a construction site, the operational manager must check the following:

- **Crane leveling.** Be certain that the crane is set up in a level manner and that it is in a position for safe rotation and operation.

- **Outriggers.** The crane's outriggers, or projecting beams that support the crane, must be extended properly for use according to the manufacturer's recommendations.

- **Crane Stability.** You must check the relationship of the weight, angle of the beam, and its radius (the distance from the crane's center of rotation to the center of the load) to the center of gravity of the load. Note especially the condition of crane loading where the load movement acting to overturn the crane is less than the movement of the crane that is available to resist overturning.

- **Electrical Hazards.** If the crane will be operating under power lines, the electric utility must be contacted and power must be cut along these lines. A clearly visible sign showing the clearance between the electrical lines and the crane in operation must be set up. A power company representative should be on site during crane operation near power lines to ensure that the lines have been properly de-energized or grounded.

11. As an operational manager at a construction site, you must be familiar with the above procedures. Why is it so important to check a crane's stability?

- **A.** to free the outrigger
- **B.** to increase rotational radius
- **C.** to prevent overturning
- **D.** to increase the load weight
- **E.** to speed up loading

12. If you are planning to set up a crane operation near power lines on a holiday, and the power company is closed that day, how should you proceed?

- **F.** Continue operations and contact the power company later.
- **G.** Set up a clearly visible sign and continue operations.
- **H.** De-energize and ground the power lines yourself.
- **J.** Continue working without cutting the lines.
- **K.** Wait until a power company representative can be on site.

New Guidelines for Food Safety Technicians

Pursuant to the new guidelines issued this week by the Food and Drug Administration (FDA), all fruits, vegetables, and herbs coming to our facility must be subjected to additional tests. In compliance with the FDA's new regulations, we must test sample items for a wider array of pathogens, particularly the new strains from soil found in many types of vegetables. Technicians in our lab will be trained to carry out these new tests.

The FDA, in accordance with the research done at the Environmental Protection Agency (EPA), is also requiring testing for two newly restricted pesticides and one newly banned herbicide. Both have very high toxicity at very low concentrations. Each sample item must be tested for the presence of these substances. The level of each toxin present must be identified and recorded. Food items that have levels above those set by the FDA and EPA must be reported to our main office, as dangerously high levels of these poisonous chemical compounds may result in banning from sale an entire lot of contaminated vegetables.

You will be receiving more detailed instructions and testing training in the next week or two. Meanwhile, please study the attached memorandum from the FDA.

13. You are a food safety technician at this food testing company. What are you testing for when you are testing food for the presence of **pathogens**?

    A.   pharmaceuticals

    B.   fertilizer

    C.   pesticides

    D.   soil

    E.   disease-causing agents

14. What does the **toxicity** of an item indicate about it?

    F.   its poison content

    G.   its nutritional value

    H.   if it contains bacteria

    J.   if it has been banned

    K.   its source of contamination

Guidelines for Plastics Recycling

Please follow the guidelines below when working with the plastics recycling machinery in our facility.

Agglomerators/Crumbers

1. Because the feed opening cannot always be adjusted to recognized dimensions due to operational difficulties, use the following combination of measures when operating this type of machinery.

   a. Make sure the feed opening is centered on the lid. The opening should be restricted to a 250 mm diameter on machines having lids up to 1,000 millimeters in diameter, and 300 millimeters for larger machines. If the machine has a square opening, the 250–300 millimeters dimension should be the maximum diagonal measurement.

   b. Make sure the feed opening is positioned at least 1 meter above the blades.

   c. Make sure the working platform is at least 1.1 meters below the level of the feed opening.

Lock-off Procedure

1. Isolate the machine from the main supply by locking off all forms of power (electrical, hydraulic, and pneumatic).

2. Use a padlock that has only one key.

3. Use a multiple hasp where several people are working. In this way, each person can fit their own lock.

4. Put a warning notice on the isolator so it is not activated.

Fire Safety

Use the guidelines below for safe external storage of highly flammable processed plastic.

   a. If the plastic pile is less than 5 meters long, the pile should be 4 meters from the facility.

   b. If the plastic pile is less than 8 meters long, the pile should be 6 meters from the facility.

   c. If the plastic pile is more than 8 meters long, the pile should be 8 meters from the facility.

---

15. As a machine operator at this plastics recycling facility, you must follow certain guidelines. During the lock-off procedure, why would you put a warning notice on the isolator?

    A. to be sure that it doesn't get activated

    B. to safely store highly flammable plastic

    C. to use a padlock that has only one key

    D. to be sure that it gets activated

    E. to make sure the feed opening is centered

16. You are regularly in charge of highly flammable materials. On your way into the plant, you notice that a pile of unlabeled material near the facility. You determine that the pile is approximately 7 meters long. How would you treat the pile of materials in order to ensure the safety of all?

    F. Make certain that the pile is 1 meter above the crumber blades.

    G. Make certain that the pile is 1.1 meters below the level of the feed opening.

    H. Make certain that the pile is fastened with a padlock.

    J. Make certain that the pile is 4 meters from the facility.

    K. Make certain that the pile is 6 meters from the facility.

Steps in Elevator Maintenance

1. Replace rusted sill strut angles at the first floor.

2. Replace drive cables with new cables, as needed.

3. Install new pit stop switches in elevator pits.

4. Clean and lubricate all metal equipment.

5. Install new rollers on roller guides, car, and counterweight.

6. Clean and lubricate sills so that the door will fit into doorframe.

7. Clean and lubricate hoist ropes. Clean hoistway door locks.

8. Check functioning of the water level detection device. Set it to 12 inches above the pit floor.

9. Activate the device. If it is working properly, an alarm should sound and the elevator will rise to the skywalk level, the highest elevation possible, where it will remain until the water level recedes.

17. You work in elevator repair and maintenance. Based on the information above, what happens to water when it **recedes**?

    A.   It increases.

    B.   It activates.

    C.   It hoists.

    D.   It decreases.

    E.   It lubricates.

18. What is the door **sill**?

    F.   repair area

    G.   the pit floor

    H.   a drainage tube

    J.   part of the doorframe

    K.   the counterweight

Answers are on page 262.

Answer Key ▪ ■ ▪

Level 3

Lesson 1 (pp. 2–9)
Skills Practice
1. B   2. G

On Your Own:
1. B	2. F	3. C	4. K	5. A	6. J
7. D	8. G	9. C	10. G	11. D	12. F

Lesson 2 (pp. 10–17)
Skills Practice
1. A   2. J

On Your Own:
1. A	2. K	3. C	4. J	5. D	6. K
7. B	8. K	9. D	10. F	11. C	12. F

Lesson 3 (pp. 18–25)
Skills Practice
1. C   2. G

On Your Own:
1. B	2. H	3. B	4. G	5. C	6. K
7. D	8. F	9. A	10. J	11. C	12. K

Lesson 4 (pp. 26–33)
Skills Practice
1. D   2. F

On Your Own:
1. C	2. G	3. D	4. G	5. E	6. F
7. E	8. J	9. C	10. F	11. B	12. J

Lesson 5 (pp. 34–41)
Skills Practice
1. B   2. J

On Your Own:
1. B	2. H	3. D	4. H	5. A	6. G
7. C	8. J	9. B	10. H	11. A	12. G

Level 3 Performance Assessment (pp. 42–50)

Item Number 1 *(Lesson 3)*

A. Incorrect: *pain killer.* The passage does not mention pain killers, but refers to antiseptics in terms of a cut.

B. **Correct:** *germ killer.* The first paragraph states that the nurse should use "an antiseptic to kill any germs in the cut," so germ killer is the right answer.

C. Incorrect: *light.* Light should be used if there is a head injury, not a cut.

D. Incorrect: *cotton pad.* The cotton pad is to be used before the antiseptic, which is described as something used afterwards to kill germs.

E. Incorrect: *sterile plastic.* Sterile plastic is not something a school nurse could give a child.

Item Number 2 *(Lesson 3)*

F. Incorrect: *double-vision.* The passage tells you that the nurse dilates the eyes to check for brain injury. Double-vision is checked as a symptom of a concussion, not brain injury.

G. Incorrect: *concussion.* Some symptoms of a concussion are described in the second paragraph. However, the word dilate refers to something the nurse does with a light to test the eyes. So concussion is not correct.

H. **Correct:** *get larger.* The second paragraph tells you that the nurse should observe to see if "the pupil does not get larger, or dilate." The definition of dilate is directly stated immediately before the term is used.

J. Incorrect: *eye movement.* Checking for eye movement is a suggested diagnostic test the nurse can do that is different from the one that involves dilating the eye.

K. Incorrect: *brain injury.* Testing pupil dilation is a way to see if there may be brain injury, but dilation does not mean brain injury.

Item Number 3 *(Lesson 3)*

A. **Correct:** *a bill.* As shown on this page, an invoice is a bill for the supplies bought from the office supply store. An invoice lists the items bought, their cost, and the total amount due.

B. Incorrect: *a list.* The form on the page does list the items bought, but it lists them to show how much the client has spent and how much money should be paid to the supplier.

C. Incorrect: *an amount.* The invoice does show many amounts of money. Its purpose is not just to list these amounts for information, however; it is to identify that these amounts must be paid.

D. Incorrect: *a purchase.* A purchase is buying something. The invoice is about a purchase that has already been agreed to for which payment is now required.

E. Incorrect: *an account.* An account is a line of credit an individual or company will have with a supplier or store. It is not an invoice.

Item Number 4 *(Lesson 3)*

F. Incorrect: *to owe.* The word is used in the phrase "Remit to," so it cannot mean "owe us this amount of money."

G. Incorrect: *to remember.* The invoice is a reminder of what was bought and how much to pay, but its main purpose is not as a reminder. The phrase "Remit to" shows that you cannot "remind to" someone, so this option is incorrect.

H. Incorrect: *to bill.* The supplier's address is written after "Remit to." So the phrase cannot mean "Bill to" the supplier. The purchaser pays the bill, not the supplier.

J. **Correct:** *to pay.* This tells the purchaser where to send the money to pay the bill. "Accounts Payable" gives you a clue that remit must mean to pay.

K. Incorrect: *to order.* The order has already been placed and delivered before the invoice is sent. So this option is not correct.

Item Number 5 *(Lesson 5)*

A. Incorrect: *You fertilize it.* The passage states that all soil prepared for planting has fertilizer added to it. So this does not apply only to bare root plants.

B. **Correct:** *You soak its roots.* The first paragraph states "If the bush or shrub you are planting is bare root, soak the roots in water for at least 45 minutes before planting."

C. Incorrect: *You compress the roots.* The passage repeats that in all cases, the roots must be spread out, not compressed.

D. Incorrect: *You make sure it is upright.* A shrub is set in an upright position while it is being planted, not before planting. This hold true for all shrubs, not just bare root shrubs.

E. Incorrect: *You remove it from its pot.* A bare root shrub comes with its roots bare, or exposed. A bare root shrub is not in a pot.

Item Number 6 *(Lesson 5)*

F. Incorrect: *Water the shrub for several minutes.* The passage states that this should be the last step after planting a bare root.

G. Incorrect: *Use your hands to tamp down the soil.* You should tamp down the soil as each layer of soil is added.

H. **Correct:** *Spread out the external roots around the plant.* The passage states that if the plant is root-bound, you should "…spread the most external roots out around the plant."

J. Incorrect: *Remove all large rocks from the soil.* The passage states that you should do this at the beginning.

K. Incorrect: *Place shovels of soil to the side of the hole.* The passage states that this should take place when you are digging the hole.

Item Number 7 *(Lesson 4)*

A. Incorrect: *Put film under the body.* Film is placed under the body in step 6. Positioning is described in step 2.

B. Incorrect: *Put patient jewelry in a safe place.* Removing the patient's jewelry is done in step 1. Positioning is described in step 2.

C. **Correct:** *Put protective mats on areas not to be x-rayed.* Adding protective mats is described in step 3, right after positioning in step 2.

D. Incorrect: *Expose the body part to the rays from the X-ray.* Exposing the body for X-ray is to occur after protective mats are placed on the body.

E. Incorrect: *Make sure the X-ray machine is at an angle.* Angling the X-ray machine is described in step 4 so it does not happen immediately after step 2 positioning.

Item Number 8 *(Lesson 4)*

F. **Correct:** *in a control room.* Step 7 states that the technician goes into the control room when the X-ray is taken.

G. Incorrect: *with the radiologist.* The technician takes the X-ray to the radiologist after the X-ray film is developed, not while the X-ray is being taken.

H. Incorrect: *adjusting the X-ray controls.* The X-ray controls are adjusted on the X-ray machine in step 5, before the X-ray is taken.

J. Incorrect: *measuring for density and detail.* The technician measures for density and detail in step 5, before the X-ray is taken.

K. Incorrect: *in a darkroom developing X-ray film.* The film is developed in step 8, after the X-ray is taken, not while it is taken.

Item Number 9 *(Lesson 1)*

A. Incorrect: *Water discharged into water bodies must be tested.* This option describes only a small part of passage content, so it is not the main idea.

B. **Correct:** *Water quality technicians test if water meets standards.* This correctly sums up the passage, which describes what a water quality technician does.

C. Incorrect: *Drinking water must meet contaminants levels.* This option is not correct because water should

not have contaminants and it is not a main idea.

D. Incorrect: *Pollutants that exceed standards must be removed.* This is not a summary of what the entire passage is about, so it is not the main idea.

E. Incorrect: *New water quality technicians will work with supervisors.* This option describes only a small part of passage content, so it is not the main idea.

Item Number 10 *(Lesson 1)*

F. **Correct:** *Drinking water must be tested to meet legal standards.* This statement describes the most important part of the technician's job.

G. Incorrect: *Technicians test water at many factories.* This statement does not refer to what the technician does.

H. Incorrect: *Technicians spend most of their time on the job.* This statement describes how technicians spend their time, but is not a detail about the type of work they do.

J. Incorrect: *Drinking water must not contain contaminants.* This statement does not directly describe the technician's main responsibility.

K. Incorrect: *Supervisors work with water quality technicians.* This statement is true, but doesn't describe the technician's work.

Item Number 11 *(Lesson 2)*

A. Incorrect: *party planner.* The passage tells you that the administrative assistant is the party planner. The caterer is mentioned in reference to providing food for the party.

B. Incorrect: *restaurant.* The passage states that the party will take place in the company reception room, not in a restaurant.

C. Incorrect: *musician or band.* The word is used regarding food and drink. Music is mentioned later in the paragraph as something other employees might have ideas about.

D. **Correct:** *cooking and serving business.* The term caterer is used to describe a company that "will cook the food, bring it to reception room, and serve food and beverages during the party."

E. Incorrect: *an organization of volunteers.* Volunteers are mentioned in relation to helping with decorations and getting the party room ready, not in relation to food, as the caterer is.

Item Number 12 *(Lesson 2)*

F. Incorrect: *volunteer.* The passage states that a coordinator organizes. Volunteers are people who offer to help out, as with decorations.

G. Incorrect: *administrator.* The letter is written by an administrative assistant, but the term coordinate refers to someone who organizes the party committee.

H. **Correct:** *organizer.* The passage tells you that the coordinator is someone who is "responsible for organizing the party committee."

J. Incorrect: *receptionist.* A receptionist is someone who greets visitors to an office. The party will be held in a reception room, but the coordinator's role is not related to that of the receptionist.

K. Incorrect: *office monitor.* The passage does not mention that anyone will be an office monitor before or during the party.

Item Number 13 *(Lesson 4)*

A. **Correct:** *Use the controls to lock the container.* Step C tells you that this is what must be done before removing the container.

B. Incorrect: *Empty the vacuum's trap.* The passage does not mention emptying the vacuum trap, which would be dangerous because it would expose the worker to asbestos.

C. Incorrect: *Monitor the amount of airborne asbestos.* The passage says that this must be done all the time, not just when removing a full container from the vacuum.

D. Incorrect: *Seal the vacuum and place it in a waste container.* The vacuum is not placed in a waste container. Only the trap container within the vacuum is placed in the waste container at the end of the job.

E. Incorrect: *Change the filter on the container.* The passage does not state that changing the filter is part of the technician's job.

Item Number 14 *(Lesson 4)*

F. Incorrect: *Put clothing and mask into the waste container.* The passage does not state that the protective clothing and mask are placed in the waste container.

G. Incorrect: *Check to see if there is any airborne asbestos.* Checking for airborne asbestos is done throughout the procedure, not after the job is complete.

H. **Correct:** *Vacuum the entire area to remove all asbestos particles.* The passage tells you in step F that after the asbestos is removed, the entire area must be vacuumed.

J. Incorrect: *Open the vacuum trap to monitor its level of asbestos.* The vacuum trap is never opened because that would release dangerous asbestos. It is not mentioned anywhere in these steps.

K. Incorrect: *Change the filter on the trap in the vacuum container.* The passage does not describe changing a filter.

Item Number 15 *(Lesson 1)*

A. Incorrect: *Surveying is used in fieldwork.* This is a detail, not a summary of the passage, which describes the job of surveyor technician.

B. Incorrect: *Most surveyors work outdoors.* The passage describes many things that surveyor technicians do. This is not correct because it does not describe very much about the job.

C. **Correct:** *Surveying involves taking land measurements.* This statement sums up what the passage is about, which is a description of the work done by a surveyor technician. So it is the main idea of the passage.

D. Incorrect: *Lasers are the most accurate surveying tools.* This option mentions one tool used in this job. It is not a summary of the passage, so is not the main idea.

E. Incorrect: *Renewable energy often involves land disputes.* This statement is not supported by any information in the passage, so it cannot be its main idea.

Item Number 16 *(Lesson 1)*

F. Incorrect: *All surveyor technicians use laser tools.* This statement is not supported by the passage, which states that surveyors also use steel tapes. Nothing in the passage tells you that all surveyors use lasers.

G. **Correct:** *Surveyor technicians may use GPS in the field.* This statement is a detail that supports the main idea, which describes what a surveyor technician does. It is mentioned in the passage as something a worker may do on the job.

H. Incorrect: *Only supervisors are able to use surveying software.* The passage states that surveyor technicians

may use software to input information gathered by measuring tools.

J. Incorrect: *Maps are used to generate land measurements.* Based on the passage, measurements taken by surveyors are used to make maps. Surveyors may consult old maps, but their job is to make newer, more accurate maps.

K. Incorrect: *Most land is bounded by angles, not straight lines.* This is not a supporting detail because it is not mentioned or supported by the information in the passage. The passage states that an angle-measuring tool may be used, but it does not say that most boundaries have lots of angles.

Item Number 17 *(Lesson 2)*

A. **Correct:** *a list of food ingredients.* Based on the passage, you can tell that a recipe tells how each dish is prepared, so it must also contain the ingredients that go into that dish.

B. Incorrect: *a list of dishes being served that night.* The passage states that the menu is the list of dishes served. The recipe is the directions the chef provides for making each dish.

C. Incorrect: *the types of food ordered for that night's meal.* The food ordered by the chef will be in the meals, but the recipe is the direction for using the food to make each dish.

D. Incorrect: *a description of the desserts.* The passage does not state that the chef makes the desserts.

E. Incorrect: *a list of the tasks to be completed before dinner is served.* The tasks performed before cooking involve more than food. The passage indicates that the recipe is the directions for making the food.

Item Number 18 *(Lesson 2)*

F. Incorrect: *soup bowl.* Based on the passage, a utensil is something used to prepare food. A soup bowl is used to serve food, so it is not a utensil.

G. Incorrect: *pie plate.* The passage does not say anything about a chef making desserts, so a chef would not use a pie plate.

H. Incorrect: *fresh fish.* Fresh fish is an ingredient in a dish prepared by a cook. A utensil is something the chef uses to prepare the food, not the food itself.

J. **Correct:** *sharp knife.* A sharp knife is a utensil, or something a chef uses to prepare food.

K. Incorrect: *refrigerator containers.* Refrigerator containers store food. They are not tools a chef uses to prepare food. A utensil is a tool used to prepare food.

Level 4

Lesson 6 (pp. 52–59)
Skill Practice
1. C   2. G

On Your Own:
| 1. D | 2. J | 3. B | 4. J | 5. B | 6. H |
| 7. B | 8. G | 9. A | 10. H | 11. A | 12. G |

Lesson 7 (pp. 60–67)
Skill Practice
1. B   2. J

On Your Own:
| 1. C | 2. H | 3. B | 4. G | 5. B | 6. J |
| 7. E | 8. G | 9. B | 10. J | 11. A | 12. H |

Lesson 8 (pp. 68–75)
Skill Practice
1. C   2. J

On Your Own:

1. B	2. H	3. A	4. H	5. D	6. F
7. C	8. J	9. E	10. H	11. C	12. G

Lesson 9 (pp. 76–83)
Skill Practice
1. D   2. J

On Your Own:

1. B	2. K	3. C	4. G	5. A	6. J
7. C	8. F	9. C	10. J	11. E	12. F

Level 4 Performance Assessment (pp. 84–92)

Item Number 1 *(Lesson 6)*

A. Incorrect: *canola oil.* This is a vegetable oil and can be used in vegan baking.

B. Incorrect: *sunflower seed oil.* This is a vegetable oil.

C. Incorrect: *corn oil.* This is a vegetable oil.

D. Incorrect: *vegetable oil.* This is a vegetable oil.

E. **Correct:** *butter or lard.* These are animal products and cannot be used in vegan baking.

Item Number 2 *(Lesson 6)*

F. Incorrect: *one; mix everything at the same time.* This is contrary to the instructions.

G. Incorrect: *two; divide the batter in half.* You do need two bowls, but this is not why. Dividing the batter is not part of the instructions.

H. **Correct:** *two: one for the dry ingredients and one for the wet.* This reflects the instructions.

J. Incorrect: *three; beat the eggs in a separate bowl.* Eggs are not used in the receipt.

K. Incorrect: *three: put the flour in a separate bowl.* This is not part of the instructions.

Item Number 3 *(Lesson 6)*

A. Incorrect: *It helps him to breathe.* This is not mentioned in the instructions.

B. Incorrect: *It relaxes him.* This is not mentioned in the instructions.

C. Incorrect: *It keeps him from seeing what you are doing.* This is not mentioned in the instructions.

D. **Correct:** *It opens his mouth.* This is consistent with the instructions.

E. Incorrect: *It restrains him.* This is not mentioned in the instructions.

Item Number 4 *(Lesson 6)*

F. Incorrect: *to soothe him.* This is not important once he has the pill in his mouth.

G. Incorrect: *to make him hungry.* This would not help with giving a pill.

H. **Correct:** *to make him swallow.* This is implied in the next sentence by the phrase "may also encourage the cat to swallow."

J. Incorrect: *to make him purr.* This would not help with giving a pill.

K. Incorrect: *to keep from getting bit.* Holding the mouth closed would help control biting, not stroking the throat.

Item Number 5 *(Lesson 7)*

A. Incorrect: *a shredding center.* There is no mention of destroying files.

B. Incorrect: *a copying center.* Copying files is not part of the process.

C. **Correct:** *a place where old records are stored.* The subject line of the memo is "Preparing files for storage," which can be used to determine the correct meaning of archive.

D. Incorrect: *the company's headquarters.* While the archives may be at the headquarters, that is not the definition of the word.

E. Incorrect: *the company mail room.* There is nothing to suggest that the files will be mailed nor stored in the mail room.

Item Number 6 *(Lesson 7)*

F. Incorrect: *unlabeled.* The memo mentions checking existing labels for accuracy, but does not mention files without labels.

G. **Correct:** *about to fall apart.* The phrase "torn or fragile" suggests that fragile has to do with being damaged or coming apart.

H. Incorrect: *plastic.* A plastic folder would not necessarily need to be replaced.

J. Incorrect: *covered with writing.* This is not suggested in the memo.

K. Incorrect: *stiff and sturdy.* This is the opposite of fragile.

Item Number 7 *(Lesson 7)*

A. Incorrect: *Some bills are damaged.* Damaged bills would not be a discrepancy.

B. Incorrect: *The drawer is secure.* A secure drawer would not be defined as a discrepancy.

C. Incorrect: *You have three $5 bills.* This does not describe a discrepancy, as this is the amount you should have.

D. **Correct:** *You have three $20 bills.* This does describe a discrepancy, as you should have four $20 bills.

E. Incorrect: *All of the cash amounts are correct.* This does not describe a discrepancy.

Item Number 8 *(Lesson 7)*

F. Incorrect: *Balance the receipts.* Receipts are not mentioned in the memo.

G. **Correct:** *Lock the drawer.* To secure means to keep safe. Locking the drawer would keep the contents safe.

H. Incorrect: *Remove the cash.* It would not be practical to remove the cash each time the sales clerk leaves the register.

J. Incorrect: *Open the drawer.* It would not make sense for the clerk to open the drawer before leaving the register.

K. Incorrect: *Sort the bills and coins.* This would also not be practical.

Item Number 9 *(Lesson 7)*

A. **Correct:** *that you are honest and respected.* This is something a customer would value.

B. Incorrect: *that you are happy in your work.* This would not necessarily make a customer feel secure.

C. Incorrect: *that you work quickly.* This also would not make a customer feel secure.

D. Incorrect: *that you are in training.* This would not comfort a customer.

E. Incorrect: *that you have a degree.* Professional identification, not a degree, indicates to the customer that you are certified to do the work.

Item Number 10 *(Lesson 7)*

F. Incorrect: *good will.* This is not the primary thing a locksmith customer would be looking for.

G. Incorrect: *humor.* This has nothing to do with doing a good job.

H. Incorrect: *anxiety.* This feeling is the opposite of what a customer would want from a locksmith.

J. Incorrect: *superiority.* This is not related to what the customer needs.

K. **Correct:** *safety.* This is what customers use a lock for and, therefore, what they expect to have provided by a locksmith.

Item Number 11 *(Lesson 8)*

A. Incorrect: *to determine if the company is making the best use of materials.* This relates to the consultants' investigation of work materials, not the labor force.

B. **Correct:** *to determine if the company is making the best use of work hours.* The consultant will analyze how efficiently the labor force makes use of its time for production.

C. Incorrect: *to evaluate the computerized information system.* This is one of the last things the consultant does, and it is mentioned in step 3. It is not related to the labor force.

D. Incorrect: *to analyze the company's financial health.* This is mentioned in step 4, and occurs after an analysis of the labor force.

E. Incorrect: *to recommend a new system of financial planning.* Likewise, this occurs in step 4.

Item Number 12 *(Lesson 8)*

F. Incorrect: *before evaluating the labor force.* The labor force is in step 2, while evaluating the computerized information is in step 3.

G. Incorrect: *after analyzing the financial health.* The financial health is one of the last things that is analyzed.

H. Incorrect: *before reviewing the use of materials.* Reviewing the use of materials is done in step 1, so nothing is done before this.

J. Incorrect: *after recommending new financial planning.* This is one of the last things done.

K. **Correct:** *after analyzing and improving systems.* In step 3, first systems are analyzed and improvements recommended, and then the computerized information systems are evaluated.

Item Number 13 *(Lesson 8)*

A. Incorrect: *Input the record without codes.* The passage states that all diagnoses must have a code.

B. Incorrect: *Mark the omission in colored ink.* It is not omissions that are marked in color, but certain changes.

C. Incorrect: *Refer the omission to the technician.* Omissions are not referred to the technician. The technician gets the file after the manager completes it.

D. **Correct:** *Look up the code and insert it in the patient record.* The passage states "if the record contains a diagnosis but no code, look up the codes in our Master Code file and insert it in the patient record."

E. Incorrect: *Use the diagnosis codes from previous visits.* Nowhere does the passage state that missing information should just be picked up from previous parts of the record.

Item Number 14 *(Lesson 8)*

F. Incorrect: *Put them in the computer file.* The technician puts the information in the computer, not the manager.

G. Incorrect: *Mark medication changes in red.* Medication changes are marked in blue.

H. **Correct:** *Mark diagnosis changes in red.* The passage states to "mark in red any changes in diagnosis."

J. Incorrect: *Mark new medication by code.* Medications are not coded, only diagnoses are coded.

K. Incorrect: *Mark the date of the appointment in blue.* Medication changes are marked in blue; the date of appointment is not marked in color.

Item Number 15 *(Lesson 9)*

A. Incorrect: *to remove bridges.* The removal of bridges is not mentioned in the memo.

B. Incorrect: *to examine loose fillings.* This is not mentioned as the use of clamps in the memo.

C. Incorrect: *to protect gums the whitening gel.* This is done with the use of the protective mouthpiece.

D. **Correct:** *to better access gums and teeth.* Clamps are used when the patient has difficulty keeping his or her mouth open.

E. Incorrect: *to increase the power of the whitening gel.* The laser light does this.

Item Number 16 *(Lesson 9)*

F. Incorrect: *The patient has loose fillings.* Loose fillings are not mentioned in the memo.

G. **Correct:** *The teeth are badly stained.* The memo states that the laser light increases the power of the whitening gel, and is used if the patient's teeth are badly stained.

H. Incorrect: *The gums are inflamed or infected.* This condition is not mentioned in the memo.

J. Incorrect: *The dentist has difficulty seeing.* This situation is not described in the memo.

K. Incorrect: *The roots require an x-ray.* Likewise, this situation is not described in the memo.

Item Number 17 *(Lesson 9)*

A. Incorrect: *Recommend remedies for problems.* Before you recommend remedies, you must test for toxic chemicals.

B. **Correct:** *Test for toxic chemicals.* The memo states that if you find air contaminants are presents in the form of gases, you should "run a follow-up test for toxic chemicals."

C. Incorrect: *Check for dust and asbestos.* You will check for dust and asbestos when you continue with the standard test because there are no air contaminants.

D. Incorrect: *Run the initial air quality test.* This is the very first thing you do and will help you find the air contaminants.

E. Incorrect: *Recommend a final report.* You will not recommend a final report until all tests have been completed.

F.   **Correct:** *when no gas contaminants exist.* The memo states that testing for asbestos and dust can only occur if no gas contaminants exist.

G.   Incorrect: *when you run a toxic chemical test.* You will run a toxic chemical test when "initial results show that air contaminants in the form of gases exist."

H.   Incorrect: *when you find air contaminants.* If air contaminants are discovered, you need to run a toxic chemical test.

J.   Incorrect: *when you find gases exist.* If gases exist, you need to run a toxic chemical test.

K.   Incorrect: *when dust and asbestos exist.* You would not be able to make this determination until you run the test.

Level 5

Lesson 10 (pp. 94–101)
Skills Practice
1. D   2. G

On Your Own
| 1. B | 2. J | 3. C | 4. K | 5. D | 6. H |
| 7. A | 8. F | 9. C | 10. J | 11. B | 12. K |

Lesson 11 (pp. 102–109)
Skills Practice
1. E   2. H

On Your Own
| 1. D | 2. H | 3. A | 4. J | 5. C | 6. F |
| 7. E | 8. H | 9. B | 10. J | 11. A | 12. H |

Lesson 12 (pp. 110–117)
Skills Practice
1. D   2. H

On Your Own
| 1. B | 2. H | 3. A | 4. G | 5. D | 6. K |
| 7. C | 8. F | 9. E | 10. H | 11. A | 12. F |

Lesson 13 (pp. 118–125)
Skills Practice
1. D   2. H
On Your Own
| 1. C | 2. F | 3. A | 4. K | 5. D | 6. F |
| 7. C | 8. J | 9. B | 10. H | 11. C | 12. K |

Lesson 14 (pp. 126–133)
Skills Practice
1. B   2. H

On Your Own
| 1. B | 2. H | 3. D | 4. K | 5. E | 6. H |
| 7. B | 8. G | 9. D | 10. K | 11. C | 12. J |

Lesson 15 (pp. 134–141)
Skills Practice
1. C   2. J

On Your Own
| 1. D | 2. F | 3. E | 4. G | 5. C | 6. F |
| 7. B | 8. F | 9. C | 10. J | 11. A | 12. K |

Level 5 Performance Assessment (pp. 142–150)

Item Number 1 (Lesson 11)

A.   Incorrect: CO_2. This is not an acronym. It is the chemical designation of the gas carbon dioxide.

B.   Incorrect: *GHG.* Though carbon dioxide is a greenhouse gas, the passage informs you that it is entered under a more precise category.

C.   Incorrect: *AWV.* AWV is the acronym for atmospheric water vapor. It is not a category of gases in the database.

D.   Incorrect: *EPA.* EPA is the acronym for the government agency, the Environmental Protection Agency.

E.   **Correct:** *LLGHG.* This acronym stands for long-lived greenhouse gases. Carbon dioxide is identified as an LLGHG, so it would be entered in this part of the database.

Item Number 2 (Lesson 11)

F.   Incorrect: *water vapor.* Water vapor is shown as AWV.

G.   Incorrect: *methane.* Methane is not given an acronym in the passage.

H.   Incorrect: *IPCC.* IPCC stands for the Intergovernmental Panel on Climate Change.

J.   Incorrect: *LLGHG.* LLGHG stands for long-lived greenhouse gases.

K.   **Correct:** *chlorofluorocarbons.* CFC is the acronym for chlorofluorocarbons.

Item Number 3 (Lesson 10)

A.   Incorrect: *because it reveals the cause of death.* The passage states that it is used as evidence, but does not state it identifies the cause of death.

B.   **Correct:** *because it forms the legal basis of the case.* The passage states that forensic evidence "may be disallowed in the legal case if it is contaminated in any way," indicating that the evidence is crucial for forming a legal basis.

C.   Incorrect: *because it reveals fingerprints that identify the criminal.* The passage does not state that forensic evidence necessarily has this information.

D.   Incorrect: *because it always contains traces of the perpetrator.* The passage does not state that forensic evidence contains marks of the criminal. You should be wary of options that use words like always.

E.   Incorrect: *because it is first sterilized for storage in contaminant-free containers.* The passage states that those who handle the forensic evidence and the storage containers must be sterile. The evidence should not be sterilized, as that would destroy important information it may have.

Item Number 4 (Lesson 12)

F.   Incorrect: *fingerprints.* The ballistics test as described in the passage does not mention that it would reveal fingerprints.

G.   Incorrect: *identification of body fluids.* The passage refers to the technician as collecting these fluids for testing, but does not state they undergo ballistics testing.

H.   **Correct:** *the type of firearm used.* The passage states that ballistics tests are conducted on the bullet and yield information about "the gun, the bullet and the conditions under which it was fired."

J.   Incorrect: *whether the bullet caused the death.* The passage states that ballistics tests are conducted on the bullet to get information, but these tests do not determine if the bullet caused the death.

K.   Incorrect: *the police interpretation of the crime.* The passage does not state what use or interpretation the police put on the results of the ballistics test.

Item Number 5 *(Lesson 12)*

A.   Incorrect: *assisting the surgeon.* The e-mail states that the perianesthesia nurse works with patients' reactions to anesthesia. It does not state that this nurse aids the surgeon.

B.   Incorrect: *administering anesthesia.* The e-mail states that this nurse monitors the patient who has been given anesthesia, but does not give it herself or himself.

C.   Incorrect: *injecting pain killing drugs.* The e-mail does not state that this nurse injects or gives any drugs to patients.

D.   **Correct:** *monitoring patients' vital signs.* The e-mail states that for "patients who have been given general anesthesia during surgery," this nurse "will monitor their vital signs" to make sure patients don't have negative reactions to the anesthetic.

E.   Incorrect: *moving patients out of recovery.* The e-mail states that the postoperative nurse does this.

Item Number 6 *(Lesson 13)*

F.   Incorrect. *arranges surgeries.* Nowhere in the e-mail does it state that a nurse has anything to do with arranging or scheduling surgeries.

G.   **Correct:** *assists before, during, and after surgery.* The e-mail describes how this nurse works with patients during all parts of the surgery.

H.   Incorrect: *treats patient complications after surgery.* The e-mail states that the postoperative nurse does this.

J.   Incorrect: *monitors the effects of general anesthesia.* The e-mail states that the perianesthesia nurse does this.

K.   Incorrect: *consults with the surgeon about the patient.* The e-mail makes no mention of any nurse consulting with the surgeon.

Item Number 7 *(Lesson 15)*

A.   **Correct:** *Research the target audience.* The passage states that before working on the design, the graphic designer must research the characteristics of the target audience.

B.   Incorrect: *Present your ideas to the client.* The passage states that this is done after the first design is created, not before.

C.   Incorrect: *Rearrange graphic elements.* The passage states that this may be done at the client's request after the client has seen and wants changes in the original design.

D.   Incorrect: *Get approval from the creative director.* The passage states that this is done only when the final design is complete.

E.   Incorrect: *Rework the colors used in the graphic.* The passage states that this is another change that may need to be made in response to the client's comments and suggestions.

Item Number 8 *(Lesson 15)*

F.   Incorrect: *the size of the ad.* The passage does not state that this is one of the design elements that may be changed.

G.   Incorrect: *the ad's distribution venue.* The passage states that the venue is what "the client has chosen," so it is not a visual element changed by the designer.

H.   Incorrect: *the ad's target audience.* The passage states that this is information obtained from the client before work begins. It is therefore not a design element that can be changed.

J.   **Correct:** *the colors used in the ad.* The passage states that changing the design elements may include "reworking the colors" used.

K.   Incorrect. *the ideas inserted by the creative director.* The passage states that the creative director only approves the final design, but does not change the design.

Item Number 9 *(Lesson 12)*

A.   Incorrect: *the fingers.* The memo states that the fingers may be involved, but they are not part of the carpal tunnel.

B.   Incorrect: *hand muscles.* The memo states that the hand muscles may be affected, but they are not the carpal tunnel.

C.   **Correct:** *a nerve sheath in the wrist.* The memo states that the carpal tunnel is "a nerve that runs through a sheath in the wrist."

D.   Incorrect: *bones in the forearm.* The memo states that these may hurt because of carpal tunnel syndrome, but they are not the carpal tunnel.

E.   Incorrect: *shoulder to wrist nerves.* The memo states that these may be painful, but they are not the carpal tunnel.

Item Number 10 *(Lesson 12)*

F.   Incorrect: *It is only used in offices.* The memo uses office equipment as an example, but does not define ergonomic as being only used in offices.

G.   **Correct:** *It relieves stress on the body.* The memo states that ergonomically designed equipment "prevents stress and damage."

H.   Incorrect: *It keeps the body immobile.* The memo does not mention any equipment that prevents the body from moving.

J.   Incorrect: *It can be used for many hours.* The memo implies that this is true, but this is not the definition of an ergonomic design.

K.   Incorrect: *It must accompany proper exercise.* The memo states that exercise may be helpful but it does not state that it must go along with using an ergonomically designed object.

Item Number 11 *(Lesson 15)*

A.   Incorrect: *Redesign the new product.* The letter does not mention that the product should be redesigned if supplies are expensive.

B.   Incorrect: *Use fewer parts in the product.* The letter does not state that the number of parts in the product should be reduced.

C.   Incorrect: *Train workers to make the parts more quickly.* The part that deals with suppliers is in steps 2 and 3. The speed at which the product is made from these parts is dealt with in step 5.

D.   **Correct:** *Purchase parts from the suppliers.* The passage states the manager must determine "if it is more cost-effective for our firm to make these new parts or to buy them from suppliers."

E.   Incorrect: *Deduct overhead from the cost of the parts.* Overhead is mentioned only in step 6, when the final cost calculations are made. Parts and supplies are discussed in steps 2 and 3.

Item Number 12 (Lesson 15)

F. **Correct:** *when costs do not decrease in time.* The passage states that the learning curve chart must show "how long it is expected to take our workforce… to make the new product." Step 5 states that if these costs "do not diminish over a reasonable time period," a new plan may need to be created.

G. Incorrect: *when "debugging" the process is too difficult.* The passage mentions "debugging" in step 4, but does not refer to it as being part of the learning-curve chart.

H. Incorrect: *when standard labor hours are too great.* The passage mentions standard labor hours in step 6. In this final step, these hours are used in a calculation. They are not described as declining or being part of the learning-curve chart.

J. Incorrect: *when factory machinery cannot be calibrated.* The passage does not state that machinery calibration is part of the learning-curve chart.

K. Incorrect: *when no suppliers have the parts you need.* The learning-curve chart does not refer to the purchase of supplies or parts, as seen in step 5.

Item Number 13 (Lesson 14)

A. Incorrect: *granite countertops.* The explanation of biobased materials within the passage informs you that these come from living things, such as plants. Granite is not living; it is a rock.

B. **Correct:** *soy-based insulation.* Soy is a plant, a living thing, so it is biobased.

C. Incorrect: *flagstone walkways.* Flagstone is not living, so is not biobased.

D. Incorrect: *solar roofing tiles.* Tiles are made of clay or other non-living materials, so they are not biobased.

E. Incorrect: *polyvinyl chloride pipes.* These pipes are made from synthetic materials, not living or biobased materials.

Item Number 14 (Lesson 14)

F. **Correct:** *if only part of the product uses recycled material.* The handbook states that this calculation is necessary to determine the weight of the recycled material relative to the weight of non-recycled material in a product or assembly.

G. Incorrect: *if none of the product components has been refurbished.* The handbook states that refurbished materials are those that are completely reused. They are not products that are made out of recycled materials.

H. Incorrect: *if the product is made only of preconsumer material.* The handbook states that both pre- and post-consumer material must be included in the calculation.

J. Incorrect: *if you cannot get documentation regarding recycled content.* The calculation is not related to documentation, only to determining the percentage of recycled material in something.

K. Incorrect: *if the materials are not obtained within the region.* The regional aspect of materials is discussed earlier in the handbook and does not pertain to this calculation.

Item Number 15 (Lesson 14)

A. **Correct:** *on the PCB.* The passage states that the CPU circuits are on the PCB.

B. Incorrect: *on the CPU.* The question asks where the CPU circuits are. The circuits for the CPU are not on the CPU, but are on the motherboard.

C. Incorrect: *on the RAM.* RAM refers to the amount of memory on the computer, not the computer's circuitry.

D. Incorrect: *on the monitor.* The monitor is a computer peripheral, meaning it is a separate device that is not part of the CPU.

E. Incorrect: *on the DVD/CD-ROM.* The DVD/CD-ROM is stated to be a disk player. It is identified as a separate drive, not a part of the CPU circuitry.

Item Number 16 (Lesson 14)

F. Incorrect: *Get a new CPU.* The passage states that the CPU is the "brains" of the computer and helps it run. It does not relate it to computer memory.

G. Incorrect: *Buy another mouse.* The mouse is a computer peripheral that has nothing to do with the computer's memory.

H. Incorrect: *Install a new DVD/CD-ROM.* The passage states that the DVD/CD-ROM is an optical disk drive. It is not the computer's memory.

J. **Correct:** *Buy more RAM.* RAM is random access memory, the memory that enables programs to run on the computer.

K. Incorrect: *Buy a new motherboard.* The passage states that the motherboard contains circuits that enable the computer to run. These circuits do not contain memory.

Item Number 17 (Lesson 15)

A. Incorrect: *when the dispatchers start the boilers.* The passage does not state that starting the boilers is involved in determining when an increase in electricity use is to be expected.

B. Incorrect: *when a current is routed from the substation.* A current that is routed from the substation is not a condition that would indicate an increase in electricity use among customers.

C. **Correct:** *when a heat wave is forecast for the area.* The passage states "weather conditions are often a good indicator of potential demand changes." If a heat wave is forecast, the dispatcher must know that people will be using their air conditioners more, so electricity use will increase.

D. Incorrect: *when the grid system is upgraded.* The passage makes no connection between upgrading the transmission lines on the grid and an increase in electricity use.

E. Incorrect: *when substations are added to the grid.* The addition of substations would not be something the dispatcher monitors and relays to the control room. It is a major investment in the utility that would be known to all.

Item Number 18 (Lesson 15)

F. Incorrect: *when use is low in one area.* The passage states that transmission be adjusted based on use, but lower use would just require less flow to that area, not rerouting.

G. Incorrect: *when there are too many substations.* The passage does not relate the number of substations to a need for rerouting. The number of substations indicates the number of areas served.

H. Incorrect: *when the circuit breakers are malfunctioning.* The passage states that the circuit breakers are in the utility company and monitored by the dispatcher. They are not related to any condition under which the dispatcher would have to reroute electricity for distribution.

J. **Correct:** *when transmission lines at a substation fail.* The passage states that a breakdown at a substation is a reason to reroute electricity around that substation, so it does not affect too many customers.

K. Incorrect: *when the voltage transformers cannot produce usable electricity.* The passage does not state that the voltage transformers produce usable electricity or that they are involved in the distribution and routing of electricity.

Level 6

Lesson 16 (pp. 152–159)
Skill Practice
1. E 2. G

On Your Own
| 1. B | 2. K | 3. C | 4. H | 5. D | 6. H |
| 7. D | 8. F | 9. B | 10. H | 11. E | 12. J |

Lesson 17 (pp. 160–167)
Skill Practice
1. B 2. G

On Your Own
| 1. C | 2. G | 3. E | 4. H | 5. C | 6. J |
| 7. D | 8. F | 9. E | 10. F | 11. C | 12. H |

Lesson 18 (pp. 168–175)
Skill Practice
1. B 2. K

On Your Own
| 1. E | 2. G | 3. A | 4. H | 5. D | 6. J |
| 7. E | 8. H | 9. B | 10. F | 11. E | 12. G |

Lesson 19 (pp. 176–183)
Skill Practice
1. B 2. G

On Your Own
| 1. C | 2. F | 3. B | 4. J | 5. E | 6. G |
| 7. C | 8. J | 9. A | 10. G | 11. A | 12. H |

Lesson 20 (pp. 184–191)
Skill Practice
1. B 2. H

On Your Own
| 1. C | 2. J | 3. C | 4. K | 5. A | 6. G |
| 7. D | 8. J | 9. A | 10. F | 11. D | 12. G |

Lesson 21 (pp. 192–199)
Skill Practice
1. C 2. F

On Your Own
| 1. D | 2. F | 3. D | 4. H | 5. C | 6. J |
| 7. B | 8. J | 9. C | 10. G | 11. A | 12. F |

Lesson 22 (pp. 200–207)
Skill Practice
1. D 2. F

On Your Own
| 1. D | 2. G | 3. E | 4. J | 5. E | 6. K |
| 7. A | 8. H | 9. E | 10. J | 11. A | 12. J |

Level 6 Performance Assessment (pp. 208–216)
Item Number 1 *(Lesson 16)*

A. Incorrect: *They will not be able to pay rent or lease an apartment elsewhere.* Paragraph 2 states that few rental properties exist *in their area.* It does not state or imply that they cannot afford an apartment in a different school district.

B. Incorrect: *Marietta will lose her job if she moves from the school district.* No clues indicate that Marietta is in any way in jeopardy of losing her job, regardless of a move. Prior knowledge may also allow you to know that most school districts employ workers from outside their districts.

C. **Correct:** *The development of their son will be disrupted because he will have to change schools.* Paragraph 2 states that they will probably be forced to move out of the district. From this, you can infer that the son will have to change schools. The fact that there is an "exceptional special-education program at his public school" leads one to believe that the son's development will suffer if placed in another (implied: not as good) program. The tone of the letter implies that they are very concerned about their son.

D. Incorrect: *They will not be able to afford the cost of professional movers.* The couple is hoping not to move at all; nowhere in their message is the cost of moving stated or implied.

E. Incorrect: *Jarrod will not be able to find work in a new city.* Prior knowledge would tell one that the family could move to a nearby town and Jarrod would keep the job that he secured in April.

Item Number 2 *(Lesson 16)*

F. Incorrect: *If necessary, Marietta will get a second job in order to keep their house.* Marietta is working extra hours at her *current* job. The letter does not state or imply that she would get a second job as well.

G. **Correct:** *Jarrod's new employer and job are stable.* Paragraph 4 tells you that his part-time job will change to a full-time job and that his new employer "has been in business for 35 years." Both of these details imply stability of the employer and his new job.

H. Incorrect: *If they are given a short reprieve on their past-due payments, they will be able to afford their current house payments beginning in July.* The couple does not ask for a reprieve or imply that they can make the same house payment that they used to make. Instead, they specifically ask for a new financing plan and tell the amount that they can pay.

J. Incorrect: *As soon as they can afford to do so, they will sell their house and rent a property in their current district.* It is clear from clues and tone that the family is desperate to keep their current home. This implies that they have no intentions of moving in the future.

K. Incorrect: *They will move when they find another school that can meet the needs of their son.* Again, the message strongly implies that they don't want to move in the future. It also implies that they are very satisfied with their son's current school and wish for him to remain there.

Item Number 3 *(Lesson 21)*

A. Incorrect: *Satisfy its members' recreational and practical interests by use of traditional and emerging technologies.* While the members' recreation interests might be satisfied by the program to a degree, the program is not considered traditional and does not use technology.

B. Incorrect: *Anticipate and meet changing needs.* The program provides information but does not anticipate or meet any changing needs of the members.

C. Incorrect: *Educate the public regarding library standards.* The program does not cover library standards in any way.

D. Incorrect: *Encourage a love of reading and learning in children.* Since it's safe to assume the employees are adults, most of them will choose adult books as their favorites, so the program will do little or nothing to affect children.

E. **Correct:** *Promote a sense of community for library patrons.* The overall principle is to allow the members of the community to get to know a little about the librarians and other staff. The first paragraph states that the library is "always trying to maintain visibility in the township and promote a sense of belonging to our patrons." These factors all imply a community-based organization.

Item Number 4 *(Lesson 21)*

F. Incorrect: *Allow homebound people to view descriptions of books online.* Viewing descriptions of books does not allow homebound people to borrow books.

G. Incorrect: *Set up book displays at local grocery stores or nursing homes.* Since the individuals are homebound, they cannot get to grocery stores or nursing homes.

H. **Correct:** *Recruit volunteers who will deliver and return books to homebound people who have placed requests by phone or online.* This solution covers all of the objectives of the program. Allowing homebound people to request specific books and have them delivered to and returned for them allows them to borrow of books of their choice. Since the organization is specified as a volunteer group, it makes logical sense that volunteers would be the ones to travel.

J. Incorrect: *Ask their relatives to pick out books for them.* This answer does not allow for books of the homebound person's choice. It also would not be a library/volunteer-run program.

K. Incorrect: *Let homebound people order books by phone or online, and then ask the library to mail the books to them.* This is not a logical choice because of the cost involved. Most volunteer groups do not have funds to support this kind of cost.

Item Number 5 *(Lesson 22)*

A. Incorrect: *when you have a headache, dizziness, or weakness.* These are not conditions that cause heat-related illness, they are symptoms of heat exhaustion.

B. **Correct:** *when the body cannot cool itself adequately.* This is the basic condition of the human body that causes heat-related illness.

C. Incorrect: *when you cannot drink enough coffee to stay hydrated.* This is not a condition that causes heat-related illness. Drinking coffee does not hydrate but rather dehydrates.

D. Incorrect: *when the body has seizures or convulsions.* This is not a condition that causes heat-related illness, rather it is a symptom of heat stroke.

E. Incorrect: *when you have dry, hot skin.* This is not a condition that causes heat-related illness. It is a symptom of heat stroke.

Item Number 6 *(Lesson 22)*

F. Incorrect: *to ensure the safety of the professor.* While the professor is obviously part of the team, the safety regulations are not for his benefit only. Moreover, as an experienced archaeologist who has worked in the field, he is aware of these regulations.

G. **Correct:** *to provide for their own safety in case of an emergency.* The students must certify that they are capable of recognizing symptoms and respond in an appropriate manner for their own safety.

H. Incorrect: *to allow travel to potentially dangerous sites.* While students are able to travel to potentially dangerous sites, this is not the primary reason for the document.

J. Incorrect: *to prepare students considering medical school.* This is not mentioned in the document.

K. Incorrect: *solely for insurance purposes.* Likewise, this is not mentioned in the document.

Item Number 7 *(Lesson 17)*

A. Incorrect: *a manager at a hotel.* A hotel manager's primary purpose is to ensure the satisfaction of the guests, not to sell them additional items or services.

B. **Correct:** *a salesperson at a store that sells men's business clothing.* A salesperson selling business attire is likely to suggest items that compliment what the customer is planning to purchase. For instance, they may suggest a shirt and tie to match a suit that the customer is buying. This increases sales and any commissions or bonuses the salesperson receives.

C. Incorrect: *a pharmacist at a drug store.* A pharmacist generally sells prescription drugs ordered by doctors. Pharmacists may suggest items to relieve symptoms that a customer asks about but usually will not suggest "extras."

D. Incorrect: *a payroll specialist at an insurance company.* A payroll specialist does not typically offer a good or service directly to customers.

E. Incorrect: *a teacher at a private school.* A teacher does not generally offer a good or service directly to customers.

Item Number 8 *(Lesson 17)*

F. Incorrect: *A public relations specialist could send press releases to several media sources at one time.* The public relations specialist uses various media sources.

G. Incorrect: *A loan officer could approve loans for clients.* The loan officer uses screening software.

H. Incorrect: *A legal assistant could schedule client appointments.* The legal assistant uses an automated calendar.

J. Incorrect: *An engineer could estimate labor needed for a project.* The engineer uses a formula/worksheet.

K. **Correct:** *A physician could quickly send a prescription directly to a pharmacy.* The doctor is placing an order for his patient. Using the point-of-sale system, the order is placed more quickly and more accurately than conventional means.

Item Number 9 *(Lesson 20)*

A. Incorrect: *All Internet access is monitored.* The policy states that the university will only monitor e-mail if there is a "reasonable suspicion" of misuse.

B. Incorrect: *Accessing the Internet for personal reasons is not permitted.* The policy states that limited and appropriate personal use is allowed.

C. Incorrect: *Internet access is limited to business use only.* The policy does not state this limitation.

D. **Correct:** *Accessing the Internet for personal use is allowed, but should not interfere with the employee's duties.* The policy makes a clear statement about accessing obscene or inappropriate sites which may result in actionable misconduct.

E. Incorrect: *Accessing the Internet is only permitted outside of working hours.* The document makes no such limitation.

Item Number 10 *(Lesson 20)*

F. Incorrect: *to expand its e-mailing list.* The policy mentions undesirable sites that the university clearly sees as harmful.

G. Incorrect: *to protect the employee from potentially harmful contacts.* The document clearly stresses individual responsibility and not protectiveness.

H. Incorrect: *to conduct research about spam mail.* Research is not at all mentioned in the policy and could only be conducted with consent of participants.

J. **Correct:** *to maintain acceptable standards of professional conduct.* The policy clearly emphasizes personal responsibility and appropriate conduct.

K. Incorrect: *to conduct market research.* The policy does not mention this as a response.

Item Number 11 *(Lesson 18)*

A. Incorrect: *final.* This is one definition of the word terminal; however, it does not make sense in the context of the e-mail.

B. Incorrect: *adding machine.* This is not a definition for terminal, nor does it make sense in the context of the e-mail.

C. **Correct:** *computer station.* In many workplaces, the term terminal is used to describe a computer station. This meaning makes sense in this context.

D. Incorrect: *fax machine.* This is not a definition for terminal, nor does it make sense in the context of the e-mail.

E. Incorrect: *register.* This is not a definition for terminal, nor does it make sense in the context of the e-mail.

Item Number 12 *(Lesson 22)*

F. Incorrect: *an opening in the side of a building filled with glass.* This is the common, everyday meaning of window, but not its meaning as it is used in the e-mail.

G. Incorrect: *a period of available time.* This is also a common meaning of window that describes an opening in one's schedule, but it does not apply to the word's use in the e-mail.

H. **Correct:** *a frame on a computer screen that displays or prompts for information.* The window that is referred to in the e-mail is a separate screen that "will prompt you to set a new password."

J. Incorrect: *an opportunity to experience something new.* This is also a meaning of window to describe a moment of opportunity, but it does not apply to the word's use in the e-mail.

K. Incorrect: *a place where questions can be directed.* Though directing questions is mentioned in the e-mail, this is not a definition of the word window.

Item Number 13 *(Lesson 19)*

A. Incorrect: *whether or not the case merits a brief.*

The rule does not entitle the Clerk to make these decisions.

B. **Correct:** *whether or not the Court has directed you to accept it.* The rule states that a brief will not be served "unless the Court directs otherwise."

C. Incorrect: *whether or not the filing attorney has also filed a written petition.* This is not mentioned in the rule.

D. Incorrect: *whether or not the brief is pertinent to the case. This* is not mentioned in the rule as a criterion for the Clerk to follow.

E. Incorrect: *whether or not the senior attorney filed the brief.* Seniority is not mentioned as a condition that entitles an attorney to be late.

Item Number 14 *(Lesson 19)*

F. Incorrect: *serve the brief anyway. The* rule provides instructions that if a brief has already been served, the Clerk need not serve it.

G. Incorrect: *seek a judgment from the court.* The matter has already been determined by procedure.

H. **Correct:** *consider the brief already served.* The rule states that if such notation appears, the Clerk should consider the brief served.

J. Incorrect: *contact the opposing party to verify.* This action is not mentioned in the rule.

K. Incorrect: *seek a contempt citation against the attorney.* This action is not mentioned in the rule.

Item Number 15 *(Lesson 17)*

A. Incorrect: *agree/disagree with a computer network.* These definitions do not make sense with the context in which the terms are used.

B. Incorrect: *accept/reject a decision about a computer network.* These definitions do not make sense with the context in which the terms are used.

C. **Correct:** *initiate/terminate interaction with a computer network.* These definitions describe what a person does when initiating or terminating interaction with the computer network.

D. Incorrect: *start/end an agreement with a computer network.* These definitions do not make sense with the context in which the terms are used.

E. Incorrect: *start/finalize a dispute with a computer network.* These definitions do not make sense with the context in which the terms are used.

Item Number 16 *(Lesson 17)*

F. Incorrect: *follow regular procedures; you will have 45 days instead of 60 days to notify the employee.* This is the opposite of what the manual states. You have more time, not less, to notify the employee of the final decision regarding a post-6-month dispute.

G. Incorrect: *classify as RECEIVED/POST-6; approve the dispute as outlined in the company policy manual.* Nowhere in the procedures does it indicate that post-6-month disputes should be classified differently than other disputes.

H. Incorrect: *follow regular procedures; you will have 6 months instead of 45 days to notify the employee.* The manual states that employee notification must take place within 60 days, which is about the equivalent of about 2 months, not 6 months.

J. **Correct:** *follow regular procedures; you will have 60 days instead of 45 days to notify the employee.* The manual states "you will have 60 days to notify the employee of the final decision." The only difference for a dispute filed 6 months after the incident is that there are 15 extra days to make a final decision.

   K. Incorrect: *request documentation; ask for verification as outlined in the company policy manual.* This is the step to take if further information is required, regardless of when the dispute is filed.

Item Number 17 *(Lesson 18)*

   A. Incorrect: *diagnose the problem.* There is no mention of a problem.

   B. **Correct:** *finish by a chemical process.* The text mentions that the "chemical reaction between the water and the cement is what cures the concrete."

   C. Incorrect: *wash thoroughly.* While water is part of the process, there is no mention of washing.

   D. Incorrect: *smooth with a trowel.* Although this might be part of preparing the concrete, it is not mentioned.

   E. Incorrect: *heal or make better.* While this is a definition of the word cure, it does not make sense in this context.

Item Number 18 *(Lesson 18)*

   F. Incorrect: *settle.* This term does not describe the meaning of weather.

   G. Incorrect: *expand.* The word expand has to do with increasing in size and does not describe the word *weather*.

   H. Incorrect: *deteriorate.* This is the opposite of the desired result.

   J. **Correct:** *endure or stay intact.* This is the desired outcome.

   K. Incorrect: *shine.* This is not usually a quality associated with concrete.

Level 7

Lesson 23 (p. 218–225)
Skills Practice
1. B   2. J

On Your Own
1. B   2. F   3. D   4. H   5. B   6. H
7. C   8. G   9. C   10. J   11. D   12. K

Lesson 24 (pp. 226–233)
Skills Practice
1. E   2. F

On Your Own
1. B   2. H   3. D   4. F   5. C   6. G
7. A   8. J   9. D   10. K   11. E   12. F

Lesson 25 (pp. 234–241)
Skills Practice
1. D   2. J

On Your Own
1. E   2. J   3. C   4. J   5. A   6. K
7. B   8. F   9. D   10. H   11. E   12. J

Level 7 Performance Assessment (pp. 242-250)

Item Number 1 *(Lesson 23)*

   A. **Correct:** *a track that doesn't measure up to standards.* The passage states that tracks that are subpar can be erased and replaced with a track of higher quality. This indicates that *subpar* means not measuring up to standards.

   B. Incorrect: *a track with too many recordings.* There is no indication in the passage that states that a track is subpar because it has too many recordings.

   C. Incorrect: *a track with musical instruments.* There is no indication in the passage that states that a track is subpar because it has musical instruments.

   D. Incorrect: *a track that measures up to standards.* The passage states that tracks that are subpar can be erased and replaced with track of higher quality. A track that measures up to standards is already of high quality and would not need to be erased or replaced.

   E. Incorrect: *a track with too few recordings.* There is no indication in the passage that states that a track is subpar because it has too few recordings.

Item Number 2 *(Lesson 23)*

   F. Incorrect: *erasing bad tracks.* The passage states that this may be done, but this does not relate to synchronizing tracks.

   G. Incorrect: *evaluating all tracks.* All tracks on a recording should be evaluated, but the passage does not state that evaluating means the same thing as synchronizing.

   H. **Correct:** *blending tracks together.* The passage states that all tracks must fit together to sound good, which means that they must be blended together precisely. This is the definition of synchronizing.

   J. Incorrect: *recording an instrumental track.* Recording an instrumental track is something that is done separately. Once this is done, the track can be synchronized with other tracks.

   K. Incorrect: *recording separate tracks.* Recording tracks separately is the first step. Once the tracks are recorded separately, they are then ready to be synchronized.

Item Number 3 *(Lesson 24)*

   A. Incorrect: *shoots the picture.* The passage does not describe the gaffer's job as shooting the picture. That is the cinematographer's job.

   B. Incorrect: *provide film for the cameras.* The passage does not refer to the person who provides the film for the movie camera.

   C. Incorrect: *make sure that all electrical equipment works.* The passage does not state that the gaffer does this job.

   D. **Correct:** *gets directions from the cinematographer.* The passage states that the gaffer gets directions from the cinematographer and conveys them to the lighting crew.

   E. Incorrect: *consults with the director.* The passage does not mention that the gaffer consults with the director. The cinematographer consults with the director.

Item Number 4 *(Lesson 24)*

   F. **Correct:** *moving electrical wires.* The passage states that the grip department places electrical wires where they should be.

   G. Incorrect: *directing the lighting foreman.* The passage states that the gaffer, not the grip department, directs the lighting director.

   H. Incorrect: *positioning the movie camera.* The passage does not state that this is what the grip does. The cinematographer positions the movie camera.

   J. Incorrect: *consulting with the film director.* The passage does not state that the grip has any consultations with the director of the movie.

   K. Incorrect: *serving as liaison with the cinematographer.* The passage does not describe liaising with the cinematographer as one of the responsibilities of the grip department.

Item Number 5 *(Lesson 23)*

A. Incorrect: *location.* The passage describes allocation in terms of giving out to different sections of the hotel, so it does not refer to anything's location.

B. **Correct:** *distribution.* The passage describes the various areas of hotel management that might get additional funds allocated to them, so allocation means distribution.

C. Incorrect: *allowable.* The context of the passage, particularly the third sentence where the word occurs, indicates that it does not mean something that is allowed.

D. Incorrect: *satisfaction.* The passage does not describe customer satisfaction in terms of the allocation of funds, as described in the third sentence.

E. Incorrect: *improvement.* The passage discusses improvements at the hotel, but improvements are not within the definition of allocation.

Item Number 6 *(Lesson 23)*

F. Incorrect: *to open it.* The passage does not imply that opening is related to configuration.

G. Incorrect: *to increase it.* The passage does state that the manager is considering increasing the size of the space referred to, but that is not a part of the configuration.

H. Incorrect: *to join it.* The passage does not state that the suggested changes involve joining rooms or spaces together.

J. **Correct:** *to arrange it.* The passage implies that the manager wants to shape the conference rooms in some way to make them more attractive to conference goers.

K. Incorrect: *to complete it.* The passage does not describe the hotel space as being currently unfinished.

Item Number 7 *(Lesson 24)*

A. Incorrect: *They have been sold.* The first paragraph describes stocks that have appreciated in value as having made money for the clients. This does not mean they have been sold.

B. Incorrect: *They have decreased in value.* The first paragraph describes stocks that have appreciated in value as having made money for the clients. This does not mean they have decreased in value.

C. **Correct:** *They have increased in value.* The first paragraph describes stocks that have appreciated in value as having made money for the clients. This means they have increased in value.

D. Incorrect: *They bring in new clients.* The first paragraph describes stocks that have appreciated in value as having made money for the clients. This does not necessarily mean they have brought in new clients.

E. Incorrect: *They have lost money.* The first paragraph describes stocks that have appreciated in value as having made money for the clients. This does not mean they have lost money.

Item Number 8 *(Lesson 24)*

F. Incorrect: *to buy and sell shares of the same stock.* When a stock is shorted, it is first borrowed and then sold.

G. Incorrect: *to borrow, buy, and sell shares of different stocks.* When a stock is shorted, the same stock is borrowed and then sold first.

H. **Correct:** *to borrow, sell, and buy back shares of the same stock.* The investor borrows the stock from another investor and then sells it in hopes that the

same stock can be bought back at a lower price. It can then be returned to the original investor, and the investor who shorted earns a profit.

J. Incorrect: *to borrow, sell, and buy back shares of different stocks.* Since shorting a stock involves borrowing and selling stocks from another investor, the investor must return the same stock.

K. Incorrect: *to buy shares when the prices are low.* While hopes of buying back shares at a lower price is part of the process of shorting stocks, it is not the only step that is involved.

Item Number 9 *(Lesson 25)*

A. Incorrect: *Note the appropriate supervisor to contact in case of an emergency.* As the supervisor, you would not need to take note of it.

B. **Correct:** *Post a floor plan that shows the nearest exit to take in case of an emergency.* The Emergency Evacuation Plan clearly states that a floor plan should be posted in order to show the nearest exit.

C. Incorrect: *Identify the proper stairwell to take to evacuate the building.* While the Emergency Evacuation Plan document does require exits to clearly be indicated on a posted floor plan, you can eliminate this answer choice because the office is on the ground floor. No stairwells are required to exit.

D. Incorrect: *Instruct all personnel to dial 555 in case of an emergency.* The Emergency Evacuation Plan document requires employees to contact security only if the alarms are broken, not for every emergency situation. Also, according to the scenario described, there is no security office to contact at the new office site.

E. Incorrect: *Designate a subordinate to oversee all evacuations.* According to the Emergency Evacuation Plan, it is the responsibility of the supervisor to oversee all evacuations, not the subordinate.

Item Number 10 *(Lesson 25)*

F. Incorrect: *Pull the manual alarm lever down; dial 555 if broken.* Because you are not in the office in the scenario described, it is not appropriate or helpful to pull the alarm, or to contact office security.

G. **Correct:** *Assist physically handicapped co-workers to safety.* It is reasonable to assist handicapped co-workers to safety, even if you are not in the office. The Emergency Evacuation Plan calls for physically handicapped employees to be assisted.

H. Incorrect: *Wait for your department supervisor to oversee the evacuation.* As supervisor, it is your responsibility to oversee the evacuation. Therefore, waiting for the supervisor makes no sense.

J. Incorrect: *Follow the floor plan to determine your exit route.* Although this would be required by the plan document if you were in the office, you are off-site, so it is not appropriate. Also, because the emergency is weather-related, leaving the restaurant should not require use of a floor plan.

K. Incorrect: *Walking calmly to avoid overcrowding in the stairwells.* Again, because you are not in the office, this choice does not make sense, especially because the emergency is weather-related and occurring outdoors. Also, there may not be any stairwells in the restaurant.

Item Number 11 *(Lesson 25)*

A. Incorrect: *to free the outrigger.* The passage does not correlate the outrigger with the crane's stability.

B. Incorrect: *to increase rotational radius.* Rotational radius is something you may change after checking stability, but it is not the main reason why you do so.

C. **Correct:** *to prevent overturning.* Bullet item 3 states that stability must be checked to prevent "overturning."

D. Incorrect: *to increase the load weight.* Load weight is part of what you check but is not the reason you do so.

E. Incorrect: *to speed up loading.* The passage does not mention how fast the crane can be loaded, nor does it relate this to stability.

Item Number 12 *(Lesson 25)*

F. Incorrect: *Continue operations and contact the power company later.* The power company representative must be present and ensure that lines are grounded before you can begin.

G. Incorrect: *Set up a clearly visible sign and continue operations.* This is one step, but the power company representative must also ensure lines are grounded.

H. Incorrect: *De-energize and ground the power lines yourself.* The power company representative is responsible for ensuring that lines are de-energized and grounded.

J. Incorrect: *Continue working without cutting the lines.* You cannot continue without cutting the lines and having a power company representative to ensure lines are grounded.

K. **Correct:** *Wait until a power company representative can be on site.* Reschedule the set up date, because a power company representative must be present before you can begin.

Item Number 13 *(Lesson 24)*

A. Incorrect: *pharmaceuticals.* The passage does not mention testing for pharmaceuticals, or drugs.

B. Incorrect: *fertilizer.* The passage does not mention fertilizer.

C. Incorrect: *pesticides.* Pesticides are discussed in the second paragraph, but not in relation to pathogens.

D. Incorrect: *soil.* The passage mentions that soil may contain pathogens, but pathogens are not soil.

E. **Correct:** *disease-causing agents.* The first paragraph indicates that the lab will be testing for pathogens, meaning that pathogens are disease-causing agents.

Item Number 14 *(Lesson 24)*

F. **Correct:** *its poison content.* The second paragraph described toxins as poisonous chemicals.

G. Incorrect: *its nutritional value.* The passage does not discuss testing for a food's nutritional value.

H. Incorrect: *if it contains bacteria.* Bacteria are pathogens, which are discussed in the first paragraph. The second paragraph deals with toxins.

J. Incorrect: *if it has been banned.* Though the second paragraph mentions that some chemicals are banned, it cannot be assumed that everything that has some toxicity has been banned.

K. Incorrect: *its source of contamination.* The passage does not discuss the source of any of the contaminants, including toxins, for which the lab tests.

Item Number 15 *(Lesson 25)*

A. **Correct:** *to be sure that it doesn't get activated.* The lock-off procedure states that a warning notice must be put on the isolator so it is not activated.

B. Incorrect: *to safely store highly flammable plastic.* This does not apply to the lock-off procedure, but rather to fire safety guidelines.

C. Incorrect: *to use a padlock that has only one key.* This is not the reason for putting a warning notice on the isolator; it is step 2 in the lock-off procedure.

D. Incorrect: *to be sure that it gets activated.* The lock-off procedure states that a warning notice must be put on the isolator so it is NOT activated.

E. Incorrect: *to make sure the feed opening is centered.* This does not apply to the lock-off procedure, but rather to working with agglomerators/crumbers.

Item Number 16 *(Lesson 25)*

F. Incorrect: *Make certain that the pile is 1 meter above the crumber blades.* This is for the feed opening.

G. Incorrect: *Make certain that the pile is 1.1 meters below the level of the feed opening.* This is for the working platform.

H. Incorrect: *Make certain that the pile is fastened with a padlock.* This is for locking the machine.

J. Incorrect: *Make certain that the pile is 4 meters from the facility.* This is for materials less than 5 meters long.

K. **Correct:** *Make certain that the pile is 6 meters from the facility.* This is for materials less than 8 meters long. Treat unlabeled material as you would highly flammable material.

Item Number 17 *(Lesson 23)*

A. Incorrect: *It increases.* Increases is the opposite of what needs to happen to the water level in order for the elevator to lower.

B. Incorrect: *It activates.* Activates does not describe what the water must do in order to allow the elevator to lower.

C. Incorrect: *It hoists.* Hoists does not describe what the water must do in order to allow the elevator to lower.

D. **Correct:** *It decreases.* Because the elevator will rise to the highest elevation until the water level recedes, it means that the elevator will not lower until the water level has lowered, or decreased.

E. Incorrect: *It lubricates.* Lubricates does not describe what the water must do in order to allow the elevator to lower.

Item Number 18 *(Lesson 23)*

F. Incorrect: *repair area.* The passage does not refer to the repair area as a place that needs to be cleaned and lubricated so that the door will fit into it.

G. Incorrect: *the pit floor.* The passage does not refer to the pit floor as a place where the door will fit into.

H. Incorrect: *a drainage tube.* The passage does not refer to the drainage tube as an item that needs to be cleaned and lubricated so that the door will fit into it.

J. **Correct:** *part of the doorframe.* The context of the sill needing to be clean and lubricated so that the door will fit into it, indicates that the sill is part of the frame.

K. Incorrect: *the counterweight.* The passage does not relate the counterweight as an item that needs to be cleaned and lubricated so that the door will fit into it.